D1452507

# DATE DUE

| | | | |
|---|---|---|---|
| | | | |
| | | | |
| | | | |
| | | | |
| | | | |
| | | | |
| | | | |
| | | | |
| | | | |
| | | | |
| | | | |
| | | | |
| | | | |
| | | | |
| | | | |

ARTHURIAN STUDIES LXX

RADIO CAMELOT

ARTHURIAN LEGENDS ON THE BBC, 1922–2005

ARTHURIAN STUDIES

ISSN 0261–9814

General Editor: Norris J. Lacy

Previously published volumes in the series
are listed at the back of this book

# RADIO CAMELOT

## ARTHURIAN LEGENDS ON THE BBC, 1922–2005

Roger Simpson

D. S. BREWER

First published 2008
D. S. Brewer, Cambridge


ISBN 978–1–84384–140–1

D. S. Brewer is an imprint of Boydell & Brewer Ltd
PO Box 9, Woodbridge, Suffolk IP12 3DF, UK
and of Boydell & Brewer Inc.
668 Mount Hope Ave, Rochester, NY 14604, USA
website: www.boydellandbrewer.com


A CIP catalogue record for this book is available
from the British Library


This publication is printed on acid-free paper

Printed in Great Britain by
Antony Rowe Ltd, Chippenham, Wiltshire

For Paddy

# Contents

# Illustrations

# Acknowledgements

As this study could not have been written without access to the Cambridge University Library and the BBC Written Archives Centre, Caversham Park, I am extremely grateful for the exemplary service I was given at both institutions.

My thanks are also due to the Ashmolean Museum; Association of Illustrators; BBC Information, Glasgow; Chris Beetles Ltd; British Library; Hastings Museum and Art Gallery; David Higham Associates; Dukes Theatre, Lancaster; Kilvert Gallery, Clyro; Newspaper Library, Colindale; Norfolk and Norwich Millennium Library; *Radio Times*; Royal Opera House, Covent Garden; Taunton Public Library; Theatre Museum, London; University of East Anglia Library; and Victoria and Albert Museum Archive.

For help and advice, I am indebted to Josian Andrew, Martin Baker, Dr Marie Denley, the Reverend Geoffrey Fraser, the Reverend Michael Gill, Sue Gill, Linda Gowans, Professor Kevin Harty, Michael D. Jacobson, Michael Jamieson, Dimitri Kennaway, Chris Lutrario, Julian May, Dr Paul Murgatroyd, Alex Noel-Tod, Brian Patten, Dr Karen Pratt, Dr Valerie Purton, Dr St John Simpson, Margaret Tarner and Professor Bonnie Wheeler.

Among the books I have consulted, I have had most frequent recourse to two: Jerome V. Reel's 'A Listing of Arthurian Music', in Richard Barber, ed., *King Arthur in Music*; and Daniel P. Nastali and Phillip C. Boardman's invaluable *The Arthurian Annals*.

Since an earlier form of Chapter 2 appeared in *Arthuriana* (Fall 2004), I am grateful to the journal for permission to reprint this material. For permission to quote other copyright matter I wish to thank Irene Bacon, BBC Written Archives Centre, Val Biro, the Eric Fraser Estate, Brian Patten, Ian Pollock, Nicholas Scarfe, the Tolkien Estate, Anne Valery and Penelope Woolfitt. Both I and the publishers are grateful to all the institutions and individuals listed for permission to reproduce the materials in which they hold copyright. Every effort has been made to trace the copyright holders; apologies are offered for any omission and the publishers will be pleased to add any necessary acknowledgement in subsequent editions.

My deepest debt is to my wife, Paddy, for her unfailing and cheerful encouragement and support for the whole project. To her this book is dedicated.

# *Abbreviations*

BBC WAC    British Broadcasting Corporation Written Archives Centre

SO             Symphony Orchestra

BBC Stations and Services

| | |
|---|---|
| A | Aberdeen |
| B | Birmingham |
| Bo | Bournemouth |
| C | Cardiff |
| D | Daventry |
| F | Forces Programme |
| HS | Home Service |
| L | London |
| LP | Light Programme |
| M | Midland |
| MP | Music Programme |
| N | National |
| NE | North-East |
| N3 | Network Three |
| P | Plymouth |
| R | Regional |
| R1 | Radio One |
| R2 | Radio Two |
| R3 | Radio Three |
| R4 | Radio Four |
| R5 | Radio Five |
| RN | Radio Norfolk |
| S | Scotland |
| TP | Third Programme |
| W | West |
| Wa | Wales |

Non-BBC Stations

| | |
|---|---|
| CFM | Classic FM |
| OW | Oneword |

The publishers are grateful to the Vinaver Trust
for generously providing a subvention towards
the production costs of this volume

# Introduction

Radio is one of the last zones to be explored for Arthurian interest. While modern research has looked far outside the traditional literary areas by investigating children's books, comics, cinema, art, music and ephemera, radio has remained largely *terra incognita*.

The medium has never had the easy glamour of the cinema, and, since the arrival of television as mass provider of entertainment and information, radio is affectionately but condescendingly regarded as 'steam radio', a curiously archaic technology belonging to the lost age, in which I grew up, of fountain pens and leather footballs. Besides, the radio medium often seems too fugitive to seize, as programmes appear to vanish into thin air never to be heard again. In the early days the cost and difficulty of cutting new discs meant that most broadcasts went unrecorded. And even when the introduction of audiotape facilitated recording many of the recordings made have since deteriorated or been discarded.

Happily, however, much of this material is still recoverable, in four main ways. In Britain the British Broadcasting Corporation has a vast archive of its activities, and though the Sound Archive is available only to BBC staff the Written Archive is open to the public. This allows researchers to read the microfiche copies of many plays, and consult the written correspondence between writers and those who commissioned or produced the work. Secondly, and crucially, the mass circulation weekly magazine *Radio Times* was launched within a year of the start of broadcasting.[1] This has not only provided a programme listing, but its informative articles about particular works and radio policies have also set the programmes within their cultural context. Throughout its existence it has also commissioned some fine drawings by contemporary artists.[2] The aural medium is thus firmly linked with printed text and pictorial illustration. My study aims to preserve this connection.[3] Thirdly, there are extant contemporary reviews, because *The Listener*, another weekly magazine published by the BBC, was established in 1929 and this provided (until it closed in 1991) perceptive, independent analysis of many radio programmes, notably music and drama, besides reprinting important talks. Lastly, since domestic tape-recorders became

---

1   The magazine was originally called *The Radio Times*, and did not drop its definite article until 1937. For convenience, however, I use the form *Radio Times* throughout. To cover the period before the first issue (30 September 1923), I have consulted the *BBC Programme Records, 1922–1926* (London: BBC, n.d.).

2   For an introduction to this topic, see David Driver, ed., *The Art of 'Radio Times': The First Sixty Years* (London: BBC, 1981); and Martin Baker, *Artists of 'Radio Times': A Golden Age of British Illustration* (Oxford: Ashmolean Museum, 2002).

3   Technical constraints oblige me, though, to omit reproduction of colour illustrations.

widely available, a good deal of private recording has been going on: my own recordings over the last twenty years are therefore used to form the basis of my fourth and fifth chapters.[4]

I have thus been able to attempt a broad survey of the programmes that dealt with the Arthurian legends across a period of over eighty years: from the birth of the BBC in 1922 up to 2005.[5] Inevitably there are some gaps and distortions. On a very few occasions, printing of the *Radio Times* was interrupted by strikes.[6] There is always the possibility, too, that an advertised programme may not have been broadcast. But both of these negative factors are sufficiently minor to be disregarded. A more serious shortcoming is the regional distortion that has probably crept in. Before the Second World War, *Radio Times* was very lavishly printed, and contained full details of almost all the programmes offered by regional stations, but after the war a unitary edition was abandoned in favour of six regional ones. Because I live, and use libraries, in south-eastern England, the issues of *Radio Times* that I have been able to consult have been those designed for this area. Programmes for other regions are not always easy to trace, as they were relegated within the London and South-East editions to very small print and paucity of detail. The problem worsened when BBC local radio began in the 1960s, for Home Service variations ceased, and these new stations assumed the regional mantle. The only detail that is given of their programmes, however, is the name of the presenter or the series title. And so, although the Arthurian legends have often been nurtured by pride in local association (in the West of England) or fuelled by nationalism (in Wales), and it is very likely that such Arthurian matter is frequently transmitted on local radio in the West or Wales, all this has remained hidden from me. Another, and even graver, deficiency is the fact that not all music is listed. In the golden pre-war days, *Radio Times* named virtually all pieces of music played, their composer and performers. Since then the practice has gradually developed of not listing 'lighter' work. Radio 1, for instance, cloaks all its pop music titles from public gaze. There is too a steadily growing cult, even on Radio 3, of celebrity being regarded as a quality pertaining to the presenter (or DJ) rather than the music or its performers. Much of the music played is now treated as a surprise dip into a bran tub or comes purportedly as a response to a special request by a listener. Inevitably great swathes of Arthurian music may have eluded me.[7]

In the case of Wagner, a certain imbalance may be detected between his stature and my relatively slender coverage. His music has always been the most

---

[4] I use an asterisk (*) to mark those dramas and features that I have listened to.

[5] The British Broadcasting Company began transmissions on 14 November 1922. On 1 January 1927 it evolved seamlessly into the publicly funded yet quasi-autonomous British Broadcasting Corporation, with a government charter that obliges it to inform, educate and entertain.

[6] Eleven weekly issues have failed to appear: nine because of strikes (in 1926, 1950, 1981 and 1983), and two because of a fuel crisis in the severe winter of 1947. See Tony Currie, *The Radio Times Story* (Tiverton: Kelly Publications, 2001), p. 242.

[7] I have consulted Alastair Mitchell and Alan Poulton, eds, *A Chronicle of First Broadcast Performances of Musical Works in the UK* (Aldershot: Ashgate, 2001), which is based on the Programme-as-Broadcast daily programme log held at Caversham, but although this contains excellent information it is strangely incomplete.

frequently mentioned Arthurian item in *Radio Times*, besides being the most popular Arthurian subject for *Radio Times* artists, and in acknowledgement of his greatness and influence I indicate the chief Wagnerian programmes near the start of each chapter, but as copious documentation of his work may easily be found in other published accounts I have chosen to devote greater attention in the present study to work that is less widely known.

As my concern is with broadcasting within Britain itself, I have made no effort to track down programmes transmitted on the BBC Empire (later World) Service. While I am very willing to notice any non-BBC broadcasts that I may encounter since independent radio stations came into official existence, in practice only Classic FM and Oneword provide enough details of their programmes as yet for the tiny Arthurian component to be visible. Essentially then my study is of the BBC. Its ethos, policies, structures and personalities have shaped and diffused the material I discuss.

In the interests of economy, and so as not to overload the reader, I have not given exact dates for all the programmes mentioned. Nor have I always drawn attention to repeats. I considered forming separate chapters for different genres (Music, Drama, etc.), but rejected this in favour of a period grouping. Division into decades would prove too piecemeal, so I have chosen blocks of about twenty years. These time categories are, of course, a convenient guide rather than an imperious *zeitgeist*.

Unlike the Green Knight I have no particular axe to grind. I hold no entrenched view about the relative worth or otherwise of any one period's Arthurian vision. Whether the Arthurian legend should or should not evolve into new forms is beside the point: it clearly has always done so; and I believe the ways in which it has accomplished this are worth noticing and understanding.

# 1

## *1922–1939: 'Loud-speakers in Lyonesse'*

'There were no loud-speakers in Lyonesse' is a well-turned phrase coined by J. B. Harker to head his *Radio Times* article of 1930.[1] The topic arose from a radio talk on modern kindergartens in *The Growth of the Child* series of the previous year.[2] Having previewed this talk Harker was prompted to recall his own very different educational background. He had attended a kindergarten himself in far-off pre-radio days, where the teacher was a former pupil of Rossetti, a friend of William Morris, and follower of 'every nice-minded, wholesome educational crank who sprang into existence in the nineties and early nineteen hundreds'. Remaining faithful to her Pre-Raphaelite principles, and with a terrific faith in the educational benefits of Malory's *Morte Darthur*, she had bestowed an Arthurian name on every child and, through a curriculum largely devoted to arts and crafts, inculcated a sense of beauty and the gentler aspects of knightly chivalry. Mervyn Wilson's *Radio Times* illustration sympathetically conveys the ambience [plate 1].

When, some twenty-five years later, Harker revisits the now forlorn scene where he had been brought up to resemble Sir Galahad, he sighs over that lost ethos, which is represented as wholly remote from the contemporary system of 'standardised lectures … and music spouted from speakers in a thousand classrooms'. The implication is that gleaming technological modernity has, alas, overpowered and displaced the once dominant culture of Arthurian legend.

Harker's view is, of course, substantially correct: by the 1920s the nineteenth-century Arthurian revival embodied in poetry and painting had spent its main force. But cultural breaks are rarely total, and, just as with many other concepts that are regularly announced as doomed – chivalry/romantic love/religious belief/nationalism/ monarchy/the novel/capitalism/civilisation as we know it/even history itself – yet have all proved unexpectedly resilient, the Arthurian legend has shown considerable versatility in adapting to changed circumstances. The history of radio broadcasting in Britain would bear this out. Three faint indications of how the legend was filtering into the new medium through the channels of commerce and/or poetry may be detected in other issues of *Radio Times*. The first is an advertisement in 1923 for the Polarphone luxury radio cabinet (Chippendale Model finely brushed in polished mahogany).[3] Fleet's lively drawing shows Arthur's knights involved in an internecine brawl because each chivalrously wishes to sacrifice his turn to listen to the crystal-set

---

1  J. B. Harker, 'There were no loud-speakers in Lyonesse', *Radio Times* (8 August 1930), 279.
2  J. B. Harker, 'Our Arthurian Days', *Radio Times* (28 June 1929), 661.
3  Polarphone advertisement, *Radio Times* (7 December 1923), 407.

headphones [**plate 3**]. While they manfully lay about each other, an unchival-
rous page grabs the phones for himself and sits under the Round Table listening
to *Children's Hour*:

> On chivalry insistent
> Each Knight was so persistent
> To sacrifice his turn to don the 'phones,
> That Arthur's table round
> Was a (K)nightly battle ground,
> And 'Children's Hour' was passed in tuneful groans.

The sales implication is that the new and expensive seven-valve Polarphone
would come equipped with a speaker that everyone in a room could listen to.
This convenience would give no further occasion for requiring either a chivalrous spirit of *noblesse oblige* or displays of juvenile self-seeking over access to
headsets.

The other two examples stem from more conventional versifying. Graham
Eltham's 'I know that near the stars' appeared in a poetic anthology taking
the 'new magic' of radio as its theme.[4] Here Eltham speculates that as radio
wavelengths may have a mysterious ability to transmit from deepest space
the lingering echoes of the great legendary stories of our civilisation, among
the great stories they relay will be those 'Of Tristan's lance against Palamides,
/ Galahad's piety, Guinever's wondering.' Similar stray breaths of Arthurian
song inform too a lavishly printed and illustrated piece by Eleanor and Herbert
Farjeon, 'A Masque of Broadcasting'.[5] This presents a tableau of the world's
history that radio now makes it possible to hear, and the cast includes some
famous names:

> Hark! The clash of Arthur's knights,
> Jousting in their mimic fights,
> Shivering a lance for fame
> And a lady making claim
>     In beauty's name.

As the clash of steel grows louder, cries are heard of 'Lancelot du Lac! A Gawain,
a Gawain!' The productions of Fleet, Eltham and the Farjeons all suggest that an
older wine was still being poured into the new bottles of radio.

## *Music*

A lingering Arthurian radio presence was most evident, however, in the field of
music. This is not surprising because live music dominated the schedules from
the outset, constituting about seventy per cent of all air time. Admittedly, in
quantitative terms very little that may even loosely be described as 'Arthurian'
was played, and, if one designated a typical BBC piece, it would probably be

---

4   'Broadcast Anthology', *Radio Times* (23 December 1930), 646.
5   'A Masque of Broadcasting', *Radio Times* (13 May 1932), 399–401.

Albert Ketèlbey's *In a Persian Garden*, as the fare provided was mainly 'light' and 'popular classical', with a regular supply of dance music. But programme planners also took their cultural mandate seriously, and consequently Percy Pitt (the Musical Director of Covent Garden Opera) was appointed Musical Adviser to the BBC in 1923 and made Musical Director in the following year. Not only did the BBC then take over sponsorship of the Henry Wood Promenade Concerts and set about developing its own symphony orchestras, but Pitt's closeness to operatic circles (he continued in his old job at the Royal Opera House!) meant that links would be fostered between the BBC and Covent Garden, and that radio would provide ample opportunity for the public to hear a wide range of operas, among them those by Richard Wagner. As a result his Arthurian works, *Parsifal* and *Tristan and Isolde*, soon entered the regular broadcasting repertoire, and became by far the most frequently played of all Arthurian music on air.[6] This runaway popularity of Wagner on radio presents a paradox.[7] Because a radio performance lacked all the visual aspects of facial expression, gesture, stage movement, costume, props, scenery and lighting that were present in a theatrical production, such a 'blind' performance might be considered a flat rebuttal of Wagner's own artistic intentions for 'music drama'. But the BBC could respond that its transmissions satisfied a strong cultural demand since most people were unable to attend live performances, and recorded forms of the entire operas were not always available: a complete *Tristan* was not issued on record until 1940, a *Parsifal* until 1951. Moreover, while a concert hall performance may be a pale reflection of the stage version, there is little to choose between them on radio. As the technical quality of radio was improved, a later critic would claim that listening on radio might even be preferred to the real thing:

> The gap between Wagner's imagination and any possible realisation of it in the theatre is so wide, that even in the devout performances at Bayreuth, one was always conscious of the uncomfortable chasm. Seated at home, one could imagine the Flower-maidens as the infinitely lovely, childish creatures described by their music; one could feel the mystery and awe of the temple-scenes without irreverently spotting Amfortas switching on the light that glows in the Grail; and one could visualise those walks up the mountain-side, so minutely and beautifully depicted in the *Verwandlungsmusik*, undistracted by the unsteady passage of a painted panorama or undamped by the mere blank of Covent Garden's red curtains.[8]

In practice, too, matters were generally made easy for listeners as most radio performances consisted of excerpts, *Parsifal* being slightly more popular in the 1920s, *Tristan* in the following decade. Predictably enough, the most frequent excerpts were the Good Friday Music or the Flower-Maidens' Scene from *Parsifal*, the Prelude and Liebestod from *Tristan*. Venues for performance could range widely: from brass band concerts where military bands made The March

6 I exclude consideration of *Lohengrin* throughout.
7 For an amusingly hostile view of opera, see Beachcomber, 'The Seven Absurdities of Opera', *Radio Times* (29 November 1929), 623. The inset cartoon by P. B. shows 'a Tristan like a large sack sagging towards an Iseult like a noisy pudding'.
8 Dyneley Hussey, 'Parsifal', *Listener* 43 (12 January 1950), 83–4.

of the Knights of the Grail *(Parsifal)* part of their standard repertoire, to opulent occasions at the Savoy Hotel, where Isolde's Liebestod was sung to the comfortably seated. Nonetheless, the performance of Wagner was often treated as a very special ceremony. This could even take the form of religious rite. *Parsifal* being widely revered as an intensely Christian work its performance was often fittingly located within the Church's liturgical calendar, during Easter Week. On a secular level, too, Wagner also retained high cultural and social *éclat*. As the advertisement for Ediswan Valves *(Radio Times,* 26 February 1926) engagingly reveals [plate 2], Wagner's Tristan and Isolde were a renowned 'Famous Association', and merely to mention them reason enough to make the public buy your product.[9]

During the prestigious annual London season of Promenade Concerts conducted by Sir Henry Wood, himself an ardent pilgrim to Bayreuth, there were special Wagner Nights on Mondays. These and succeeding Wagner broadcasts were regarded as showcase events, talked up in *Radio Times* with advance publicity, helpfully explanatory articles on the Arthurian content, photographs of associated medieval and Pre-Raphaelite paintings, a wealth of handsome modern illustrations and even an imposing special cover by Clixby Watson devoted to a *Parsifal* concert [plate 4]. Besides numerous short extracts, the BBC also began broadcasting entire acts of these operas from Covent Garden: Acts 2 and 3 of *Tristan* were given as early as June 1923 and Act 3 of *Parsifal* in February 1924. Such events were only sporadically repeated until the early 1930s, but from then on acts from *Tristan* were broadcast a couple of times a year. When Bruno Walter, who was then the chief conductor of the German seasons at Covent Garden, conducted one such performance in 1931 it was signally marked in *Radio Times* by Donia Nachsen's drawing – the first for a live broadcast of this work [plate 5]. Many others would follow [plate 6].

As for performances of the entire operas, a breakthrough was achieved by the broadcast in 1928 of a concert performance of *Parsifal* by the National Orchestra under Sir Henry Wood at the Queen's Hall, London, which lasted for two hours. This concert version was repeated six times in the 1930s. One of these performances is marked by Elizabeth Rivers's bold design, the first specially commissioned serious illustration for an Arthurian subject in *Radio Times* [plate 7]. *Tristan*, though, was not made available in a concert version, so an entire broadcast performance of this opera had to wait until 1936, when the sensible arrangement was contrived whereby individual acts were relayed from Covent Garden on three separate nights over a period of a fortnight. This was, in fact, an outstanding operatic production, for it was superbly conducted by Fritz Reiner, featured Lauritz Melchior, who was regarded as the 'best Tristan of his time', and it marked a triumphant London début as Isolde for the great Norwegian soprano, Kirsten Flagstad.[10] These landmark broadcasts were heralded by significant illustrations from C. W. Bacon (for Act 1) and Clixby Watson (Act 2) [plate 8].

In marked contrast to the widespread diffusion of Wagner, the major home-

---

9   Ediswan Valves advertisement, *Radio Times* (26 February 1926), 477.
10  *The Times* (19 May 1936), 14.

grown operatic work, John Dryden and Henry Purcell's 'dramatick opera' of *King Arthur* (1691), received slender attention. It had fallen out of favour since the mid-nineteenth century, and even such excerpts as the lovely 'Fairest Isle' aria were broadcast only very occasionally until 1933 onwards. Full production has always been problematic because it requires two casts: actors and singers. A rare revival had been staged at Cambridge in 1928 (and the text published), but this was not broadcast. For this omission there was perhaps good reason: the undergraduate soloists may have 'worked manfully', but it 'was hardly to be expected that they could do justice to the main airs'.[11]

Nonetheless, despite the dearth of staged productions there was a much livelier tradition of concert performances, the standard being set by the celebrated Birmingham one in 1897, and it was in this form that the work most effectively reached the air from a variety of provincial sources. As early as 1925, a one-hour condensation was presented from Aberdeen by the 2BD Operatic Choir and Wireless Orchestra under Arthur Collingwood. Two years later a couple of comparable performances took place: another one-hour version by the Harold Brooke Choir at Bishopsgate, London, and a more substantial version running to an hour and three-quarters that came from the Birmingham Station Opera and Chorus under Joseph Lewis. From the Leeds Choral Union and SO under Norman Stafford in 1931, there ensued another shortish version (70 minutes), before the period's major performance took place in 1935 at the Queen's Hall, London, given by the BBC SO under Adrian Boult. This was treated as a very significant revival, worthy of a full-page preview article in *The Listener* by the eminent musicologist Edward J. Dent, who observed that the work was 'still comparatively unknown'.[12] Another preview followed in *Radio Times* by Julian Herbage, a stalwart of the BBC's music staff, who was in charge of the production.[13]

Herbage arranged Purcell's score, cut out Dryden's contribution, and substituted a blank verse narration written by Michael Creswell, which was delivered by two actors in evening dress: King Arthur's own role thus disappeared entirely, an omission which, Herbage conceded, 'may seem strange'. In this way the whole work amounted to only an hour and fifty minutes. The music critic William McNaught praised the orchestra and choral singing, and commended the producer's attempt to 'give something better than a straightforward concert performance', but he felt that the English soloists used were inadequate, and the need to darken the hall in order to project limelight on to the narrators had deprived him of his customary pleasure of reading the score.[14] A spin-off from the production was, however, Herbage's instrumental *Suite: King Arthur*. This proved a viable method of featuring Purcell's music rather than Dryden's verse, and was played occasionally thereafter.

A second British choral work received a singular revival in 1927, when Sir Frederick Cowen's *The Water Lily: A Romantic Legend for soli, chorus and orchestra*

---

11  A. K., 'Purcell's King Arthur at Cambridge', *Musical Times* 69 (1 March 1928), 255–6.
12  Edward J. Dent, 'Purcell's King Arthur', *Listener* 14 (4 December 1935), 1037.
13  Julian Herbage, 'Dryden's King Arthur Composed by Purcell', *Radio Times* (6 December 1935), 13.
14  William McNaught, 'King Arthur', *Musical Times* 77 (January 1936), 68–9.

was performed by five soloists, the Cardiff Repertory Chorus and Station SO under Warwick Braithwaite (C 30 January). Though first performed at the Norwich Festival in 1893, where it had earned appreciative reviews, Cowen's cantata seems to have been little known since then, and, as it has escaped the attention of even Arthurian bibliographers, it now deserves a closer examination.[15] *Radio Times* provided a helpful summary, which I quote to preserve the flavour of the age:

In the PROLOGUE, after an Orchestral Introduction, Sir Galahad (*Tenor*), wandering in the forest near King Arthur's Court, is greeted by a rustic band of men and maids, who sing of the joyous coming together of lovers. This reminds him of a dream in which he saw a lovely face in the heart of a water-lily. 'Come from glade, or bower or stream, / Lovely lady of my dream!' he begs, and in answer airy spirits appear, sent by the goddess Norna (*Contralto*) to bring him a vision of her whom he would fain see again. He falls asleep, and in a dream sees a ship, whereon is seated an Egyptian Princess, Ina (*Soprano*). She sings that she is journeying to where her lover waits for her – 'at Britain's Court.' Sir Galahad awakes.
SCENE 1. The magician Merlin (*Bass*), seeing Ina's ship approaching, causes a storm to break upon it. It sinks, and Merlin is beginning to lament his rashness, when Norna appears, and tells him how grave is his act, since Ina is awaited at the Court of King Arthur. Norna summons a magic boat, and sets forth to seek Ina.
SCENE 2. Ina  has been cast up, alone, on one of the Scilly islands. She laments her fate. Norna arrives and rescues her.
SCENE 3. On the coast of Cornwall Merlin awaits them, with a swift car drawn by swans, which transports Ina to Caerleon.
SCENE 4. At Arthur's Court, a tournament is about to begin. The arrival of Merlin's car creates great excitement. Ina is presumed to be dead, and flowers are strewn upon the car. Merlin suggests that the King's knights shall try by touch to revive her. 'For so may pass to her the kindred life of him, her destined lord.' Many knights do so without success, but at Galahad's touch she revives, and joins her lover in a joyous duet.[16]

Cowen had avowedly based his story on Wordsworth's late poem, 'The Egyptian Maid; or, The Romance of the Water Lily' (1835), and had followed the original narrative quite faithfully.[17] One important structural change is, however, made: he prepares us for the final outcome, and gives the narrative a more satisfactory shape, by opening with Galahad's dream, whereas in Words-worth's poem this key event had been retained (clumsily) until the final dénoue-ment. Cowen, too, makes more of the Egyptian Princess: he gives her a name

---

[15]  Frederick Cowen, 'The Water Lily: A Romantic Legend for Soli, Chorus and Orchestra. Words by Joseph Bennett', in *Programme of the Norfolk and Norwich Twenty-fourth Triennial Music Festival* (London: Novello, Ewer, 1893), pp. 13–27. A favourable preview and review appeared in *Musical Times* 34 (September 1893), 521–3; and (November 1893), 658. It was praised too in *Eastern Daily Press* (7 October 1893), 5. The autograph MS is in the British Library: BL Add MS 50767, 118ff.
[16]  *Radio Times* (30 January 1927), 205.
[17]  William Wordsworth, 'The Egyptian Maid; or, The Romance of the Water Lily', in *The Poet-ical Works*, ed. Ernest de Selincourt (London: Oxford University Press, 1904), pp. 369–74.

and a singing role. In Wordsworth she had been nameless and mute. A minor name change also occurs: Wordsworth's Nina, the Lady of the Lake, becomes more Wagnerian, the goddess Norna. Joseph Bennett's libretto takes up an occasional Wordsworthian phrase ('a vessel seems to hang in air'), and follows quite closely the overall meaning of Wordsworth's stanzas, but recasts the diction and syntax into simpler forms more suitable for singing. The result reads banally (as do most libretti), but Wordsworth's original is also very thick ankled (in Tennyson's perspicuous phrase). What was most modified was the underlying theme. Wordsworth's poem is conceptually underpinned by a religio-philosophical schema, in which Merlin represents the destructive propensities of a mechanistic outlook and the Egyptian Maid a beautiful unregenerate paganism – Wordsworth bigotedly condemns the 'idol' on her boat's prow – that must be awakened by Christian inspiration (Nina/Galahad). Cowen will have none of this, however, and creates a simpler tale in which love is quite enough:

> At the prow, where the lily gleams,
> Stand thou, O Love, and cry
> To the wandering storms that they flee
> From the path of thy votary;
> Fair shall it be, as the beams
> In the blue of a Summer sky.  (p. 27)

So much for the words. As for the music, we have to rely on the reviews of the 1893 première, which comment on the difficulty of the work, both for vocalists and instrumentalists, and the constant use of *leitmotiven*. A strong Wagnerian influence may thus be assumed. Though lacking 'the swing of broad phrases with which vocalists can make their best effect', the love music glowed 'with the richest and most varied harmony', the choruses were 'masterpieces in dramatic *ensemble*', the skilful and suggestive supernatural scenes displayed the 'most fitting orchestral figuration and colour'. Overall, it was 'an unquestionable success', perhaps indeed 'a triumph.' As for the broadcast version, this may have been, as *Radio Times* pointed out, 'somewhat shortened' to fit the allotted slot of an hour and a quarter, but it represents a major early flowering of Arthurian music on air.

Radio also featured important Arthurian choral work by a third British composer: Rutland Boughton. Boughton's deep involvement with the Arthurian legend took idiosyncratic and original forms. His *Bethlehem*, a recreation of the medieval Coventry Nativity Play, bestowed Merlin's name, for example, on one of the Wise Men, and he attempted an ambitious cycle of Arthurian operas. His direction of annual summer festivals at Glastonbury from 1914 to 1926 provided the opportunity to mount what he dreamt of as an English equivalent of Bayreuth, and despite having very limited resources and facilities he contrived to stage four of his projected six Arthurian operas. Even when this project collapsed his music would still enjoy some limited access to broadcasting. Though the 1920s witnessed only a single performance of *Bethlehem* – Boughton complained that the BBC was boycotting his music on political grounds – during the 1930s not only *The Immortal Hour* (his tremendous London success) but also his version of the Tristan legend received noteworthy air time. Boughton's opera, *The Queen of Cornwall*, which was based on Thomas Hardy's recently completed drama, *The Famous Tragedy of the Queen of Cornwall* (of which more later), was staged at Glastonbury in 1924 and 1925. Certain excerpts from it (particularly the Overture) were first broadcast in 1932 and occasionally repeated, but the major breakthrough came with a performance in 1935 of the entire opera (or music drama, as Boughton termed it), in a special version arranged for broadcasting by the composer, with the Wireless Chorus and BBC Orchestra conducted by Albert Coates. In *Radio Times* an illustration by C. Walter Hodges evoked a romantic image of Tintagel, the setting for Boughton's tragic work.

Previewing this performance in *The Listener*, Francis Toye (who judged the work from reading the score) pronounced himself wholly unsympathetic to Boughton's aesthetic theories and ultra-left politics, but warmly praised his ability to write 'admirable tunes possessing individual quality and, as a rule, perfectly suited to their context'.[18] Though sometimes 'naïve', Boughton was, he thought, significant because he had 'sincerity, allied with naturalness, and a love and understanding of the theatre exceptional among British musicians'. Managing without the score, but having listened to the broadcast, the forthright W. R. Anderson dissented.[19] Conceding that the work had 'some attractive tunes', he disliked the 'long declamatory periods', the manner in which the voices dominated the orchestra, and judged that there was a fundamental mismatch between the styles of the music and the poetry. But Boughton's music continued to be played. Later that year, for example, he was invited to conduct the BBC Midland Orchestra in a special concert dedicated to his work. For this he chose excerpts not only from *The Queen of Cornwall* but also from his new Arthurian opera, *The Lily Maid*. A further short item, 'Sir Galahad', was awarded a performance in 1938 (N 27 September). This was oddly described (*Radio Times* has its vagaries) as a folksong, but it was surely the setting he had composed in 1898 of Tennyson's famous lyric.

Like Boughton, and perhaps with greater justification, Arnold Bax felt neglected by the BBC, complaining regularly to the new head of BBC Music, Adrian Boult (he had succeeded Pitt in 1930), that his own compositions were not being broadcast frequently enough.[20] He appears to have had a case. His tone poem *Tintagel*, which had its first public performance in 1921 and was issued on record in 1930, does not seem to have been premièred on air until 1931. Preceded by a full-page article by Richard Church (*RT*, 24 April), it was then played by BBC SO under Basil Cameron. But it still was not heard very often: I can trace only half a dozen other performances in this period. What proved far more popular was another work of similar title but for brass band by a member of the BBC music staff: Denis Wright's *Symphonic Suite: Tintagel*, which included sections named 'King Arthur', 'Merlin' and – surprisingly – 'Elaine' (What was *she* doing *there*?). Such bands were heavily featured in those days, and Wright's piece was regularly played by military or industrial ensembles.

---

[18] Francis Toye, 'Rutland Boughton and his Music', *Listener* 13 (30 January 1935), 203.
[19] W. R. Anderson, 'Wireless Notes', *Musical Times* 76 (March 1935), 223.
[20] Lewis Foreman, *Bax: A Composer and his Times*, 2nd edn (Aldershot: Scolar Press, 1987), pp. 275–6.

More esoterically, there was in 1938 a complete performance (spread over nine months) of Riccardo Zandonai's opera *Francesca da Rimini* (based on Gabriele D'Annunzio's play, of which more later), which has important allusions to the Lancelot–Guenevere story. And intriguingly, there were four renditions of 'Lancelot' from Leon Adam's *Deux airs de ballet* (1912), performed thrice by military band, once by girl *siffleuse*.

What the BBC also tapped into was a strong regional culture, which delighted to express itself in local festivals and civic pageants. A fine example of this was a Thomas Dunhill piece, which stemmed from music he had composed in 1925 for W. Graham Robertson's *The Town of the Ford*, a pageant play for Guildford, Surrey.[21] Dunhill then reworked the score into his *Guildford Suite* of six movements, the third of which featured The Fair Maid of Astolat. When performed on radio in 1927, Dunhill provided an accompanying description:

> Sir Launcelot, guest of Sir Bernard of Astolat (which, according to tradition, stood where Guildford now stands), is departing with his men-at-arms for the great joust at Camelot. Elaine, sick with unrequited love for him, and lured by the mysterious song of the river, sets forth, amid the lamentations of her bower maidens, upon her last journey to him who will come to her no more.[22]

This suite (and particularly this movement) proved relatively popular, being played another half-dozen times before the war.

A similar pageant was held at Taunton in 1928.[23] Here the Arthurian associations were even stronger, for the legend supports the entire narrative of the town's development. Opening with a modern return of King Arthur on the barge, who appoints the three accompanying queens to oversee the defence of country, customs, law and freedom, it closes with Arthur entrusting Excalibur to the Bishop of Winchester as a symbol of Christian continuity. This pageant also found some limited access to the air. The Mayor of Taunton gave an overall account (C 1928), and the specially composed music by Laurance E. Tanner, which included an *Entrance of King Arthur*, was later given a concert performance by the Former Bristol Hippodrome Orchestra (W 1933).

The BBC's regional stations, besides, presided over the performance of at least four new Arthurian compositions. In 1927 Susan Spain-Dunk, whose works were regularly heard at the Proms in the 1920s, conducted the Henry Wood SO in the first performance of her *Poem for Orchestra – Elaine*, a tone poem based on Tennyson's *Idylls*, which was repeated in a Bournemouth Municipal SO concert in the following year. The same year witnessed the première of a composition by a pianist in the Cardiff Station's Orchestra, Hubert Pengelly's *Tristram and Iseult*, with the composer as conductor and Margaret Wilkinson as soprano soloist. Next year the Birmingham Studio Augmented Orchestra under Joseph Lewis premièred Stanley Wilson's *Scena: The Quest of the Grail*, for tenor voice and

---

21  Thomas Dunhill, *The Town of the Ford: A Pageant Play*. Vocal Score by W. Graham Robertson. Op. 66 (Guildford: Andrews, 1925).
22  *Radio Times* (28 April 1927), 167.
23  M. F. Cely Trevilian, *Defendamus: A Pageant of Taunton, 1928*. Music by Laurance E. Tanner (Taunton: Goodman, 1928).

orchestra, while the same orchestra presented Frederick Bye's *Tone Poem – Merlin* in 1930.

In addition to publicising the new, radio afforded at least nonce perform-ances in the mid-1930s to revivals of older orchestral works, such as J. D. Davis's *Symphonic Poem: The Maid of Astolat* (played 1933), E. W. Naylor's *Scena: Merlin and the Gleam* (1934) and the American Edward MacDowell's *Symphonic Poem: Lancelot and Elaine* (1935).

As for lyric music, much was based on nineteenth-century verse. Settings of Tennyson poems occurred quite steadily. Among these, Frederick Nicholls's 'Elaine's Song' was heard most frequently, but Armstrong Gibbs's 'The Lady of Shalott' and Christopher Edmunds's setting of the same poem were also played, as were Julius Harrison's setting of William Morris's 'Near Avalon'; Vincent Thomas's versions of Arthurian poems by Ernest Rhys; and Eric Fogg's 'King Arthur's Sleep', which was a setting of Leigh Henry's attractive lyric.[24] Another main source was Welsh verse. Here two items recurred most often: W. S. Gwynn Williams's settings of T. Gwynn Jones's *Eisteddfod* prize poem, 'Ymadawiad Arthur' [The Passing of Arthur] and Silyn Roberts's 'Arthur yn cyfodi' [Arthur is Arising], but there was also a sprinkling of other songs such as Vera Henry's 'Arthur gyda ni' [Arthur with us], a setting of a Howell Elvet Lewis poem, and Vaughan Thomas's 'Caledfwlch' [Excalibur].

One jovial song heard time and again throughout the period had a protean resilience. Known variously as 'King Arthur's Sons/Servants/Men' it was described as traditional or Old English, as a North Country/Lancashire/Dorset-shire/students' song, and attributed to an arrangement by Roberton/W. G. Whit-taker/Rutland Boughton/Harold Sykes/J. K. Lees /Broadwood/T. Keighley or to a printed source in *Daily Express Community Song Book* or *New Fellowship Song Book*. Heard less often, but of comparable genre, was 'When Good King Arthur Ruled This Land' and a modern ballad pastiche by Reginald Redman to words by E. R. Appleton: 'Three Kings of Somerset.' The second of these kings is Arthur, and the (now forgotten) associated stanza runs:

> King Arthur held his tourneys
> In Avalon's fair vale,
> And Glastonbury's ancients
> Relate the stirring tale.
> That Arthur still is living
> And soon will come again
> With all the Knights of Chivalry
> Ariding in his train.[25]

Of a living Arthurian tradition in more contemporary musical idioms, there was less evidence. I can spot only one citation of 'Avalon' (presumably Al Jolson's song); the sole work that received repeated performance in whole or

---

24  Thomas's *Song-Settings of Poems by Ernest Rhys* included 'The Song of Dinadan', 'Alis, la belle pilgrim', and 'The Sword Song of Geraint'.
25  Reginald Redman, *Three Kings of Somerset. Song*. Words by E. R. Appleton (London: Cramer, 1933).

part was Billy Mayerl's *Legends of King Arthur: six impressions for pianoforte*. (The six sections were: Prelude, Merlin, Lady of the Lake, The Passing of Arthur, The Sword Excalibur and Guinevere.) Composed perhaps as early as 1919, however, this light classical work recalls Grieg and MacDowell rather than the age of syncopation.[26] As Mayerl played the piano regularly (and stylishly) on the BBC, he invariably performed the work himself.

In addition to all the named music above, there was a great undertow of incidental music (discussed below), which was commissioned to accompany dramatisations of Arthurian literature.

## The Historical Arthur

In contrast to the considerable range of Arthurian music, the number of programmes dealing with the historical Arthur was rather exiguous, amounting to an average of only one programme a year.

That there was some attempt at an academic examination of evidence for the existence (if any) of Arthur is shown by general talks such as M. C. Sharpe's *Arthur and the Round Table* in *Scholars' Half-Hour* (Bo 1924) or Professor R. M. Hewitt (of University College, Nottingham)'s *The Legend of King Arthur* (Nottingham 1927), while an identically titled talk in the school programmes by the Reverend F. Ives Cater (1927) was probably academically conceived, too. More commonly, a study of Arthurian fact took as its starting point a particular regional focus in the West Country. In the very first year of British broadcasting, Frederick Bligh Bond spoke on *Old Buildings* (L 1923). As he had just achieved distinction (or notoriety) for his archaeological methods at Glastonbury (he claimed to have used psychical insights to aid his discoveries), it is likely that his own work at Glastonbury would have been mentioned.[27] More orthodox accounts of that town would doubtless have been provided by Una Rodenhurst (Newcastle 1924) and Laura Hird (Manchester 1927), and in Irene Gass's approach to the Arthurian story from a Somerset angle for *Children's Hour* (W 1930), though Alice M. Buckton's talk, *St Michael's Tor*, was imaginatively venturesome in the opinion that Joseph of Arimathea had buried the Holy Grail at the foot of the Glastonbury hill (C 1930). More authoritative would have been Margaret E. Riley's *Early Romances of the West of England: King Arthur in Fact and Fiction* (P 1930) and two talks by the distinguished local historian Charles Henderson: *Cornwall and the Cornish* (London 1928) and *Tintagel Castle and the Legend of King Arthur* (P 1930). On the other hand, W. P. Drury's *The Vanished Land of Lyonesse* (P 1925) leaned more heavily on Tennyson's poetry than on historical research. There was, besides, S. P. B. Mais's cursory travelogue, *The Atlantic Coast of Cornwall* (N 1932), but the major talk, and one that fortunately found permanent form in *The Listener*, was Geoffrey Grigson's classic *King Arthur and Tristan*

---

[26] See Peter Dickinson, *Marigold: The Music of Billy Mayerl* (Oxford: Oxford University Press, 1999), pp. 107–8.

[27] See William W. Kennawell, *The Quest at Glastonbury: A Biographical Study of Frederick Bligh Bond* (New York: Garrett, 1965).

*in the West* (W 1936), which begins by showing that Arthur's own association with Tintagel and other Cornish venues is literary rather than historical, but then goes on to expound Professor Joseph Loth's theory that the Tristan legend has a much firmer Cornish origin, which is identifiable through the names of characters and sites.[28]

Local interest in current archaeological excavations, too, gave rise to informed investigations at Caerleon by Ifan Kyrle Fletcher (C 1929) and Nevile Watts at South Cadbury (W 1933). Specific claims for other areas are infrequent, though Hester Paton Brown devoted three *Children's Hour* programmes to the case for an Arthurian Scotland (S 1935), Monica Marsden recounted the story of *The Knights who Sleep beneath Castle Richmond* (North 1935) and G. Arbour Stevens's *The Fascination of Brechfa* celebrated that Welsh locale as the centre of Merlin's magical control over Britain (Wa 1937), in a programme promoted by a powerful C. W. Bacon illustration in *Radio Times* [**plate 9**].

The lines between fact and fiction, regional pride and patriotic over-enthusiasm were not always clearly determined. In a Welsh language broadcast, for instance, the Reverend J. L. Williams held up Arthur and St David as the two ideals that have shaped Welsh national and religious character, Arthur having 'not only conquered the enemies of Wales, but taught the people to dedicate the national movement to the idea of freedom' (W 1933).

All these concerns were with the Arthur of Britain; the Breton aspect seems to have been ignored. Indeed the sole Continental foray that I have come across is one of Isaac Williams's *Travel Talks on Art* (C 1928), in which he features Innsbruck, and focuses on the statue of King Arthur in the Nine Worthies series there (*Radio Times* supplied the relevant photograph).

## Reading and Adapting 1: Medieval Literature

Medieval Arthurian literature per se received little critical attention on air, a noteworthy exception being Professor Mary Williams's talk on *Geoffrey Arthur, or Geoffrey of Monmouth* (W 1930). Scant scholarly treatment seems to have been awarded to Malory except for Professor James Moffat's brief consideration of Caxton's edition (Glasgow 1927). The *Morte Darthur* was instead given occasional readings. The first occurred in a mixed programme of music and verse, when S. Fowler Wright (already a prolific Arthurian poet himself) recited passages from 'The Tale of Sir Gareth' (B 1924). The other two Malorian excerpts arose in 1928, when an unnamed extract was read by Oliver Baldwin during the interval in Debussy's opera *Pelléas et Mélisande* (L), and the story of 'How King Arthur was wounded in the fight and how he died' was given during an interval in a symphony concert (C).

But Malory was, *pace* J. B. Harker's lament over lost Lyonesse, given considerable prominence in children's programmes until 1930. Since Late-Victorian times abridged book versions had been widely available, and during the 1920s this availability continued, whether through reprints of older editions or in newly

28  *Listener* 16 (9 September 1936), 477–9.

prepared texts for schools or private leisure reading. Some evidence supporting the continuing popularity of Arthur may be found in a source that is fictional but carries the ring of authenticity: Richmal Crompton's bestseller *William – the Bad* (1930). When William, a most unbookish scapegrace hero, is given a copy of *King Arthur and the Knights of the Round Table* as a birthday present from a friend's aunt, he is induced to read it only by a spell of continuously wet weather. By degrees, however, he and his friends are so gripped by the story that they resolve forthwith to set out as knights and go 'rightin' wrongs'.[29] The rest of the novel details their attempts, concluding with the immortally pugnacious sentiment: 'William's only feeling on the matter was one of regret that he never really finished the fight with Pelleas' (p. 259). The BBC added to this stock of juvenile Maloriana not by adapting already published work but by commissioning its own, both for schools (educational) and for *Children's Hour* (fun). Within the first year of broadcasting, *Children's Hour* carried a five-part series, *Legends of King Arthur*, written by the incongruously named Leonard Badman (L June–July 1923). A little later the schools programme followed suit by hosting the Reverend A. Austin Foster's talk on Malory (A 1926). There is evidence besides that production of such programmes was significantly audience-led, for, in a survey asking young listeners what topic they would choose to listen to, 'King Arthur' topped the poll.[30] The outcome was a major serialisation, *Stories of King Arthur* by C. E. Hodges (Uncle Peter), read for *Children's Hour* by Uncle Rex (R. F. Palmer) in fifteen instalments (L 1926). Next year the Mary Williams who was later to give a talk on Geoffrey of Monmouth varied the focus by writing a five-part series for schools on *Heroines of the Arthurian Legends* (Swansea 1927). This was shortly to be supplemented by an eleven-part serialisation of the Arthurian legends (L 1928) as part of a schools programme featuring 'Great Stories from History and Mythology', written by the Director of the Education Section, J. C. Stobart, and Mary Somerville. Soon after, Margaret M. Kennedy (celebrated later as author of *The Constant Nymph*) produced for *Children's Hour* her three-part *Kynge Arthur and Certeyn of his Knights*, which recounted the story of the two swords, the treachery of the Fairy Morgan and the adventures of Sir Launcelot (D 1929). Marjorie Barber then selected three more tales from Malory (Gareth, Elaine, Morte d'Arthur) in a single programme for her schools study of the writer (L 1930), before another significant series was created for *Children's Hour* by Lawrence du Garde Peach, an exceptionally prolific writer of radio drama (for adults and children). Peach wrote a set of five short plays (two featuring Arthur, and one apiece for Launcelot, Balin and Galahad) that were first broadcast by the Western region but then rapidly repeated by London (1930–31). Their success is indicated by the fact that they would also find more permanent form by appearing as an illustrated book in 1940.[31] Curiously, this burst of Malorian radio enthusiasm died away after 1931. For the remainder of the decade I can trace only two similar programmes: *How Lancelot came North*,

---

29  Richmal Crompton, *William – the Bad* (London: Macmillan, 1984 [1930]), pp. 1–2.
30  *Radio Times* (3 December 1926), 562.
31  L. du Garde Peach, *Knights of the Round Table: Five Plays from the Arthurian Legend*, illus. Evelyn Simpson (London: Pitman, 1940).

a story told by 'The Owl' for *Children's Hour* (North 1934), and Rhoda Power's account of Arthur in a schools *World History* series (N 1938). Though this latter is claimed as a 'history', the inclusion of Excalibur and Mordred points to its true character as a dramatisation of Malory.

Arthurian works that predated Malory were heard but, as they presented linguistic problems for most listeners, they were commonly given in very modernised versions. Chaucer's treatment of the Loathly Lady story appeared very early in broadcasting history in a *Children's Hour* adaptation of *The Wife of Bath's Tale* by Leonard Badman (L 1923), and then in Dryden's version, when it was accorded what should have been a fine reading by Edith Evans and Michael Redgrave (L 1931). The language of *Sir Gawain and the Green Knight* posed far greater difficulties. Even though the twentieth-century rehabilitation of the work was under way with Tolkien and Gordon's edition of the text (1925), and a few translations and retellings had already been published, it reached the air only in the guise of juvenile literature, in the form of *Children's Hour* adaptations by Stuart Vinden (M 1937) and Eileen Atherton (Wa 1938).[32]

The strong emphasis on regional broadcasting allowed Wales to play a prominent role in the diffusion of its Arthurian heritage. In addition to the music and talks discussed above, Welsh language broadcasting had enabled Magdalen Morgan to present in *Children's Hour* a three-part version of *The Adventures of Sir Owen* (taken from *The Mabinogion*) and one on *Y Greal Santaidd* (W 1931).[33] Moreover a series of schools programmes was created by T. Rowland Hughes (who was to earn some renown as a novelist), which was later published as *Storïau Mawr y Byd* (1936) and included an account of Arthur and *Y Saint Greal* (adapted from Malory).[34] Hughes's name will recur also in later contexts, but the most remarkable 'Welsh' treatment was in English and by F. O. Miles, a nine-part sequence of burlesque accounts: *Y Mabinogion as modern film producers might see it* (C 1929). Starting with 'The Story of Geraint and Enid as filmed by D. W. Griffith', it went on to 'The Story of Peredur and the Addanc as filmed by Fritz Lang', 'The Story of Peredur as filmed by Douglas Fairbanks' and 'The Story of Blodenwedd as filmed by Cecil B. de Mille'. Not only the loudspeaker but also the film camera had come to Lyonesse.

### Reading and Adapting 2: Post-Medieval Literature

Though Renaissance treatments of the Arthurian legends did not loom very large on radio, and Spenser's *Faerie Queene* was out of high critical favour between the wars, it nonetheless formed the subject of four talks in the 1920s. Two of these were for juveniles: by Marion Henderson in *Children's Corner* (Glasgow 1925) and J. C. Stobart and Mary Somerville in a schools broadcast (L 1928); but more academic talks were given by Miss K. E. Brooks in *Scholars' Half-Hour* (Bo 1925) and Professor A. E. Morgan (Sheffield 1925). Elsewhere, the attraction of its local

---

32  Stuart Vinden, *The Story of Sir Gawayne and the Green Knight*; Eileen Atherton, *Gawayne and the Green Knight*.
33  In all discussions of *The Mabinogion* I consider only the Arthurian tales.
34  T. Rowland Hughes, *Storïau Mawr y Byd* (Aberystwyth, 1936).

historical focus probably decided the production of Eleanor Farjeon's account of *Queen Elizabeth at Kenilworth* (HS [M] 1938), a feature that most likely included some reference to George Gascoigne's *The Princely Pleasures* masque (and its Arthurian personae) that was originally mounted for the royal visit.[35]

Some interest was paid, as has been shown above, to Dryden's *King Arthur*, but this was largely owing to its association with Purcell's music. As for nineteenth-century poetry, it is not very easy to discover what was read on air because *Radio Times* does not always list individual poems. Although John Betjeman (already a well-known broadcaster in the late 1930s) certainly referred to R. S. Hawker's *The Quest of the Sangraal* in his programme on that poet (W 1939), the producer had to impress upon Betjeman that Hawker should not be presented 'as a figure of fun', and the speaker duly toned down his talk.[36] Nonetheless, the excerpt printed in *The Listener* is facetiously titled 'Sermons that ruined the carrot crop', and is concerned only with the eccentricities of Hawker's personal life (posing as a mermaid on the seashore, and so on).[37] It is unknown whether the three programmes on William Morris included any of Morris's fine Arthurian verse (D 1929; N 1930; W 1934). The only Arthurian poet that definitely received regular attention was Alfred Tennyson. His great Victorian reputation may have recently slumped among literary critics, but on radio he seems to have been the most frequently read poet after Shakespeare, which suggests that he remained widely appreciated beyond the avant-garde circles of Bloomsbury and Academia. Among the many Tennyson poems broadcast, many were Arthurian. A literary ballad such as 'The Lady of Shalott' proved, of course, a congenial form for radio presentation and well suited for lady elocutionists. As Muriel Spark's novel reminds us, Miss Brodie recited it in the late afternoon to her Edinburgh pupils of the 1930s 'to raise their minds before they went home'.[38] On air the poem was not only recited by Norah Campbell (Belfast 1925), Gladys Ward (D 1928) and Enid Hewitt (S 1934), but it was 'declaimed' by Marian Taylor to music by Wilfred Bendall (Ne 1925), arranged for three voices by Peter Slade (M 1937) and set variously to music by Christopher Edmunds and C. Armstrong Gibbs. Moreover, The Lady (or her alter-ego, Elaine of Astolat) served as inspiration for commonly heard orchestral works by MacDowell, Boughton, Dunhill, Wright, Spain-Dunk and Davis. She was, in fact, a vivid Arthurian icon for the times. Even more surprisingly, in view of the hostility of contemporary academic critics, *Idylls of the King* was not neglected either, for selections were broadcast on at least thirteen occasions. The choice of *Idyll* was quite varied: three apiece came from 'Gareth and Lynette' and 'Morte d'Arthur', two apiece from 'Guinevere' and 'The Coming of Arthur', and three from unnamed idylls. Only three of these programmes were aimed at children, consequently the typical audience was adult, as indeed it was for 'The Lady of Shalott'. Since very little other

---

35  It is possible that L. du Garde Peach's *Children's Hour* play, *Kenilworth Castle* (R 1936), also included some mention of Gascoigne's masque. However, L. Edith Thomas's *Kenilworth Castle: The Round Table* (HS [M] 1939) dealt instead with a quasi-Arthurian tournament of 1279. This was an episode from her lively script for an historical pageant being mounted at Kenilworth that week.

36  Bevis Hillier, *John Betjeman: New Fame, New Love* (London: John Murray, 2002), p. 155.

37  *Listener* 21 (23 February 1939), 407–8.

38  Muriel Spark, *The Prime of Miss Jean Brodie* (Harmondsworth: Penguin, 1965 [1961]), p. 21.

Arthurian verse seems to have been recorded in *Radio Times*, Tennyson emerges as the sole English survivor in the early twentieth century's reaction against Victorianism and Pre-Raphaelitism.

In broadcast twentieth-century verse merely a few Arthurian traces remained, and these were in Welsh. Not only was the key modern Welsh Arthurian poem, Thomas Gwynn Jones's *Ymadawiad Arthur* [The Passing of Arthur], heard frequently in a musical setting (see above) but the verse itself received a rare radio tribute by Frank Eames, when he recalled hearing that poem and Robert Silyn Roberts's *Trystan ac Esyllt* at the National *Eisteddfod* in 1902 (W 1936). Extracts from a later *Eisteddfod* winner, the Reverend William Morris's *Ogof Arthur* [Arthur's Cave], were also broadcast (W 1934).

As for the Arthurian novel, only two items are of note. The first, and minor one, was a talk by Ifan Kyrle Fletcher on the Welsh associations of Thomas Love Peacock (C 1928), which most probably incorporated some discussion of his Arthurian novel, *The Misfortunes of Elphin*. The second, and more significant, was the serialisation of T. H. White's *The Sword in the Stone* within a year of publication (N June–July 1939). Marianne Helwig made a six-part dramatisation, and Benjamin Britten (who liked the novel) was engaged to write incidental music. The part of Merlyn was acted by Robert Farquharson, Wart by Robin Maule, and Archimedes the Owl by Carleton Hobbs. Produced by John Cheatle, it was transmitted on Sundays at just after five o'clock, thereby targeting largely a young and/or family audience. Evidently promoted as a star attraction by the BBC, it was signalled by a series of closely illustrative line engravings by Robin Jacques every week in *Radio Times* [**plate 10**]. Like Britten, Jacques admired the novel, remembering it as 'imaginative and different'.[39] The major twentieth-century Arthurian work of prose fiction had thus gained early and distinguished recognition on radio.

## Reading and Adapting 3: Drama

The BBC's Drama department (headed by Val Gielgud – the brother of John – from 1928) was one of the corporation's chief artistic strengths. Following a policy of broadcasting plays that had already been presented in the conventional theatre, its scope ranging from Shakespeare to contemporary European drama, it employed a distinguished repertory company of actors (supplemented by guest stars), and its audience was wide. Among the plays selected, a few were Arthurian. The first of these was Stephen Phillips's *Paolo and Francesca*, which qualifies as 'Arthurian' because the eponymous lovers confess their mutual love while reading the story of Launcelot and Guenevere.[40] First produced (highly successfully) in 1902, it may be regarded as Very-Late-Romantic in character, and it was therefore rather an old-fashioned choice for radio performance, a

---

[39] Driver, *The Art of 'Radio Times'*, p. 112.
[40] Stephen Phillips, *Paolo and Francesca: A Tragedy in Four Acts* (London: John Lane The Bodley Head, 1899).

reminder of the then conservatism of the medium.[41] Slightly shortened to just under an hour and a half, it was provided with incidental music by Percy Pitt (L 20 June 1928). Within a year another play on the same theme was broadcast: D'Annunzio's *Francesca da Rimini*, in an English translation by Arthur Symons (L 13 March 1929).[42] More colourful, passionate and violent than Phillips's play, it is also much more 'Arthurian'. The audience here is well prepared for the crucial reading, as a jester had earlier told the tales of Arthur and the Round Table to the court at Rimini, where a room was frescoed with the story of Tristan's fatal love; and a copy of the Lancelot book that had been left prominently open on the set at the Malatesta court was read by Francesca to her ladies. *Radio Times* made sure that listeners would not miss the allusions, either, by providing a summary and a reproduction of Dante Gabriel Rossetti's watercolour of the lovers' first kiss. The BBC would return to this story in 1938, when Zandonai's opera, based on D'Annunzio's play, was performed (see above).

In contrast to these studio productions, the BBC also provided outside relays. Among them was a broadcast from Malvern, in Worcestershire, of Henry Fielding's *Tom Thumb the Great*, performed by Sir Barry Jackson's Malvern Festival Company, produced by H. K. Aycliff, and with an arrangement by Ernest Irving of the original music. Allowed a running time of over two hours, this would doubtless have been a very competent performance in terms of both acting and music, as Ernest Thesiger, a leading actor, starred as King Arthur, and Herbert Carruthers conducted the orchestra (M 11 August 1932).

In marked contrast to Fielding's eighteenth-century burlesque, toward the end of the period the Welsh Regional Service mounted another signal revival: two dramas by Ernest Rhys that were much closer in spirit to Phillips and D'Annunzio. Originally staged in 1908 but newly adapted for radio by Dafydd Gruffydd, *Enid: A Lyrical Play* and *The Quest of the Grail* were broadcast on 27 November 1937 and 19 April 1938 respectively, both with the music by Vincent Thomas that had accompanied their London premières.

## Making it New

Although the main thrust of BBC Drama was to transfer works from the conventional theatre, it also commissioned pieces written specifically for radio. One of the most notable works introduced in this way was a play prepared for broadcasting by Alice M. Buckton. After some years of teaching and writing in London, Buckton had settled in Glastonbury in 1913 on buying the Chalice Well. She had arrived there at about the same time as Boughton, and co-operated with him in his first Festival, but their relations were uneasy and they soon parted artistic company. Whereas Boughton moved around the country periodically, and left Glastonbury for ever in 1927, she made the place her home until shortly before her death in 1944, and was very influential in restoring the

---

[41] J. P. Waring, *The London Stage 1900–1909: A Calendar of Plays and Players*, 2 vols (Metuchen, N.J. and London: Scarecrow Press, 1981), 1: 147.

[42] Gabriele D'Annunzio, *Francesca da Rimini*, translated by Arthur Symons (London: Heinemann, 1902).

town as a religious and cultural base, establishing a hostel, and developing an arts-and-crafts centre, besides writing and staging masques, mysteries and pageants. Notwithstanding her interest in ancient forms of drama, she was also instrumental in making a film, *The History of Glastonbury*, for which she wrote a scenario presenting the town's development by means of a pageant. Though the film proved technically inadequate, it is interesting to see her then turning her creative energies to the new technology of radio, and creating the first Arthurian play designed for the medium. Her scheme was ambitious and employed music specially written by Warwick Braithwaite, the conductor of the Cardiff Station Orchestra (and later conductor of the National Orchestra of Wales). The play was called *Arthurian Legends 1. The Wooing of Guinevere* (C 28 June 1925), and was performed by the 5WA Radio Players and the Station SO conducted by Braithwaite. Sadly no record survives of the text, but a useful plot outline was printed in *Radio Times*:

| I | 'The Lament of Uther' | Braithwaite |
|---|---|---|
| Scene 1 | Woman's Bower in Camelot | |
| Scene 2 | Council Chamber at Camelot | |
| Scene 3 | Outside Castle Gates of Camelot | |
| | Arthur in his tent | |
| II | 'Merlin' | Braithwaite |
| Scene 4 | The Queen's Apartments, Camelot | |
| Scene 5 | Arthur receives Guinevere in the Forest | |
| Scene 6 | On the shore of the Isle of Avalon | |
| | Sailors await the arrival of the King and Queen newly wedded | |
| III | 'Arthur' | Braithwaite |
| Scene 7 | Arthur takes Guinevere to the Mountain Height of Avalon | |
| Scene 8 | Arthur brings Guinevere into the Royal Palace at Wedmore | |
| IV | 'Guinevere' | Braithwaite |

According to a preview in *The Western Mail*, Buckton had planned a series of six works on this theme to be given at monthly intervals.[43] No trace is extant, however, of these intended sequels, but in the following year Braithwaite conducted a performance of his own *Prelude, 'Excalibur'* (C 1926), a work that may be related to either the above work or a sequel, and Buckton later contributed an item, 'Avalon: An Arthurian Legend', to a concert entitled *Legend Land* that was conducted by Braithwaite and included works by Wagner and Boughton (C 16 February 1928).[44]

Buckton's high seriousness found no immediate successor. Original plays in the main clutch that followed were short and intended for children. Three selected Gareth as hero: Dorothy Eaves's *Gareth: The Welsh Boy who Became a Knight* (C 3 July 1930), Dorothy Champion's *Fairhands: A Play about Gareth, Prince of Orkney* (W 23 January 1931) and Basil Ashmore's *Sir Gareth the Fair* (N 21 September 1938). The latter play freely acknowledges its debt to Tennyson's

---

[43] *Western Mail* (27 June 1925), 13.
[44] It may also be related to Braithwaite's opera *Pendragon*, which he had completed by 1939. See Donald Brook, *Conductors' Gallery* (London: Rockliff, 1945), p. 32.

*Idylls*, while Carmen's attractive illustration in *Radio Times* suggests a comple-mentary Pre-Raphaelite ambience [plate 11]. Three other pieces took their inspi-ration from folklore. M. Melville Balfour's *The Watcher of the West* was 'a tale of Cornwall and King Arthur' (W 27 June 1935) while both T. Rowland Hughes's Welsh play, *Ogof Arthur* (Arthur's Cave) (W 15 August 1934), and a King Arthur episode ('The Caves') in the young Christopher Fry's serial *The Tall Hill* (R 3 December 1939), seem to have taken up the Sleeping King motif.

Another group used the Arthurian legend as an object of burlesque humour. Dorothy Worsley, a Welshwoman writing in English (and married to a BBC variety producer), is the main figure here. She invented a new knight, Sir Goahead, and gave him a serially adventurous career, such as fending off a giant in hobnail boots to rescue a beauteous damsel, and encountering a dragon 'with a pynke spotted necktye' (W 1933). These exploits were then either adapted or extended by Worsley into a one-hour play for an adult audience, *The Adven-tures of Sir Goahead*, which told how the gallant knight was banished from 'Ye Table Rounde and meeteth ye speckled sea serpente', all of which was ironically billed as 'another unpardonable intrusion of *The Children's Hour* into the evening Programme' (W 9 March 1934). Lewis Hart provided an appropriate drawing for *Radio Times* [plate 12].

Continuing to work this seam, Worsley presented a series of 'Legendary Lampoons For Your Amusement', the first of which was *King Arthur and Ye Table Rounde*, a 'Musical Distortion' featuring music by Mai Jones (W 19 February 1937). The quality of Worsley's prolific work was often privately questioned by her BBC employers for not being 'of the desired standard', and 'not ideal for *Children's Hour*'.[45] She was accused of culling her jokes 'from stock sources', she used too much alliteration, her work had 'a suggestion of cheapness ....' On the other hand, it did 'seem to be fairly popular', and *Children's Hour* organisers complained that it was 'extremely difficult to get comic stuff at all'. Though they tried to limit her contributions to one a month, they continued to employ her for many years to come. According to BBC files she was also paid for her contribu-tion to a comparable skit by Mary Cardew and Peter Lonsdale in the episode devoted to 'King Arthur and his Knights' within their *Tale Twisting* series, though *Radio Times* does not record her contribution to this (R 27 February 1936).

A number of programmes by other hands flirted with the concept of Merlin as sage or mage.[46] Naunton Davies's one-act comedy, for example, bestowed his name on a tailor in *The Village Wizard* (C 21 October 1929), and a like playfulness of fancy informs Henrik Ege's *Depression Over Fairyland*, for which Eric Fraser provided a fitting illustration (N 11 September 1931, repeated 1933). Doubtless, however, Ege would claim that a serious message was intended. Described in *Radio Times* as a 'fantasy' with music by Robert Chignell, the theme is that Fairy-land is suffering from an economic downturn because modern children are more interested in technology than in fairies:

---

45  BBC WAC: Dorothy Worsley file.
46  See 'Merlin', a story (Newcastle 1925), 'Merlin', a legendary story (?) (Newcastle 1926); and Cassius's talk 'The Message of Merlin' (P 1925). Merlin (E. Whitnall) answered questions in the *Why?* series (N 1935), and there was a *Children's Hour* programme by Helen M. Enoch named *Magic in the Air: From Merlin to Aladdin* (M 1935).

Babes of four with clockwork brains
Make their parents buy them trains;
Fairy tales they do not understand.
When we hope to catch them dreaming
They are wide awake and screaming.
Times are very bad in Fairyland.

Among the dramatis personae is listed the Head Wizard to King Oberon, named
Merlin (Stuart Robertson). As in so many other allusions to him in this period
he is probably treated as a slightly comic figure. I assume – no script is extant
– that he will, however, assert his magical power to demonstrate the supremacy
of Imagination over drab mercantile reality. For a less humorous treatment we
must turn to another product of the Cardiff studio, *Tristram*, a forty-minute
dramatisation of the legend. This included some music from Wagner, but was
largely the work of Charles Fisher, a young journalist from Swansea (R [Wa] 10
December 1937). Produced by T. Rowland Hughes, it had added point in acting
as preview for an upcoming *Eisteddfod* whose chair poem would have Tristram
and Iseult for theme.

But the period's greatest Arthurian venture had an even wider significance. In
1936 D. G. Bridson, a major BBC writer-producer, was preparing a new play on
the theme of the Round Table for presentation at Christmas. As incidental music
was required, an offer was made to Arnold Bax, presumably on the strength of
his *Tintagel*, but Bax declined because he did 'not want to have to work at all
strenuously' as he felt 'rather tired musically'.[47] Rutland Boughton was then
approached, who said he liked the script, but was wary about spending too
much time on music that would be unsuitable for later concert performances.[48]
Bridson tried to win him over by suggesting that music from Boughton's Arthurian operas could be recycled into this play, but no agreement was reached, and
eventually the commission was handed to Benjamin Britten, his first from the
BBC. In the meantime it had been decided to hold the programme over until the
following year, so Bridson used the breathing space to adopt 'a more ambitious
treatment'. The completed play would consist of eighteen scenes, each prefaced
by a verse link, cover the Arthurian story from the Sword in the Stone until
the Last Battle, be produced by Val Gielgud, and employ a distinguished cast
including Leon Quartermaine (Arthur), Esmé Percy (Merlin), Michael Redgrave
(Galahad), with Robert Farquharson and Ion Swinley as narrators.[49] Incidental
music would be performed by the London SO and BBC Chorus conducted by
Clarence Raybould. The event was signalled in *Radio Times* by a rousing James
R. Hart illustration [plate 13] and a full-page article by Bridson, who claims that
his play combines the historical Arthur with the poetic, and will 'give a new
significance to the stories of both'. *King Arthur* was broadcast on 23 April 1937
(N) and repeated the following night (R).

Bridson was an experienced writer for radio, and his treatment was in many

---

47  Foreman, *Bax*, p. 307.
48  BBC WAC: Bridson file.
49  BBC WAC: typed playscript of D. G. Bridson, 'King Arthur'.

ways very well devised. Aware that such a play lasting an hour and a half not only needed the support offered by excellent music but also differing methods of narrative, he alternates between prose for the dramatic scenes and various verse forms, spoken by four different narrators, for the linking passages. Later Bridson expressed his great satisfaction with Britten's contribution, but the composer did not reciprocate. His diary records that, although he feels his music 'comes off like hell', he was highly irritated by the actual play:

> its stilted dialogue, a pale pastiche of Malory – its dull Tennysonian poetry, & not nearly as good as that either – and its complete divorce from realities or humanities.[50]

Britten's dismissal of both the style and the content of the play has some justification. He is right about the dullness of the Malorian prose scenes, and there are certainly many echoes of Tennyson (and William Morris) present: from the latter's 'The Defence of Guenevere', for example, Bridson borrows the Queen's parable about having to choose between two differently coloured cloths (pp. 46–7). But elsewhere the verse is usually more varied than Britten suggests. It opens with a bold assertion of Bridson's:

> Time lays no finger upon the flowers of honour,
> Rust shall not arrogate their glittering armour
> Who, in the clear pursuit of righteousness, played well their part.   (p. 1)

This passage, repeated twice at key moments later in the play, supplies a thematic counterpoint to the play's main thrust – the dangers of pride. Unlike Tennyson, who portrays a blameless king, Bridson sees Arthur rather than Guenevere as the prime agent of Camelot's destruction. Not only does he sin with the wives of his enemies, while hypocritically prompt to have his wife burnt alive, naked, and in public, but he is also fatally flawed with the sin of pride. This pride is symbolised in a highly original (and effective) scene where Arthur unsheathes Excalibur and flamboyantly discards the scabbard to signify his defiant declaration of war against Rome. As a narrator later comments:

> The scabbard of the King, and all the virtue
> Merlin had said of it, is flung aside.
> But thoughtless disregard sets little store
> By Merlin or his counsel, as the pride
> Of boundless power spurs the King on, and will
> To conquer throws discretion to the flame
> Of wild ambition, as all prudence falls
> Prey to a ravening appetite for fame.   (p. 20)

It is odd that Britten (who shared Bridson's pro-appeasement policies) thought the work completely divorced 'from realities', for the play is blatantly designed to reflect the politics of the contemporary European crisis. Its action is over-

---

[50] *Letters from a Life: The Selected Letters and Diaries of Benjamin Britten 1913–1976*, ed. Donald Mitchell and Philip Reed, 2 vols (London: Faber & Faber, 1991), 1: 486.

shadowed by the question of the morality of war. Arthur is a bluff imperialist whose overweening pride leads Britain into an unjustifiable foreign campaign against Rome, thereby inducing his impoverished people to enlist only 'to better poverty in the fortunes / Of a successful and outrageous war' (p. 20), the sad result being to bring his people to 'death in worthless causes' (p. 60). Contemporary appeasement arguments are surely placed in the mouth of the hermit who declares, 'Your quarrel is unjust and your war unhallowed. … Defence of liberty is just, Arthur, but never a war of conquest' (pp. 21–2). Moreover, Bridson's play was broadcast just before the coronation of King George VI (12 May 1937), an event brought about by the sudden abdication of Edward VIII: the programming on St *George's* Day had acquired additional significance. Bridson therefore contrives to be not only a critic of Arthur but also patriotic and royalist, distinguishing between an errant monarch and a virtuous. His play has two coronation scenes (the first in London, and a very detailed later one in Rome), both of which adumbrate the 1937 occasion (the first British coronation to be broadcast on radio); and the play's closing promise of an Arthurian Second Coming evidently looks forward to the new reign of George VI, who will preach a gospel of peace rather than war:

> But as another King, I shall come – a King who shall rule justly and righteously, and who shall restore to our great country its ancient freedom, its ancient happiness.   (p. 61)

The play had faults. As with many similar works, it attempts to compress too much of the vast Arthurian story into ninety minutes, but its greatest weakness is the uneasy balance between Malory and modernity. This is accurately pinpointed by Grace Wyndham Goldie's review in *The Listener*.[51] Though she found the work 'impressive', and particularly admired Farquharson's 'magnificent delivery of the ringing verse description' of Lancelot's escape from Guenevere's tower, she thought Bridson had fatally compromised in his approach. Three-quarters of the play was a rehash of Malory's narrative, with its concomitant ethic, while the remainder tried to endow the material with a modern ethical viewpoint and a contemporary significance. Moreover the Grail episodes appeared a tedious distraction from the main story. All this gave the work 'a curious unevenness of texture'.

When attempting to secure Boughton's co-operation, Bridson had held out the prospect that the play would pass into the 'classic' stage and, revived annually, would attract an audience of ten million listeners a year. This did not ensue. Britten's incidental music has been turned into an orchestral suite and is heard again on modern radio, but the broadcast play has never been repeated, and the text languishes in the archives at Caversham. Two reasons suggest themselves for this total neglect. The first is that Bridson's version was rapidly overtaken, and outclassed, by the appearance of T. H. White's *The Sword in the Stone* (1938). The second is that the onset of the Second World War made Bridson's

---

[51]  Grace Wyndham Goldie, 'Broadcast Drama: King Arthur', *Listener* 17 (28 April 1937), 12.

pro-appeasement play seem outdated and out of touch with the heightened military mood of the country. A new spirit in Arthurian drama was required, and this need was rapidly met by the timely commissioning of Clemence Dane's *The Saviours* (see Chapter 2).

# 2

## 1940–1959: 'The envy of the world'

### Music

The Second World War curtailed BBC broadcasting of Wagnerian opera immensely as the composer was regarded with deep political disfavour in Britain. Between 1940 and 1945 *Radio Times* lists only half-a-dozen excerpts from *Tristan*, and an irreverent comedy sketch by Bernard Miles, *The Truth about Tristan* (F 1941). *Parsifal* fared slightly better in that a one-hour concert version by the BBC SO under Sir Adrian Boult was broadcast on Good Friday 1940, and lengthy excerpts conducted by Sir Henry Wood in the following year, but otherwise only about eight short excerpts were listed on air during the war years. And even if the BBC had been willing to relay these operas from Bayreuth, they could not have done so because neither was staged there during those years, the only operas performed there during the war being *The Ring* and *The Flying Dutchman*. Moreover, production at Bayreuth was then suspended for the first five years of peace.[1]

The BBC was not, though, entirely baulked by this hiatus, for the new Third Programme (extolled as 'the envy of the world') soon exercised its designated artistic freedom from strict programme scheduling.[2] This meant that it could broadcast a whole opera or play regardless of length. It accordingly mounted its first *studio* performance of *Tristan*, which was sung in German, with Marjorie Lawrence as Isolde and Arthur Carron as Tristan, and was conducted by Sir Thomas Beecham (24 October 1946). This broadcast was cursorily dismissed by W. R. Anderson ('so much of the singing was unsteady that I found it hard to enjoy the texture'), and Dyneley Hussey had a few reservations, because the cuts made followed the practice of the stage, and were inappropriate for radio; but though the soloists would perhaps have struggled on the Covent Garden stage, he believed that their performance on radio was excellent, and the orchestral playing was superb.[3] Thereafter, expensive foreign relays were routinely set up for *Tristan*, live from Zurich under Hans Knappertsbusch, with Kirsten Flagstad

---

[1]  Geoffrey Skelton, *Wagner at Bayreuth: Experiment and Tradition* (London: Barrie & Rockcliff, 1965).
[2]  A former BBC producer, Peter Laslett, used this phrase in 1977. It was later quoted as epigraph, and adopted as book title, in Humphrey Carpenter, *The Envy of the World: Fifty Years of the BBC Third Programme and Radio 3, 1946–1996* (London: Weidenfeld & Nicolson, 1996), p. v. The 'world' may well have been envious, but in Britain only about 2 per cent of listeners tuned in to the Third.
[3]  W. R. Anderson, 'Round About Radio', *Musical Times* 87 (December 1946), 371. Dyneley Hussey, 'Broadcast Music', *Listener* 36 (31 October 1946), 608–9.

as Isolde, singing 'with more emotional expression than of old' (TP 5–8 June 1947), and again, under Otto Ackermann (TP 26 June 1949), while *Parsifal* was recorded from Cologne under Richard Kraus (TP 2 January 1950, repeated 31 March).[4]

This last mentioned was the production that led Dyneley Hussey to aver that listening to a radio performance could be more enjoyable than attending one at the theatre.[5] Nearer to home, *Parsifal* was twice performed again at Easter by the BBC SO under Boult (HS 4 April 1947 and 13 April 1949). *Radio Times* illustrations were provided by Tom Poulton [plate 14] for the first, and by Dorothea Braby for the second.

From then on, the BBC covered all the Covent Garden productions of these two operas: *Tristan* in 1950, 1951, 1953 and 1958; and *Parsifal* in 1951 (when Kirsten Flagstad took the role of Kundry) and 1959 (for which Eric Fraser supplied a compelling *Radio Times* drawing [plate 15]).

Moreover, as soon as post-war activity was resumed at Bayreuth – even though radio could not adequately convey a sense of the radically new stage sets introduced there by Wieland Wagner – the BBC broadcast recordings of the 1951, 1952, 1954 and 1956 festival performances of *Parsifal* (the great conducting era of Knappertsbusch), and the 1952, 1953 and 1957 (twice) performances of *Tristan*. A 1955 production of *Tristan* by the Stuttgart State Orchestra at the Royal Festival Hall, London, was also slotted in. *Radio Times* and *The Listener* continued to provide authoritative critiques, a notable example being Martin Cooper's talk suggesting that the new Bayreuth productions, which stripped Wagner of his nationalist fustian and 'misleading theatrical façade', had surprisingly revealed his work to have greater spiritual significance and a more 'universal validity' than had previously been apparent.[6] Considerable publicity continued to be given to Wagner, too, by means of previews and reviews, such as Hans Keller's '*Tristan* and the Realism of Adolescence', which preceded its musical analysis by tracing the opera's influence on a recent film, *The Young Lions*, wherein Marlon Brando is seduced by the wife of his C.O. to the strains of *Tristan*.[7] However, overall BBC policy was now modified: Wagnerian opera was broadcast more often in its entirety, but far fewer extracts were played than in pre-war days.

Extracts from Purcell continued throughout the war at roughly the previous rate and, shortened to an hour and a quarter, Herbage's arrangement of the whole opera was presented in a studio production by Stephen Potter in 1943. This employed a text reshaped by Clifford Bax. McNaught found this solution unsatisfactory, believing that the best method would be to 'scrap Dryden, except for a few verses that have become wedded to famous tunes, and somehow or other work the musical numbers into an entirely new drama or verbal pageant'.[8]

---

4    Dyneley Hussey, 'Broadcast Music', *Listener* 37 (12 June 1947), 931–2.
5    Hussey, 'Parsifal', 83.
6    Martin Cooper, 'Wagner as Christian or Jungian Myth: Reflections after Bayreuth' (TP, 26 January 1959): reprinted in *Listener* 61 (29 January 1959), 216–17.
7    Hans Keller, 'Tristan and the Realism of Adolescence', *Listener* 59 (5 June 1958), 957. Keller would soon become a very important figure in the BBC's Music Department. By 1977 he could claim that he had been 'in charge of more or less everything, with the sole exception of opera': quoted in Carpenter, *Envy of the World*, p. 198.

Reductions of the dramatic text would prove the norm. Though J. A. Westrup's seminal study of Purcell (1937) had argued that *King Arthur* was 'a singularly satisfying work' and needed a stage presentation, for a concert performance without the dialogue was 'ridiculous and meaningless', and though the opera was staged twice in the post-war years (Cambridge 1949, Nottingham 1956), neither production was broadcast, presumably because both were by amateurs.[9] Instead the BBC relayed four concert versions. The fullest of these was conducted by Constant Lambert, and included the speaking roles of Arthur (Ralph Truman) and Merlin (Felix Felton) together with a narration by Derek Hart. For this broadcast Third Programme allocated a generous two hours, though W. R. Anderson noted the omission of the 'famous hit at parsons and tithe in the harvest song' (TP 23 January 1949).[10] Thereafter, the customary curtailment was enacted. This policy found support in Arthur Jacobs, whose review of the Cambridge production urged the need for 'a simplified performing edition' that would sacrifice 'some reverence for the text'.[11] W. Gillies Whittaker and Jane Dawkins, too, regarded the whole work as 'too fantastic and bombastic to be staged today'.[12] Accordingly their new edition in 1951, which was aimed at the needs of 'Schools, Girls' Clubs and Women's Institutes, and Youth Clubs', rearranged and revised Dryden's text in order to reshape it as an operetta. Meanwhile on air, Herbage's version at the Albert Hall (HS 21 February 1951), a performance that ran for an hour and a half, was prefaced by Herbage's full-page article in *Radio Times* explaining that he had on this occasion dispensed with the two narrators, and slimmed down Dryden's text to focus on Purcell's masque scenes.[13] This was a mistake in the view of Arthur Jacobs:

> it would have been better to preserve some semblance of dramatic representation – if necessary, by having a new narration written, suitable for declamation between the items by an actor in the role of Chorus.[14]

The 1953 performance under Anthony Bernard (TP 6 June) ran to only an hour and three-quarters, and again highlighted the Purcell component, but in Herbage's 1959 version (HS 17 June) the suggestion by Jacobs seems to have been taken up, and a linking narration was commissioned from the poet Louis MacNeice (a major BBC producer-writer). MacNeice apparently tackled it 'in the spirit of, and with some textual debts to, Dryden', and his narration, according to Herbage, 'set the seal of success on the performance, … every critic picked it out as the high spot of the evening'.[15] And it was indeed to be widely used in future.

8   W. McNaught, 'Broadcast Music', *Listener* 29 (13 May 1943), 580–1.
9   J. A. Westrup, *Purcell* (London: Dent, 1937), pp. 136–7.
10  W. R. Anderson, 'Round About Radio', *Musical Times* 90 (March 1949), 83.
11  Arthur Jacobs, 'King Arthur at Cambridge', *Musical Times* 90 (September 1949), 326–7.
12  *King Arthur and the Saxons: An Operetta or Cantata by Henry Purcell*. Designed and arranged by W. Gillies Whittaker and Jane Dawkins (London: Oxford University Press, 1951), p. [i].
13  Julian Herbage, 'King Arthur, or the British Worthy', *Radio Times* (16 February 1951), 11.
14  Arthur Jacobs, 'The BBC's King Arthur', *Musical Times* 92 (April 1951), 182–3.
15  'A Restoration Gloss on King Arthur', *The Times* (18 June 1959), 15. BBC WAC: MacNeice file, letter from Herbage to MacNeice. A later critic would, though, think it an 'unfortunate

However, this opera was prized for more than aesthetic criteria. Highly regarded as a very British piece in both composition and subject matter, *King Arthur* was often treated as a national icon. The wartime production of 1943, for example, went out significantly on 3 May, which was marked as the official St George's Day that year, with the *Radio Times* cover promoting the performance by displaying Eric Fraser's very martial image of a majestically defiant Arthur. Continued performance, too, of 'Fairest Isle' during the war surely signalled a comparably patriotic intent. The 1951 production at the Albert Hall, given by the BBC SO under Boult, chimed in neatly with the Festival of Britain held later that year. Recordings from this performance were played eight times a day at the Festival itself throughout the summer, because BBC Television Pavilion chose to illustrate its modern studio procedure with a model transmission of extracts from *King Arthur*, using costume and scene designs by Michael Ayrton, and with speaking roles for Michael Hordern as King Arthur, Geoffrey Wincott as Merlin, and Noel Dryden, a descendant of the poet, as John Dryden.[16] In complementary fashion, the 1953 performance was a flagship event scheduled for the week of Queen Elizabeth II's coronation, and at the 'Land of Hope and Glory' concert given on Coronation Day, Jennifer Vyvyan sang 'Fairest Isle'. (The Arthurian echoes of this royal event were still ringing the next day in Gilbert Harding's follow-up programme, *And now it's over*, when James Robertson Justice would read a story about the coronation of King Arthur at Pentecost [HS 3 June 1953].)

Boughton's operatic ventures received much less attention. *Bethlehem* earned a wartime performance (1941), but only a couple of excerpts were played from *The Queen of Cornwall* until the whole opera was revived in 1950 by the BBC Opera Chorus and Orchestra, conducted by Stanford Robinson, with Sylvia Fisher (Iseult) and Denis Dowling (Tristram) (TP 24 February). Reviewing the year's broadcasts for a Penguin musical guidebook, the composer Harry Dexter commended the opera as 'a remarkably fine work', and regretted that it was no longer performed on stage.[17] The *Musical Times* reviewer, too, was very warm in its praise. This 'tuneful, straight-hitting work' sounded even better than it had done 'in the gallant Glastonbury days', he thought.[18] 'The composer's bold sweep and graphic show seemed to exhilarate his singers, by whom he was hearteningly served.' Further assessment of the gallant Glastonbury days was to be provided some four years later, when Boughton's entire achievement at the Glastonbury Festival from 1914 to 1926 was made the subject of a fifty-five-minute programme on the Home Service's West region (11 May 1954).

A notable wartime performance took place of Maurice Jacobson's choral setting, *The Lady of Shalott, for tenor, chorus and orchestra*. Composed in 1942, it received its broadcast première by the Sale and District Musical Society conducted by Clarence Raybould (HS 29 January 1944). The piece drew praise

---

solution' because of the constant interruptions from a narration that was alien to the music's style and often too mocking in tone (*Times*, 5 November 1964, p. 16).
16 BBC WAC: T14/440.
17 Harry Dexter, 'Music Over the Air', in *Music 1951*, ed. Ralph Hill (Harmondsworth: Penguin, 1951), pp. 220–32 (p. 226).
18 W. R. Anderson, 'Round About Radio', *Musical Times* 91 (March 1950), 100.

from eminent critics of the day, both Thomas Dunhill and Eric Blom claiming that Jacobson was the first prominent composer to tackle Tennyson's poem success-fully.[19] Intriguingly, too, a dance tune by Frederick Curzon, called *Lancelot Two-Step*, made its appearance in a show by Phil Cardew and his Orchestra (LP 1951). But generally the performance of most other English Arthurian works dwin-dled. Wright's *Tintagel Suite* was apparently given no wartime listing (doubtless the brass bands were more pressingly engaged) and Bax's *Tintagel* was neglected in the early post-war years, performances picking up again only in the mid-1950s. The 'King Arthur' ballads enjoyed a wave of popularity in the early 1940s (perhaps their ebullience matched the national mood), but were little heard later. Most light Arthurian music, in the style of Dunhill, Mayerl or the Tennysonian and Welsh songs, underwent a similar decline.

But if British light music wilted, greater attention was now paid by the Third Programme to work from further afield, both operatic and orchestral. For example, Zandonai's opera *Francesca da Rimini* was heard again, this time on gramophone records from an Italian radio recording conducted by Antonio Guarnieri (TP 25 May 1954). Music Department was demonstrating pioneering qualities by giving, for instance, a first broadcast performance to an English translation by Clifton Helliwell of Frank Martin's dramatic oratorio *Le Vin herbé*, which was based on Joseph Bédier's version of the Tristan legend, and combined serial technique with Late-Romantic tonality (23 January 1948).[20] It was similarly adventurous in broadcasting a performance of Joseph Guy Ropartz's *La Chasse du Prince Arthur* (1948), by a Dutch orchestra conducted by Charles Münch, and in awarding an English première by the BBC SO under Boult to Paul Ladmirault's 'Prelude: *Tristan and Iseult*', which had been written some twenty years earlier for a dramatisation of Bédier by Louis Artus (24 September 1949). Even more significantly it relayed Olivier Messiaen's towering *Turangalîla Symphony* from its first performance in Britain (26 June 1953), followed by a talk on the work by Felix Aprahamian. A useful reminder of the BBC's bravery in welcoming the revolutionary piece is unwittingly supplied by Anderson's very hostile review of it. Messiaen was, he claimed, a 'deadly bore', his symphony a 'childish to-do'.[21] The first *public* performance in Britain followed a year later and was also broadcast (TP 12 April 1954).

What is more, the BBC could claim responsibility for creating new Arthurian music by the commissioning of Phyllis Tate's cantata *The Lady of Shalott* to mark the tenth anniversary of the Third Programme. Though played without a break, her work consists of four sections: a Prologue marked *Allegretto simplice*; a *Moto perpetuo* for the Lady's weaving; an *Alla marcia* for the arrival of Lancelot; and a *Barcarolle*, in which the viola makes its first appearance, leading into an Epilogue.[22] Premièred on 24 October 1956, under the direction of Walter Goehr, Tate's setting for tenor, viola, two pianos, celesta and percussion received, however,

[19] Cited in article (December 2005) by Julian and Michael Jacobson on 'Maurice Jacobson' website: musicweb-international.com.

[20] Joseph Bédier, *Le Roman de Tristan et Iseult* (Paris, 1900).

[21] W. R. Anderson, 'Round About Radio', *Musical Times* 94 (August 1953), 359–60.

[22] Information from Alan Frank's programme notes for the performance at the King's Lynn Festival, 24 July 1961: *Eleventh Festival Programme, 22 to 29 July* (King's Lynn, 1961), p. 21.

mixed reviews. *Musical Times*, seeing no need for a setting of Tennyson's 'pale romance', believed the result merely parodied Britten. *The Times*, too, objected to the choice of poem, and found the word-setting 'not always effective', but conceded that the texture was consistently attractive. Most positive was *The Listener*, which, while admitting that the shape of Tennyson's verses 'seems to be a handicap', praised Tate's imagination and her 'assured handling of a large composition'.[23]

In addition to the above, there was once again a great deal of incidental music that was commissioned to accompany dramatisations of Arthurian literature. This will be noticed below.

## The Historical Arthur

The earlier local interest in the historical Arthur received a new impetus at the outset of the Second World War in Douglas Cleverdon and Felix Felton's topical series *The Land We Defend*. Their 'West Country' episode, which went on air during the Battle of Britain (HS 5 August 1940), homed in on the legend's continuing patriotic relevance:

Now when the enemy threatens us again, we remember all that it [The West Country] stands for – the heroic deeds of Drake and Sir Richard Greville, perhaps, and the old Arthurian legends of Tintagel and Glastonbury. ...

But, remarkably, the earlier amateur interest in the historical Arthur expressed in many regional talks fell away. Blake Briars's *Was King Arthur a Cumbrian?* (NE 1956) was a rare exception. Nor did children's programmes, apart from L. du Garde Peach's account of Joseph of Arimathea at Glastonbury (HS 1949) and Jean Sutcliffe's *King Arthur* (HS 1959), dwell on these matters. And it was not until the early 1950s that a cluster of academically informed talks addressed the issue. Three of them stemmed from Donald Boyd's project for a sequence examining well-known stories in the light of modern historical and archaeological knowledge. Named *Myth or Legend?* this twelve-part series (HS 1953–4) was produced by Michael Stephens in co-operation with Glyn Daniel, who was then enjoying considerable celebrity on television shows, and was, with Mortimer Wheeler, hugely instrumental in widening the popular appeal of archaeology. Daniel's introductory talk, *Lyonesse and the Lost Lands of England*, which set out his distinction between 'myth' and 'legend', would touch only sparingly on the Arthurian associations, but both R. F. Treharne's *Glastonbury* and Jon Manchip White's *Tristan and Iseult* gave, within the constraints of their fifteen-minute accounts, attractive and academically sound expositions of their topic. All these talks were then published in book form.[24]

Of even greater moment was the Third Programme's commission of a twenty-minute talk, *Who Was King Arthur?*, by the great Celtic scholar, Kenneth Hurlstone

---

23 Hugh Ottaway, 'Radio Notes', *Musical Times* 97 (December 1956), 646. 'A Cantata for Radio', *The Times* (25 October 1956), 3. Dyneley Hussey, 'Half Sick of Shadows', *Listener* 56 (1 November 1956), 727–8. The broadcast was recorded and repeated in 1959.
24 G. E. Daniel, et al., *Myth or Legend?* (London: Bell, 1955).

Jackson (8 October 1954). Aiming at an intelligent, though non-specialist, audience Jackson evaluated the evidence of the early Welsh and Latin records, concluding cautiously that there 'may have been a great leader of the Britons called Arthur', that the battle of Badon 'was probably fought at some unknown hill in southern England', and that Arthur was perhaps killed 'in a civil conflict'. Repeated four months later, Jackson's definitive talk was then given more permanent form by publication in *The Listener* before being worked into his chapter for R. S. Loomis's *Arthurian Literature in the Middle Ages*.[25] A month afterwards Home Service pursued the matter with a comparably academic discussion on *The Historical Arthur* (23 March 1955) by C. A. Ralegh Radford (the excavator of Tintagel), C. L. Mathews and John Morris (the historian who was later to write *The Age of Arthur*).[26] And, in a 1958 programme on the legends and archaeology of Glastonbury (N3 22 April, repeated HS September), Radford would be joined by a youngish Geoffrey Ashe, who had published his first Glastonbury study in the previous year.[27]

That is not a large tally for twenty years of broadcasting. But if the BBC gave scant regard to the historical Arthur, it compensated by providing much ampler coverage of creative work arising from the Arthurian legends.

### *Reading and Adapting 1: Medieval Literature*

In contrast to the international repertoire of broadcast music, literary programmes had a different focus. Despite the wide availability of English translations in print, I cannot trace any broadcast in these years devoted, for example, to Chrétien de Troyes, Marie de France, Gottfried von Strassburg or Wolfram von Eschenbach. When these names did crop up, it was almost wholly within the context of Wagnerian opera. Concern with the medieval Arthurian legend remained firmly rooted in the British tradition.

Certain types of Malory programme persisted, but the three-part adaptation for schools of Howard Pyle's Malorian retelling (HS 17–31 May 1944) introduced two new features: it was taken from an already published source, and was probably the first American handling to be heard in Britain. It is possible that the source and the stories selected (Arthur's coming, the King of Camilard's plea for assistance, and the fight between the White and Black Knights) were regarded as having important political resonance because of America's popularity as a vital military ally during the Second World War. This version was followed by a pair of four-part adaptations of Malory: by Moira Doolan (HS 1952) and then by Robert Gwyn for *Children's Hour* (HS [Wa] 1952).[28]

Extracts also continued to be read aloud, mainly for adults. *Morte Darthur* featured, for instance, in Henry Ainley's reading of 'The Death of Arthur' as

[25]  *Listener* 53 (17 February 1955), 285–6. Kenneth Hurlstone Jackson, 'The Arthur of History', in *Arthurian Literature in the Middle Ages: A Collaborative History*, ed. Roger Sherman Loomis (Oxford: Clarendon Press, 1959), pp. 1–11.
[26]  John Morris, *The Age of Arthur: A History of the British Isles from 350 to 650* (London: Weidenfeld & Nicolson, 1973).
[27]  Geoffrey Ashe, *King Arthur's Avalon: The Story of Glastonbury* (London: Collins, 1957).
[28]  Moira Doolan, *King Arthur*; Robert Gwyn, *Knights of the Round Table*.

'described by' Malory and Tennyson (HS 1944).[29] His comparison was then carried over into a Forces Educational Broadcast entitled *Legends of Arthur* (LP 1946). Similarly a later schools series featured a reading of Malory's 'The Passing of Arthur' (HS 1950) four months after a reading of Tennyson's poem of the same title. Alvar Lidell read an extract titled 'How Sir Galahad joined the Round Table' (TP 1947) and a further brief reading of Malory by R. H. Ward ensued (HS [W] 1952), prefaced by a Laurence Housman talk, *The Truth about the Round Table*. But a new direction had already become evident. Marking this heightened level of treatment was a talk by Jacob Isaacs on *Sir Thomas Malory* (TP 3 August 1947), a prompt response to Eugène Vinaver's landmark edition in that year of *The Works of Sir Thomas Malory* from the Winchester manuscript discovered in 1934. In turn this edition inspired two major radio adaptations by Douglas Cleverdon: *The Death of Arthur* (TP 9 April 1952, repeated July, and 1953) and *The Quest of the Holy Grail* (TP 3 June 1953, repeated October, and 1955). Generous time allocations (two hours, and an hour and a half respectively) and a distinguished cast (Robert Harris as Lancelot, Carleton Hobbs as the King) were accorded these consciously prestigious occasions, both specifically based on the Winchester text, and both featuring specially commissioned musical scores by the then very highly regarded atonalist P. Racine Fricker. In *The Listener* J. C. Trewin, a Cornishman who was well disposed to Arthurian material, nonetheless found fault.[30] Despite the magnificent speaking, it remained a 'reading' and never became 'a very dramatic occasion'. By the time the 'great final passages' arrived, they lost their excitement because one's ear had been dulled. Serial form, he suggested would be preferable, for though 'thirty minutes of Malory can be superb; two hours can become a superb monotony'.

The treatment of *Sir Gawain and the Green Knight* reveals a similar pattern to Malory broadcasts. For schools Margaret Millar completed a two-part dramatisation (HS 1950, repeated 1953), but a major development then occurred with the commissioning of J. R. R. Tolkien to provide a verse translation. As long ago as 1925 Tolkien had collaborated with E. V. Gordon in publishing an edition of the medieval text, and had probably begun a verse translation in the 1930s or 1940s.[31] News of this reached Bridson at the BBC, who suggested to Tolkien that Wilfred Pickles and a Manchester cast could read the poem on air.[32] Although it was agreed that production should take place in the second half of 1951, a considerable delay occurred, because Tolkien did not have the translation ready until July 1953. This translation proved very faithful to the original, following it virtually line-for-line, and preserving much of the alliterative verse form. Envisaging the production as a broadcast poem, Tolkien maintained that it should be read by a single voice, and that this should be his own ('It's my pidgin. If you don't let me read it we can wash out the whole thing.').[33] P. H. Newby (novelist and Controller of TP), who had initially favoured Dylan Thomas as reader, had

---

29  A letter in *Radio Times* (27 February) expressed disapproval of the 'hash' of mixing Malory and Tennyson in this way.
30  J. C. Trewin, 'Broadcast Drama', *Listener* 47 (17 April 1952), 647.
31  Humphrey Carpenter, *J. R. R. Tolkien: A Biography* (London: Grafton, 1992), p. 146.
32  BBC WAC: Tolkien file, letter from Bridson to Tolkien, 28 July 1950.
33  BBC WAC: letter from Tolkien to Newby, 4 August 1953.

the difficult task of persuading Tolkien to accommodate himself to the require-
ments of a radio format, to allow more than one voice in the broadcast, and to
split the series into four not five instalments. Newby had his way. Six voices
(none of them Tolkien's) were used over the four broadcasts (6–30 December).
What had been designed as an introductory talk, confining itself to the poem's
theme rather than its stylistic qualities, was delayed by Tolkien's indisposition,
and finally broadcast only at the end of the series. In all, however, the BBC had
achieved a notable coup, for this verse translation never reached print during
Tolkien's lifetime. Not until 1975, as an outcome of the international craze for
*The Lord of the Rings*, was a publication assembled by Christopher Tolkien from
materials among his father's papers.[34]

A kindred mixture of scholarship and popularisation surrounded *The Mabinogion*. On one hand, Tudur Watkins dramatised *The Lady of the Fountain* for *Children's Hour* one St David's Day with music by Arwel Hughes (HS 1943), but the
early post-war period also saw a remarkable cluster of academic programmes. As
part of a symposium on Welsh literary history – probably the most distinguished
Arthurian series ever given on radio – W. J. Gruffydd gave a talk on *The Arthurian Legend and The Mabinogion*, outlining the relationship between Welsh tales
and the Continental development of Arthurian romance, and suggesting that
the folklore tradition of Arthur as popular hero had adopted the mythological
traditions of the 'Great Youth' (HS [Wa], early 1947).[35] A highly important new
translation by Gwyn Jones led quickly to increased radio interest in the Welsh
Arthurian stories, in that Third Programme hosted a talk by Jones, followed by
a reading of his translation of *Culhwch and Olwen* (16 January 1950).[36] Jones then
gave the talk again in revised form (TP 10 June 1951) and provided a new one
on *Three Arthurian Romances* (TP 20 June 1950) with readings by Arthur Phillips.
The older and more widely known translation by Lady Charlotte Guest was,
however, retained in Home Service, where a feature on her life was presented
by Harry Green (HS [Wa] 24 September 1950), while a schools series on *The
Mabinogion* also included a retelling of *The Adventures of Peredur* (HS 1951). This
mini-Welsh revival was continued by a translation by W. M. Merchant from a
Welsh version of *The Seven Sages of Rome* (TP 21 July 1952, repeated 1954).

Two rather uncommon items for children should also be noticed. J. Jefferson's
story, *The Grave of Vortigern*, was read by Arthur Bush in the *Stories Old and New*
series (HS 1947), while *The Awntyrs of Arthur* made an appearance in a regional
*Children's Hour*, when Bertha Lonsdale retold the story of *King Arthur and the
Churlish Knight of Tearne Wadling* as part of a series on folklore and legends of
the North (HS [N] 1954).

Finally, the Third Programme was once again splendidly initiatory in its

---

34  Carpenter, *Tolkien*, p. 146. *Sir Gawain and the Green Knight, Pearl and Sir Orfeo*, tr. J. R. R.
    Tolkien, ed. Christopher Tolkien (London: George Allen & Unwin, 1975). This includes a
    slightly shortened version of Tolkien's radio talk on pp. 2–6.
35  The talk was printed in *Welsh Review* 6: 4 (1947), 244–8.
36  Gwyn Jones and Thomas Jones, trs, *The Mabinogion: A New Translation from the White Book of
    Rhydderch and the Red Book of Hergest*, illus. Dorothea Braby (London: Golden Cockerel Press,
    1948). This was a limited edition. A year later it was published in Dent's Everyman Library,
    replacing Charlotte Guest's translation.

commissioning of Nevill Coghill's modernisation (and resulting popularisation) of *The Canterbury Tales* – the Arthurian *Wife of Bath's Tale* being given its first broadcast, in a dramatisation by Stephen Potter, on 2 December 1946 (repeated 1947 and 1949). Reviewing the opening broadcast of the series, Martin Armstrong makes the valid point that, whereas it is not difficult for a modern reader to tackle Chaucer's Middle English text, listening to the original now presents problems for many. Coghill's necessary adaptation was, he felt, 'dazzling.'[37] Read aloud, Chaucer's virtues – 'the minuteness and precision of his visual detail, his sly humour, the perfection of his art as portrait-painter and story-teller' – emerged with 'astonishing brilliance'. Chaucer, he concludes, 'writes superbly for the radio'. Encouragingly, an audience of two million was achieved.[38] As in the case of Tolkien's *Sir Gawain*, radio performance had not only scooped publication in book form but had been the primary goal.[39]

## Reading and Adapting 2: Post-Medieval Literature

There was no sign, however, of a recovery in the academic fortunes of Spenser's *Faerie Queene*. A stray reading by Pamela Browne from Book 1 (HS 1945), which may have incorporated Arthurian incident, was given, but the sole major Spenserian presentation was a production by Louis MacNeice for the poet's quatercentenary in 1952. This seems an occasion when a BBC writer-producer's own taste certainly influenced the selection and handling of material, for MacNeice had long championed the importance of Spenser against a then hostile critical environment. Consequently twelve hour-long programmes were devoted to a dramatised reading of the epic poem, and Valentine Dyall took the part of Prince Arthur in three of these (TP 6 and 27 October, 1 December).

As before, Tennyson was more read than any other Arthurian poet, and the readers included such accomplished performers as Flora Robson, Margaret Rawlings, Valentine Dyall and Marius Goring. 'The Lady of Shalott' was selected on many occasions: for schools (1942, 1946, 1952, 1957), for general listening on the Home Service (1945) and even the Third (1950, 1952), besides being set to music by Tate and Jacobson (see above). Nonetheless, a *Listener* critic could still find the poem 'too sweet, too effortless, too lacking in astringency'.[40] 'Morte d'Arthur' (or its later form, 'The Passing of Arthur') was heard too in schools programmes (1953), *Woman's Hour* (1950) and other general broadcasts (1944). 'Sir Galahad', by contrast, figured only once, in a selection made by John Bryson (TP 1950), and the *Idylls* were scarce. A typically hostile reaction to them is voiced by Stephen Williams, who claims that 'glittering as they are with lovely, lustrous decoration', they 'seem somewhat faded and impotent to us now'.[41] Douglas Cleverdon, however, produced a reading of 'Guinevere' (HS 1945) and the

---

37 Martin Armstrong, 'The Spoken Word', *Listener* 36 (31 October 1946), 608.
38 According to *Archive Hour* (R4 21 October 2000).
39 Coghill's translation was published by Penguin in 1951.
40 Martin Armstrong, 'The Spoken Word', *Listener* 43 (29 June 1950), 1111.
41 Stephen Williams, 'The Legend of the Grail', *Radio Times* (15 April 1949), 6.

Forces programme that undertook an overall comparison between Malory and Tennyson (see above) must have addressed the *Idylls* in some wise. So too with A. L. Rowse's talk, *Tennyson in Cornwall* (HS [W] 1947). A slight indication of Tennyson's incipient return to modern critical regard came with W. W. Robson's talk on him in *The Poet and His Public* series (TP 1957), though the regard was likely to have been unsympathetic from this Leavisite critic.

A few glimmerings suggest that other Victorian verse was being salvaged. Fifteen minutes of extracts from Swinburne's *Tristram of Lyonesse* were read by Christopher Pemberton in 1944 (HS); Bridson took special pleasure in arranging for two William Morris poems to be read by Margaret Rawlings: 'The Defence of Guenevere' (TP 1951) and 'King Arthur's Tomb' (TP 1951); and Matthew Arnold's *Tristram and Iseult* finally achieved an airing in a schools broadcast (HS) of 1957. Furthermore, a notable episode from Thomas Love Peacock's Arthurian novel, *The Misfortunes of Elphin*, was adapted by Michael Kelly as *Sea Flood* and provided with music by Arwel Hughes (HS 1 May 1950).

Probably the only nineteenth-century Arthurian piece certainly to achieve mass circulation via radio was the most significant prose fiction of its age to take up the legend: Mark Twain's burlesque, *A Connecticut Yankee in King Arthur's Court*. This was 'freely adapted' for radio by Wallace Geoffrey as *A Yank at the Court of King Arthur*, and serialised in seven weekly episodes (LP November–December 1946). *Radio Times* promotes this version by printing two photographs of the leading actor (Douglass Montgomery), suited in armour but smoking an anachronistic pipe and using a modern phone. Twain's popularity was probably enhanced too by the distribution in 1949 of a film version by Paramount Pictures starring Bing Crosby. Unlikely as it sounds, a radio broadcast was made from a cinema performance of this (LP 1949), and a selection of music from the film was soon to reach the Light Programme, one song – 'Busy Doing Nothing' – even becoming a hit record.

A new production of Wallace Geoffrey's adaptation was broadcast in 1954 as a single play, with music by John Hotchkiss and a prefatory *Radio Times* drawing by Norman Mansbridge, which reveals a contemporary sartorial updating [plate 16]. As it formed part of the popular *Saturday Night Theatre* series (HS 14 August), it would doubtless have attracted a wide audience, though J. C. Trewin did not find it a memorable performance, and thought Twain's novel was 'never very hilarious'.[42]

Despite the fact that other Arthurian films continued to be shot, none of them seems to have been noticed in *Radio Times* until the release of *The Black Knight* prompted a talk by its director, Tay Garnett, about his filming it in Spain (HS 5 February 1954).

Twentieth-century Arthurian fiction, though, was increasingly recognised. T. H. White's *The Sword in the Stone* returned to radio in a new guise. His Arthurian 'fantasy' had, in Marianne Helweg's view, 'gradually increased in stature and fame, so that it can now almost be called a classic'.[43] Helweg, who had made

---

42  J. C. Trewin, 'Broadcast Drama', *Listener* 52 (19 August 1954), 299.
43  Marianne Helweg, 'Merlyn's Magic Again', *Radio Times* (16 March 1952), 6. By this time she had changed her name from Helwig.

the serial adaptation of the novel in 1939, was so delighted by Francis Dillon's rediscovery of Britten's complete score for that broadcast, which was presumed destroyed in the bombing of the music library, that she determined to make a new adaptation. Although T. H. White had sold all rights in the book to Walt Disney, the latter agreed to waive his copyright and to grant permission for the BBC to mount a single new broadcast. Helweg then turned the novel into a ninety-minute drama, reusing the Britten score, which Walter Goehr would conduct. Dillon was, fittingly, appointed producer, Peter Ustinov took the part of Merlyn, Jeremy Spenser that of Wart, Patience Collier was Madame Mim, Norman Shelley played Sir Ector, and Geoffrey Wincott King Pellinore (HS 16 March 1952). Bruce Angrave supplied two stylishly witty drawings for *Radio Times* [plates 17, 18].

It may seem strange therefore that no adaptation was made of *The Sword in the Stone*'s successor, *The Once and Future King*. When this came out in 1958, its publishers (Collins) suggested that it would be a good choice for BBC serialisation on *Woman's Hour*, but the suggestion fell on stony ground. In 1958, the editor of *Woman's Hour* (Joanna Scott-Moncrieff) wrote to her Deputy Editor, M. A. Hart:

> I have only brushed through *The Sword in the Stone*, and while I feel that we should search ceaselessly for the unusual and fresh in serials, I doubt that listeners could suspend disbelief to the point required.[44]

Miss Hart was uncompromising in her reply. The book was 'unreadable in [her] opinion! In any case, readers without the background would lose the point.' And the matter was closed.

Other slighter works were, however, adapted. Chief of these was a witty short story by Anthony Armstrong, *Sir Borloys and the Dark Knight*. This deservedly popular piece had originally appeared in the *Strand Magazine* (1933), was twice published in collections of Armstrong stories (1942, 1945), and included (with a minor bowdlerisation) in a children's Christmas anthology (1946) before adaptation by Elfrieda Paxton for a twenty-five-minute *Wednesday Matinée*, with Hilary Wontner as Borloys and Carleton Hobbs as the Dark Knight (HS 30 April 1947).[45] It is a slightly saucy tale of how an overweight and ineffectual knight ('a minor segment of King Arthur's Round Table') is duped into helping the Dark Knight's beautiful daughter elope but is then trapped into marrying her unattractive sister, though he takes some comfort in the culinary pleasures of his future father-in-law's table. As the extant script reveals, Armstrong's playful narrative and crisp dialogue were smoothly transferred to the medium of radio.

Also converted was Helen Clare's children's novel, *Merlin's Magic*, an allegorical fantasy wherein the Arthurian characters (representing human imagination) defeat extraterrestrial worshippers of modern technology.[46] This tract for

---

44   BBC WAC: internal memo, 13 September 1958.
45   BBC WAC: typed playscript of Anthony Armstrong, 'Sir Borloys and the Dark Knight'. The original story had appeared in Anthony Armstrong, *The Pack of Pieces* (London: Michael Joseph, 1942), pp. 48–64; in his *The Naughty Princess* (London: Macdonald, 1945), pp. 45–59; and in *The Children's Christmas Gift Book* (London: Odhams, 1946), pp. 80–98.
46   Helen Clare, *Merlin's Magic* (London: Bodley Head, 1953).

the times was adapted by Nan Macdonald in four parts for *Children's Hour*, with David Markham as Merlin (HS 25 April–4 May 1956). Though never as central to the main theme as in Clare's novel, there is some comparable material in another novel serialised for *Children's Hour*, John Masefield's *The Midnight Folk*, whose young hero pays a dream visit to Arthur's court, where he jousts with the Black Knight (HS 1958). Other children's programmes would continue to retell the traditional folktales loosely associated with the Arthurian world. A wartime schools programme on Tom Thumb had the customary episode involving his stay at Arthur's court (HS 15 October 1942); a later version by Muriel Levy went out in *Children's Hour* (HS 19 July 1946), as did F. W. Harvey's verse fantasy with music by Reginald Redman, *Jack the Giant Killer* (HS 7 January 1945).

Novelists writing for a more adult audience received scant attention. None was read or dramatised, but C. A. Lejeune gave an appreciation of Arthur Machen (TP 1948) while Frederick Bradnum at one time considered adapting John Cowper Powys's *A Glastonbury Romance* for radio before sensibly reaching the conclusion that the novel was too unwieldy.[47] The chief exception to the general neglect was Charles Williams, who received significant notice by forming the subject of a talk by T. S. Eliot (TP 1946) that was reprinted in *The Listener*.[48] Addressing himself to a general audience, Eliot did not recommend Williams's 'later and best' poems (i.e. the Arthurian ones) because they did not make easy reading. Though he conceded that *Taliessin in Logres* is 'absorbing after we have got the hang of what he is after', he recommended people to start with the novels, especially the Grail novel, *War in Heaven*. The latter was discussed, too, by Walter Allen in *Book Talk* (HS 1947). All his novels were featured besides in a C. S. Lewis programme (TP 1949) and, soon after its publication, Glyn Daniel promptly reviewed the joint Lewis–Williams production, *Arthurian Torso*, which explicates Williams's Arthurian poetry (HS [W] 1949).[49]

Some other twentieth-century verse was slightly more prominent. T. S. Eliot was, for example, heard reading *The Waste Land* in a recording he had made in America some three years previously (TP 14 December 1949). But easily the most noteworthy venture was the introduction of David Jones's two great prose-poems that rework significant themes from Malory and *The Mabinogion*. Jones's path to radio was undoubtedly smoothed by the fact that two of his close friends (Harman Grisewood and Douglas Cleverdon) were BBC employees of some standing. Cleverdon's first adaptation of *In Parenthesis* would have run for about ninety minutes, and was, remarkably for such a 'difficult' work, scheduled for mainstream broadcasting on 11 November, Armistice Day, 1939. But the outbreak of war on 3 September resulted in a rapid reorganisation of all planned broadcasts, and so the programme never went ahead.[50] Cut to forty minutes, it was later listed for 10 November 1942 in the Home Service. At the last moment,

47  BBC WAC: Bradnum file, memo from Bradnum to AHD (S), 22 January 1957.
48  T. S. Eliot, 'The Significance of Charles Williams', *Listener* 36 (19 December 1946), 894–95.
49  A. H. W. Smith cites a musical work based on Williams's verse, Robin Milford's *The Summer Stars: A Masque*, a shortened version of which was broadcast (HS [W] 1957): 'Update IV: a Supplementary Bibliography of Twentieth Century Arthurian Literature', *Arthurian Literature* 10 (1990), 135–60 (150).
50  Douglas Cleverdon, 'David Jones and Broadcasting', *Poetry Wales* 8: 3 (1972), 73.

however, the broadcast had to be cancelled to make room for a speech by Winston Churchill.[51] This pause made BBC authorities wonder whether a work articulating the horrors of trench warfare was 'in accord with the prevailing mood'. They decided it was not, and production was shelved. Four years later, peacetime having somewhat relaxed the mood, Cleverdon returned to the material, and produced an extended version of ninety minutes for the Third Programme, with an introduction by David Jones, and with 'several superb quasi-liturgical interludes' composed by Elizabeth Poston (19 November 1946). In spirit, Cleverdon's adaptation is very faithful. He bowdlerises just a little, but his insertion of an occasional proper name helpfully points up the Arthurian allusions for a listener. Although his abridgement may seem severe in reducing the original by about three-quarters, this length was probably the maximum possible for the attention of a modern radio audience. Despite the difficulties created by Jones's esoteric references and fractured syntax, the broadcast was apparently successful in communicating the pathos of his theme and the forcefulness of his peculiarly individual idiom. Coupled with music and sound effects, it seems to have made for powerful listening. So powerful, in fact, for Jones himself that listening to it precipitated another mental breakdown.[52] Within the BBC the production was considered a very effective exploitation of the medium. As Nest Cleverdon recalls, 'Who could forget Dylan Thomas reading the "Boast of Dai"?'[53] It was submitted (albeit unsuccessfully) for the Prix Italia, and very quickly repeated in a new live production (December 1946). Philip Hope-Wallace noted that the broadcast had many of 'his critical colleagues in ecstasy', and he himself found it 'more immediately moving than one would have believed'.[54] In the matter of 'mechanics and mimicry' it was 'absolutely first-rate', but his praise, nonetheless, sounded a more cautious note in wondering whether the sound version gave sufficient help in clarifying its overall structure for those listeners who had not read the book, for the tension of radio drama, which depends on anticipating the next move, differs from 'the backward and forward-looking curiosity which hold[s] your eye to the printed page'.

Nine years later a new production, lasting two hours, was mounted with Richard Burton taking the leading part of Private John Ball. Though Dylan Thomas was dead by that time, Cleverdon had fortunately preserved a recording of his famous delivery of the Boast of Dai Evans – the recording of the rest of the 1946 production had been destroyed – and so this was inserted into the new production (TP 30 January 1955). This time Cleverdon ensured that the performance was recorded and preserved. Both Thomas and Burton told Cleverdon it was the greatest production they had ever taken part in. Jones, however, did not approve of the broadcast; he would, according to Nest Cleverdon, have liked to have his poem 'read aloud, very slowly and monotonously, by himself'. Douglas

---

51 This was a key Churchill speech after Montgomery's victory at El Alamein, a turning point of the Second World War: 'Now this is not the end. It is not even the beginning of the end. But it is, perhaps, the end of the beginning': *The War Speeches of The Rt. Hon. Winston S. Churchill*, ed. Charles Eade, 3 vols (London: Cassell, 1951–2), II: 343.

52 Douglas Cleverdon, 76.

53 Nest Cleverdon, 'David Jones remembered', in *David Jones, 1895–1974: A Map of the Artist's Mind*, ed. Merlin James (London: Lund Humphries, 1995), p. 61.

54 Philip Hope-Wallace, 'Broadcast Drama', *Listener* 36 (28 November 1946), 766.

Cleverdon's enthusiasm for Jones, though, remained undimmed and, within a year of the publication of *The Anathemata*, this too was adapted (TP 5 May 1953), and twice repeated (1954 and 1958). For this Cleverdon used the pre-recorded voice of Dylan Thomas, who was then away in America on a recital tour. Jones is said to have liked Dylan Thomas's reading in this. Cleverdon himself believed that Diana Maddox's rendition of the Lady of the Pool's thirty-minute mono-logue 'was one of the greatest radio performances' that he had ever heard.[55] In Nest Cleverdon's opinion, her husband's productions had acted as an intro-duction to Jones's work for many people who might otherwise have had no knowledge of it. Two other programmes followed rapidly: a feature about Jones's work, compiled by Goronwy Rees, in which David Jones, T. S. Eliot and Nicolette Gray were among the speakers (HS [Wa] 29 October 1954); and, for good measure, a talk on the artist-poet given by another friend of Jones, H. S. Ede (TP 20 December 1954).

Another leading contemporary poet was featured in the *New Poems* series. After a wartime visit to Cornwall, Henry Reed had written a four-part 'Tintagel', which made an intricate examination of the 'perpetually recurring story' of the Tristan legend. These four parts would appear separately in periodicals and anthologies but, as all four parts were broadcast in an arrangement for five speakers (HS 7 December 1944), the poem thus made its first complete appear-ance on air, before publication in book form in 1946.[56] Yet such an event remained a rarity.

## Reading and Adapting 3: Drama

Once again, the BBC's strength was displayed in adaptation of stage plays from a rich variety of sources. At the simplest level, it was prepared to mount new productions of plays it had broadcast many years previously. This was the case with Stephen Phillips's *Paolo and Francesca*, which had originally been produced in 1928, but was given a new adaptation by Jon Manchip White, produced by Hugh Stewart (HS 6 October 1952). As the title of White's *Radio Times* preview ('A Verse Play from the Lumber Room') indicates, Phillips's reputation had fallen into neglect.[57] White himself follows contemporary fashion in deprecating the moral timidity of the author, and disliking the 'Pre-Raphaelite element' in the play: White's comparison of Francesca with 'a figure from a stained glass window by Burne-Jones' is intended to be pejorative. Nevertheless he still finds the work 'impressive and enjoyable', for Phillips could always contrive to bring off the big scenes, and over the whole play there hangs 'the sombre, brooding, Websterian quality at which the dramatist aimed, and which recalls the rich haunting sadness of Tchaikovsky's tone-poem'. Laurence Scarfe's illustration in *Radio Times* adds the elegance of a formalised Pre-Raphaelite setting **[plate 19]**.

Welcoming this revival of the work, J. C. Trewin thought that the broadcast

---

55  Douglas Cleverdon, 79.
56  See Henry Reed, *Collected Poems*, ed. Jon Stallworthy (Oxford: Oxford University Press, 1991), p. 158n.
57  *Radio Times* (3 October 1952), 11.

proved the play's force 'as a piece of direct narrative', and he observed that few modern verse dramatists could match Phillips's resounding lines, which were memorably delivered by William Devlin (as Giovanni, Tyrant of Rimini), who governed the performance in 'a richly sombre study'.[58] On the debit side, however, White's adaptation had excised many of the play's once-celebrated phrases, and neither Alan Badel (Paolo) nor Claire Bloom (Francesca) were convincing. Nor could the medium of radio convey 'the visual *coup de théâtre* when Giovanni parts the curtains before the dead are brought in and the play fades on its Websterian echo'.

But this was the only revival; all other plays were new to radio. Regional sentiment may be responsible for the airing of *Lancelot* by James Bridie, who was then the leading Scottish dramatist with a string of London West End productions to his name. Written in 1939, it had not reached the stage until October 1945 at the Glasgow Citizen's Theatre (of which institution Bridie was a joint founder). It was perhaps written with a London Old Vic performance in mind, but that body had rejected it despite support for the play from Laurence Olivier.[59] Later performed only 'a time or two as a pageant', it was courageous of the Scottish Home Service to broadcast it in an adaptation by J. L. Galloway in an eighty-minute production by Moultrie R. Kelsall (21 April 1947). On the page its modern spoken idiom seems adequately lively, and it includes some refreshingly discordant voices of chattering, gossiping and grumbling from servants and peasants, but critics at the Glasgow première were surely correct when they found little coherence in the drama's development.[60] It opens promisingly enough in the aura of 1930s eugenics, with Merlin striving to 'increase the sum of human happiness' through creating 'the best kind of man'. Already he has mated Uther with Ygraine to produce the Age of Chivalry. Now he will mate 'the best Knight' with the daughter of Pelleas (a religious crank) to produce Galahad. But after Lancelot has been given a spiked drink to make him procreate with the handsome yet stupid Elaine, the play changes direction, Merlin soon disappears into a rock, and the conventional Lancelot–Guenevere story banally takes over.

The Third Programme's first venture into the Arthurian stage domain was greatly innovatory in welcoming an avant-garde work by Julien Gracq. His four-act play *Le Roi Pêcheur* had been published in 1945 but not performed in France until 1949, when the 'critics were unjustly brutal' to it.[61] All the more adventurous therefore for the BBC to have commissioned an English translation (*The Fisher King*) by Rollo H. Myers and E. J. King Bull, and to have supplemented it with incidental music by Elisabeth Lutyens, a leading serialist composer. It was broadcast on 19 April 1949, repeated the following month, and revived two years later (March 1951). An abbreviated version of Gracq's foreword was also read by Pat Butler (TP 19 April 1949, repeated May). In this bleak and deeply original interpretation of the legend, Percival's achievement of the Grail is frustrated not

58   J. C. Trewin, 'Broadcast Drama', *Listener* 48 (16 October 1952), 655.
59   See Winifred Bannister, *James Bridie and His Theatre* (London: Rockcliff, 1955), pp. 162–4.
60   James Bridie, 'Lancelot: A Play in Two Acts', in *Plays for Plain People* (London: Constable, 1944), pp. 1–78.
61   Norris J. Lacy, ed., *The New Arthurian Encyclopedia* (Chicago and London: St James Press, 1991), pp. 211–12.

only by the eunuch Klingsor (fat as a capon) but also by two unexpected adversaries: the hermit Trevrisent, and Amfortas, the Fisher King himself. Trevrisent expresses his own 'distrust' of the Grail story, and believes Percival (Andrew Faulds) is far too presumptuous in appointing himself Grail finder:

> The blood of Christ is a good excuse for the Grail, but I am not satisfied. I don't trust this old skin into which new wine has been so strangely poured. I see it as a snare, an image, badly restored – an age-old temptation to purchase redemption.[62]

In place of Percival's lonely pride, he urges more social forms of seeking salvation: being just and honourable, doing our duty according to our station, giving alms to the poor, and praying with our fellow men. Realising that the long-awaited Pure Fool is at hand, Klingsor (Esmé Percy) enters the castle of Montsalvat in disguise to frighten Amfortas with the threat of displacement by the new hero. Though ostensibly rebuffed by Amfortas, Klingsor's aim is achieved because Amfortas grows aware that he does not really want his present sufferings to cease, for they give him a meaningful central role at Monsalvat, and provide a comforting hope for his knights ('it *is* an occupation to have a sick person in the house', p. 63). Consequently, despite Kundry's pleading (she is unselfishly ready to sacrifice herself for Percival), Amfortas succeeds in foiling Percival by telling him that achievement of the Grail will mean the destruction of selfhood, and the concomitant death of Kundry (Jill Balcon). Appalled at the prospect of this terrifying aridity, Percival refuses to ask the necessary question, and departs. As Amfortas knows, however, 'This mad ardour for the Grail has not been quenched. Another will come' (p. 83). Warders on the walls of Montsalvat then resume their watch for deliverance. The play's circling ambiguities continue. It is likely that this work, though deemed a failure on stage, is much better suited to the medium of radio, where the lack of external action is an asset rather than a hindrance, where its interchange of metaphysical debate can receive a necessary concentration from the listener, and where its richly orchestrated diction can evoke the oppressive somnolence of the lifeless corridors of the Grail castle. In *Radio Times* Stephen Williams recommended the free adaptation by Myers and King Bull, which 'may annoy the professors and rule-of-thumb academicians' but would please everyone who liked to hear 'easy and natural English'.[63] Listening to a revival in 1951, Philip Hope-Wallace thought it contained 'several first-rate performances', and was 'well worth while'.[64]

A second French work about the Grail had an even more distinguished provenance in that it was written by Jean Cocteau and translated by W. H. Auden. The original, *Les Chevaliers de la Table Ronde*, had been performed in Paris in 1937. Auden's translation (*The Knights of the Round Table*) was also intended for stage production, and was provided with alternative passages for radio, but this hoped-for staging was held up until 1954, whereas BBC did the promised

---

62  BBC WAC: typed playscript of Julian Gracq, 'The Fisher King', tr. Rollo H. Myers and E. J. King Bull, p. 35. An English translation of this play seems never to have been published.
63  Williams, 'Legend of the Grail', 6.
64  'Broadcast Drama', *Listener* 45 (15 March 1951), 435.

broadcast as planned (TP 22 May 1951, repeated July 1951 and April 1953).[65] Produced by Peter Watts, the play featured Clive Morton as Arthur, Alan Judd as Lancelot, Patrick Troughton as Galahad, and Joan Matheson as Guinevere. Like Gracq's, Cocteau's interpretation is idiosyncratic in plot, and allegorical in intent. While the evil enchanter Merlin manipulates the court through a demon that assumes a series of false personae, the Grail represents reality. When this Grail is ultimately revealed by Galahad, the court is forced into sunlight, and many previously hidden unpleasant facts (such as Lancelot's and Guinevere's adultery) become known. 'Everyone must', says Galahad, 'always pay, pay in his person and in his actions.'[66] The subtext for Cocteau, it is claimed, is that the play is a parable of his own long battle against opium addiction: the message is that weaning oneself of magical substances is necessarily painful.[67] Unhappily, this skewing of the allegory appears forced and, though on the surface the play flows well in Auden's lively idiomatic version, the action seems overly contrived, and lacks the deeper structural logic of, for example, Cocteau's *La Machine Infernale*. If the purely aural effect of radio worked well for Gracq, it does not generally suit Cocteau's play. Anticipating this charge the *Radio Times* preview claimed that some of these scenes were easier to represent on radio than on stage. For instance, the scene in which the King's 'tortured imagination conjures up the voices of Lancelot and Guinevere and they reveal their guilt in a conversation within the King's mind' would be 'enhanced by radio production'.[68] But this play relies heavily on visual witticism, on chess pieces realigning themselves, sliding chairs, self-opening and self-closing doors, and so forth. The loss of stage costume is felt particularly in the many disguise scenes, when the demon's appearance in the role of the False Gawain, the False Guinevere or the False Galahad can be detected only through vocal means: too great a reliance is then thrust on to Auden's trick of making the False personae slip into Cockney accents. Even *Radio Times* had to admit the difficulty that this doubling posed for a radio producer. 'Without vision', wrote Philip Hope-Wallace in *The Listener*, 'a whole dimension was lacking – fatally, it seemed to me.'[69] Nonetheless, he concluded charitably that he was 'glad of the chance to hear it.' Previewing the 1953 repeat, Peter Forster was more positive. He admired the 'characteristic Cocteau idiom of naïve knowingness', and considered that the final scene was, though in prose, 'the very stuff of dramatic poetry'.[70]

The Grail theme was pursued, at a very considerable remove, in an adaptation of *The Thistle and the Grail*, an early novel by a leading Scottish writer, Robin Jenkins.[71] Three years after publication it was dramatised by John Keir Cross, and produced by James Crampsey, for the Scottish Home Service as part of the *Annals of Scotland* series (11 February 1957). The novel gives a moving

65 See Humphrey Carpenter, *W. H. Auden: A Biography* (London: Unwin, 1983), p. 368.
66 Jean Cocteau, 'The Knights of the Round Table', tr. W. H. Auden, in *The Infernal Machine and Other Plays* (Norfolk, CT: New Directions, 1963), pp. 179–291 (p. 290).
67 Bettina Liebowitz Knapp, *Jean Cocteau* (New York: Twayne, 1970), pp. 106–7.
68 C. N., 'Cocteau's Camelot', *Radio Times* (18 May 1951), 10.
69 'Broadcast Drama', *Listener* 45 (31 May 1951), 891.
70 P. F., 'At the Court of King Cocteau', *Radio Times* (17 April 1953), 21.
71 Robin Jenkins, *The Thistle and the Grail* (London: Macdonald, 1954). All quotations are taken from a later edition: (Edinburgh: Polygon, 1994).

account of life in a decaying industrial town near Glasgow, for whose economi-
cally depressed citizens value is centred on 'the mysterious masculine sacra-
ment' (p. 63) of football, a game that was invented for exercise and recreation,
but is now 'our only substitute for a faith and purpose' (p. 166). As the narrative
focuses on how the local team (the Thistle) wins the Junior Football Cup, and
thereby brings about a degree of social redemption, that prize trophy is described
on four occasions as a Grail (pp. 47, 169, 214, 287). The complex moral ironies of
Jenkins's three-hundred-page novel are, however, largely sacrificed to the time
constraints of the ninety-minute radio version. In the novel, the first reference
to the Grail is made by the new minister of the kirk, who proposes to lead a
religious revival by preaching to the football crowd at half-time, and jocularly
suggests that this public sermon might regenerate the team's fortunes on the
pitch: 'The Cup, like the Holy Grail itself, is there for the winning' (p. 47). Thereafter, the four brief Grail references that reinforce this analogy are all made by
the omniscient narrator, and arise quite appropriately from the novel's continual
exploration of the quasi-religious aspects of Scottish football. Moreover the fans'
obsession is set within a broader ironic frame through contrast with the 'heret-
ical' stance of those men who scorn the activity, and the womenfolk, who are
sensibly aware that it diverts money from their families' needs. The radio adaptation, however, is organised less subtly. Though three brief Grail references are
made by the narrator (Tom Smith), and one by the minister (Russell Hunter),
the prominent introduction of the theme is given to another local character, a
reprobate ex-miner, called Tinto (Eric Wightman), who defends his partiality for
'the lassies':

TINTO:        There was other than me that liked the lassies.
RAB:          And wha was that, Tinto?
TINTO:        Rabbie Burns for one. And King Arthur's Knights, ye wee
              illiterate scab, Rab Nuneaton! I'm maybe an old tramp but
              I've read a book or two in my time. It was through the lassies
              that they found the Grail, and by the glory we might find it
              too!
ARCHIE:       What Grail? Ye're daft, Tinto!
TINTO:        The Cup, my mannie!   (p. 16)

A little later he confides to his friend Crutch:

TINTO:        I'm an old man and I'm not far off the pauper's burial ground
              up bye, but if we just had the Cup I could die happy, like Sir
              Whatever it was with the Grail.
CRUTCH:       Och, you and your Grail!   (p. 31)

Similarly caught up in this metaphor, the pub landlord too promises free drinks
on the day the Thistle win the Grail (p. 85). Because a key player is induced to
join the team through love for a local girl, a lassie may, as Tinto intimated, be
regarded as performing a vital role in achieving the quest, for the Grail/Cup
is duly won, and news of this victory is whispered over the grave of the dead
tramp.

But if Jenkins's novel had adroitly secured the reader's willingness to believe in the numinous quality of football, the radio play does not, for the Grail concerns placed in the mouth of the tramp and the landlord are so blatantly contrived that the play slips temporarily into folksy sentimentality. Yet, despite this failing, and some mild bowdlerisation of language, enough of Jenkins's deeply humane psychological insight survives in other areas of the broadcast to make this work a valid, though minor, reappropriation of the Grail legend.

In 1956 two much more substantially Arthurian plays had been broadcast, both adopting Tristan as subject and both produced by Charles Lefeaux, who had taken the role of Sir Hector in the pre-war production of Bridson's *King Arthur*. Thomas Hardy's *The Famous Tragedy of the Queen of Cornwall* was not a new work, having been written in 1923, and premièred in Dorchester shortly afterwards. Though the text was published in that year, further performances were very rare and a proposed broadcast from the Dorchester production had not occurred, so Lefeaux's choice of the play for radio (TP 28 February, repeated April) was a significant event.[72] Hardy's aims are radical in both content and technique. By observing the Greek unities of time and space, he condenses the action to one hour (on radio it was given only forty-five minutes), and contrives to get all this action to Tintagel by freely adapting traditional sources: thus he brings Iseult the Whitehanded from Brittany in search of Tristan, and makes Mark the victim of Iseult of Cornwall's dagger, before she takes a Tosca-like leap to her death. In revolt against the theatrical conventions of his day, Hardy specifies that his play should have no scenery, and is intended for performance by amateur actors. This proved problematic at the Dorchester production. As contemporary reviewers observed, the delivery of Hardy's gnarled alliterative diction required the skill of professionals.[73] In this respect the radio performance was doubtless superior, for its cast was professional, and included Mary Morris (Iseult), Rachel Gurney (Iseult the Whitehanded) and Gordon Davies (Tristram). Even the finest actor would, however, be stretched in delivering such lines as:

> She's glode off like a ghost, with deathy mien;
> It seems towards the ledge – yes, she – the Queen.[74]

Incidental music was composed by Norman Demuth. In the absence of any review in *The Listener* – a useful reminder of how much out of favour this play was – one may speculate that the medium of radio was very appropriate for Hardy's minimalist intentions, but it is uncertain how radio would have compensated for the loss of one of the stage play's few strengths: the dramatic tension created by the hidden watcher (the jealous Iseult or the murderous Mark) whose presence is seen by the audience.

The second Tristan play also had strong roots in amateur drama. It had stemmed from a recommendation by Cornish County Drama authorities that

---

72  Harold Orel, *The Final Years of Thomas Hardy, 1912–1928* (London: Macmillan, 1976), p. 105. The proposed BBC broadcast was cancelled at the last moment: see *The Collected Letters of Thomas Hardy*, ed. Richard Little Purdy and Michael Millgate, 7 vols (Oxford: Clarendon Press, 1978–88), VI: 224n.

73  Keith Wilson, *Thomas Hardy on Stage* (London: St Martin's Press, 1995), pp. 125–8.

74  Thomas Hardy, *The Famous Tragedy of the Queen of Cornwall* (London: Macmillan, 1923), p. 170.

Festival of Britain Year (1951) should be marked by the presentation of a Tristan play at the open-air Minack Theatre near Land's End.[75] The merits of three versions were debated: Hardy's *Queen of Cornwall*, Masefield's *Tristan and Isolt* (which had already been staged at the Minack in 1939) and an unnamed 'American version of the story' (by which Amory Hare's *Tristram and Iseult* [1930] was perhaps meant), but the final decision was to commission a new work, *Tristan of Cornwall* by Nora Ratcliff, which, unlike Hardy's brief version, became a four-act play with a full treatment of the story from the time of Tristan's second visit to Ireland. Though drawing heavily from Bédier's retelling, she does make some alterations. Her Iseut has loved Tristan from the start, and is understandably dismayed when he claims her as a bride for Mark; the well-intentioned Brangwayne then hopes to put matters right by giving Tristan the love drink.[76] Although Ratcliff's method of relating some key scenes (such as the wedding night) only in flashback can often make the narrative needlessly obscure, she can effectively exploit the dramatic confrontations between characters, by presenting them in the manner of a pre-Wagnerian opera, with sharply distinguished soloists and a background chorus. She also works hard at making the most of her theatre's picturesque location, with frequent reference to the sea, rocks and sky in her verse, so that these natural features provide a richer context, resonance and authenticity for her play's action. Undoubtedly assisted by the grandeur of its stage setting, the production received some national attention. *The Times* carried an impressive photograph on its back page, and Trewin in *Punch* called it 'an exciting theatrical night'.[77] The question of a broadcast was then taken up by the BBC. Although Third Programme's John Morris rightly condemned Ratcliff's 'extremely weak' verse, trite imagery, cliché-ridden dialogue and her failure to provide 'some new interpretation of the legend' or a relation 'to contemporary themes', the Home Service accepted the play by February 1953, and Ratcliff made some revisions, though, as she was to admit to Lefeaux, by exploiting the visual possibilities of the Minack theatre she had 'probably reduced its value as a radio script'.[78] Meanwhile, news of a forthcoming new work by Ratcliff at the Minack, *Arthur of Britain*, resulted in this too being shown to the BBC. Here rejection was summary, Cynthia Pughe, the Drama Script Reader, submitting a negative report on this 'pedestrian effort'. Nonetheless, Helena Wood made an adaptation of *Tristan of Cornwall*, the play was cast with Yvonne Mitchell as Iseut and Peter Coke as Tristan, while incidental music composed by John Greenwood included the setting of two lyrics from the play: 'Iseut ma drie' and 'There were four knights of Cornwall'. Eric Fraser contributed an attractive illustration for *Radio Times*. When the broadcast eventually went ahead (HS 16 April 1956), Trewin's judicious appraisal registered his disappointment.[79] Despite the fine voices in Lefeaux's production, the text failed to 'become memorable speech', and although the play offered a 'reasonable, direct narrative, making discreet

[75] See Denys Val Baker, *The Minack Theatre* (London: George Ronald, 1960), pp. 46–50.
[76] BBC WAC: typed playscript of Nora Ratcliff, 'Tristan of Cornwall'.
[77] *The Times* (11 August 1951), 8. 'At the Play', *Punch* 221 (22 August 1951), 216.
[78] BBC WAC: Ratcliff file.
[79] 'Drama', *Listener* 55 (26 April 1956), 526–7.

use of a chorus', the imagination did not flash: the play needed the special visual setting that it had once enjoyed on the Cornish coast.

## Making it New

At a much lighter level, the BBC commissioned comedies such as Philip Phillips's *The Three Princes* (HS 1940, repeated 1941), a twenty-minute 'modern addition to the lore of knight-errantry' that included Merlin and the Witch of Wookey Hole; and children's plays such as K. T. McGarry's *Merlin's Wand*, 'another adventure of Grimalkin, the witch's cat, based on a Lancashire legend' (HS 1942). *King Arthur's Tree*, a Tintagel story by Alison Uttley, probably went out on *Children's Hour* (c.1947).[80] Some details survive, too, of Lester Powell's *Sir Lancelot and the Little Hands*, which was devised as a thirty-minute *Wednesday Matinée* (HS 1 January 1947). *Radio Times* denotes a setting at Astolat for this, and lists Merlin among the cast. Unhappily, the script is not at Caversham, but a summary is. From this we learn that:

> the jongleurs and chroniclers who recorded the adventures of the Knights were much the same sort of people as those in the film industry, and that ballad-making was just as highly industrialised. In short that Camelot was the Hollywood of the times in which King Arthur lived. We see the dirty methods by which they get the fair Deirdre to sign a contract on behalf of her niece Shirlee.[81]

Two episodes in the influential comedy series *The Goon Show* took up aspects of the legend: 'The Spectre of Tintagel' (HS 1956) and 'King Arthur's Sword' (HS 1958); and numerous comedy programmes from other sources probably contained many such minor sketches, but they have gone unrecorded.[82] Yet, far more importantly, the BBC became a major patron for new serious plays, and helped to develop the genre of radio drama, which gave rise to some exceptional (and non-Arthurian) triumphs, such as Dylan Thomas's *Under Milk Wood* and Samuel Beckett's *All That Fall*.

The most important new commissioning was Clemence Dane's *The Saviours*. This was a series of seven sixty-minute plays, in verse and prose, which had a resonantly urgent topicality. As Dane signalled in her *Radio Times* preview:

> If ever an Arthur were needed he is now ... it becomes clear that Arthur has in a sense already returned, and will always return, whenever young Britons rise up to fight for the preservation of the people's right, for a purer justice and a stronger, cleaner land.[83]

---

80  The story was the leading item in *Uncle Mac's 'Children's Hour' Book*, ed. Derek McCulloch (London: Purnell, [1947]), pp. 1–18. The title page says that all the stories had been broadcast in *Children's Hour*, but I cannot trace the date of this story's broadcast. According to BBC WAC records, an Alison Uttley talk, *King Arthur's Country*, was broadcast, however, in the Pacific service on 29 November 1947.

81  BBC WAC.

82  Spike Milligan, *More Goon Show Scripts* (London: Sphere, 1974), p. 15.

83  Clemence Dane, 'The Men Who Saved Our Land', *Radio Times* (22 November 1940), 5.

Begun during the London Blitz, the series opens with a *Merlin* (HS 24 November 1940), in which Saxon invaders of Ancient Britain are firmly equated with Nazis (Rowenna [Lydia Sherwood] is a 'German Frau', her Druid priest a 'German spy'), while the burning of Vortiger's castle is given the horrific immediacy of the modern incendiary bombing of London.[84] Dane's sentiments are – understandably enough – hyper-patriotic: her central figure is not Bridson's proud and lustful ruler but a messianic Arthur who represents Britain's 'indestructible spirit' (p. v). As the eponymous hero of the second part, *The Hope of Britain* (HS 29 December 1940), he takes immediate control of armed resistance against the Saxons, and achieves victory after ten years of fighting. Merciful to the families of the Picts who had traitorously collaborated (signifying Celtic nationalists of a later day?), he then establishes a model welfare state for his countrymen. His downfall is due not to any sin of his own but to the treachery of his nephew (and official heir) Modred (Valentine Dyall), who seduces Queen Wenhaver (Lydia Sherwood again!). After the Last Battle, Arthur sails back to Avalon, where he had once been raised by Morgan, but there is no doubt of his eventual return. This imminence is implied by the Arthurian leitmotif in all further plays in the sequence. Merlin serves as linking narrator in each episode of this national pantheon: King Alfred has read about Arthur, and plays Merlin's harp (*England's Darling*, HS 2 February 1941); Merlin lends a disguise to Robin Hood (*The May King*, HS 9 March 1941); Essex knows Merlin's *Prophecies* and rides to Tilbury 'like Arthur waked from Avalon' to meet Queen Elizabeth, a descendant of Arthur (*The Light of Britain*, 4 May 1941); Nelson is the 'King who has come again and saved his people' (*Remember Nelson*, HS 19 October 1941); while in the final play the Unknown Soldier of the First World War is ultimately synonymous with the wounded Arthur himself (*The Unknown Soldier*, HS 11 November 1942). This final synthesis would be movingly conveyed too, in very contrasting ways, by the vignettes of Eric Fraser [plate 20] and Dorothea Braby [plate 21] in *Radio Times*.

The drama gains an imaginative dimension from Dane's verse, for her attempted lyrical evocation of an English countryside, embodying order, peace and prosperity, provides a bitterly effective contrast to the destruction wrought by fierce dynastic competitiveness. Moreover Dane's success in matching the mood of the time may be noted, as the last two dates indicate, by the fact that her plays were carefully scheduled to appear on or near appropriate national anniversaries, such as Trafalgar Day and Armistice Day. The entire series soon reached print, and in the Coronation Year of 1953 three of her episodes (including *The Hope of Britain* and *The Unknown Soldier*) were revived on air (with Alexander Davion as Arthur, and Mary Wimbush as Wenhaver), evidently deemed suitable for national and royal celebration and observance.

Writing many years later, Val Gielgud emphasised the importance of Dane's achievement. Though the series was 'uneven', he considered *England's Darling* and *The Unknown Warrior* 'as outstanding among broadcast plays.'[85] A more

---

[84] Clemence Dane, *The Saviours: Seven Plays on One Theme* (London: Heinemann, 1942), pp. 10–11.
[85] Val Gielgud, *British Radio Drama 1922–1956: A Survey* (London: Harrap, 1957), p. 100.

captious note was, however, sounded by Grace Wyndham Goldie.[86] Slightly resistant to such an 'occasion-tailored, moral-pointing' drama, she objected to the insertion of incongruous modern concepts into medieval stories:

> [Dane] made Arthur ... an early Socialist standing for the rights of labour against Big Business, and though, for all I know, there may be excellent evidence to support this, yet the effect of sticking a modern conception of democracy into a medieval story was as incongruous in its effect as if she had crowned a suit of fifteenth-century armour with a black bowler hat.

Even more unsatisfactory in Goldie's opinion was that the Arthurian legend itself lacked a middle section to match the excellent beginning and end. This structural weakness had made the subject 'a death-trap for a whole succession of playwrights from Comyns Carr in the 1890s to D. G. Bridson in 1937'. Nonetheless, she draws attention to the production's notable quality as radio drama. It was, for instance, excellently cast, with Leon Quartermaine as Merlin and Lydia Sherwood as Wenhaver, while the 'surprising' selection of Marius Goring as Arthur was 'most successful of all':

> Arthur is only too apt to be a bore. An actor who specialises in nobility would have been almost bound to make him one. Mr Goring's power gave him the arresting reality which he should have and which he so often lacks.

Richard Addinsell's incidental music fitted the play, while Val Gielgud's production particularly 'suited the microphone' in its handling of time, and showed how radio could free the imagination above the 'dead level of the physically possible'. The sole weakness was that this imaginative freedom was given inadequate scope: for example, when Arthur's sword sang, instead of emitting a strange new sound, the sword's song was merely a powerful baritone delivering 'Who holds me holds Britain!'

Radio's eminent suitability for spoken verse would help to reinstate verse as an accepted medium for drama, and among the many verse dramas that were commissioned were highly original works by Henry Treece, a leading figure in the Apocalyptic movement, which rebelled against 'social reporting', and promoted the revival of myth. His *The Dark Island* (TP 1948) had described the Roman invasion of Britain. For this he then composed an Arthurian sequel: *The End of a World*, a sixty-minute dramatic interpretation by a dozen voices (nine male, three female) of the coming of the Saxons to Romanised Britain. Despite its Arthurian surface derived from Nennius and *The Welsh Triads*, the new play was, according to Dafydd Gruffydd of the Drama Department (Wales), more fundamentally concerned with the eternal struggle between Good and Evil or Light and Darkness. Its verse showed, in his view, a great improvement over that of the earlier work; it had fine dramatic quality, and was excellent for broadcasting because it created colour and movement easily, and was comprehensible at first hearing. Gruffydd was very keen to mount his own production of this, claiming that as Treece was Welsh (a half truth), and his subject and treatment 'essen-

[86]  Grace Wyndham Goldie, 'Heroes on Sunday', *Listener* 25 (2 January 1941), 28.

tially Celtic', a Welsh production would 'be able to do it full justice'.[87] Though
the Welsh Home Service was prepared to broadcast it, Gruffydd suggested
that the play's quality entitled it to a Third Programme performance. In the
London drama department, it largely won the support of E. J. King Bull, who
recommended its acceptance subject to some revision, for it was too wordy, and
needed a stronger focus on the narrative line, in particular a clearer explanation of Medrawd's role.[88] But these recommendations were rejected by the Head
of Third Programme, Harman Grisewood, who judged that, unlike the verse
of Charles Williams or David Jones, the work was commonplace in language
and characterisation, lacked poetic intensity and made no fresh or profound
investigation of the Arthurian subject.[89] His negative conclusions were endorsed
by Leslie Stokes and Laurence Gilliam.[90] The upshot was that Third resolved
to reserve its judgement until a successful broadcast was mounted elsewhere.
A broadcast therefore went ahead on the Welsh Home Service (12 April 1949).
A couple of years later, Mollie Greenhalgh tried to have it revived on Third, but
her proposal was promptly turned down by Donald McWhinnie.[91]

However conflicting these evaluations may appear, all of them seem to be
justified. The language has considerable range and power in conveying the
sensuous beauty of the turning year, an imagery that structurally underpins the
thematic development from Late-Roman languor, to the dream of Camelot, and
the threat from Saxon violence. There is too a modicum of dramatic tension owing
to a finely struck balance between differing viewpoints: the Woman's scorn of
the invaders, and the Man's more sympathetic understanding of the hunger-
driven Saxons. There is some evidence besides that the specially commissioned
music by the distinguished Welsh composer Grace Williams was well integrated
with the verbal script, and would have enhanced the work's effect. Occasionally
too the Arthurian tradition is freshly reworked, as in the variant on Taliesin's
reincarnation boast:

> I left the coal-face later, man,
> The tin bath on the hearth,
> My Blodwen in the rocking chair.
> I bowed my head in the raw Spanish sun,
> 'Guadalajara' was my requiem.[92]

But more commonly the verse appears blunted; the long laments and panegyrics
are too diffuse and unlocalised. We listen to a set of moving variations upon
the Welsh stories, but without deep understanding: for we need to know why,
for example, Medrawd treacherously kills his kinsman Arthur just before the

87   BBC WAC: memo from Dafydd Gruffydd to Head of Drama, 23 November 1948. Treece was
     born and raised in Staffordshire; his mother's family had moved there from Wales.
88   BBC WAC: memo from E. J. King Bull to Head of Drama, 14 December 1948.
89   BBC WAC: memo from Harman Grisewood to Head of Welsh Programme, 26 November
     1948.
90   BBC WAC: memos from Leslie Stokes (of Third Programme), 23 December 1948; and from
     Laurence Gilliam (Head of Features), 2 February 1949.
91   BBC WAC: memo from Mollie Greenhalgh to Charles Lefeaux, 31 December 1951; and from
     Donald McWhinnie to Play Department, 31 December 1951.
92   BBC WAC: typed playscript of Henry Treece, 'The End of a World', p. 29.

battle against the Saxons at Camlan. Its success must therefore be considered as limited.

The second Arthurian work by Treece faced a similar rough passage before finding partial acceptance. His *Tristram and the Watchers* was initially submitted to Third, where Cleverdon pronounced it 'competently written' but 'rather dull'.[93] Once more, it is E. J. King Bull's assessment that seems shrewd, pinpointing what he thought the weakness of the play: it lacked a high climax, and the final moral uttered by the Three Stones was not strong or deep enough. On balance, though, he thought that the play should, after some revision, be broadcast on Third.[94] His proposal was, however, overruled by Harman Grisewood, who found the piece 'situationally rather commonplace', and the verse 'no more than just about alright'.[95] So, once more, the play was produced by Dafydd Gruffydd for the Welsh Home Service (11 January 1950). Treece had hoped to use music by Grace Williams again, but this seems not to have happened: a memo from the Head of Welsh Programmes indicates that the only sound effect employed was 'a gust of wind'. Written immediately after the performance, this memo to Harman Grisewood suggests that the latter might like to reconsider the play for the Third, subject to some slight revision. This revision would entail cutting out the 'character of the Watcher, who is the symbol of Fate, and expanding the idea of conflict between the three characters.'[96] Even though Treece made these changes, Grisewood does not seem to have shifted his position, and the revised version, containing about 'twenty-five per cent of new verse' and known as *The Tragedy of Tristram*, went out on the Welsh service again (6 October 1950). Accepting his fee for this new broadcast, Treece probably found pleasure in mentioning that T. S. Eliot had suggested that this verse play should be made the nucleus of his next collection for Faber.[97] As a copy of the earlier version is not available at Caversham, it is on the printed form that we must now rely.[98]

The shortcomings of *The End of a World* are no longer evident in this second drama. In plot, Treece adheres mainly to the Bédier version, but presents it solely through the ghosts of Tristram, Mark and Yseult Blanchemain, who are compelled to re-enact in soliloquy and dialogue their tragic involvements. By the introduction of newly invented domestic detail, however, Treece brings distinctness and life to these personae: Tristram is fiercely proud of his sons, while Yseult of Ireland, we are told, suffers from wrinkles, roughening hands, and the lack of children in the house. Moreover, Treece's drama skilfully exploits the potential of radio: a stage production involving only ghosts in such a static plot might verge on the ludicrous, but on radio these disembodied voices, set on the borders between dream and reality, are wholly engaging, and the temporal fluidity of the broadcasting medium allows frequent flashbacks to earlier key moments in the tragedy. Crucially, Treece's robust blank verse is rhythmically

[93] BBC WAC: undated memo from Cleverdon to Laurence Gilliam.
[94] BBC WAC: memo from E. J. King Bull to Head of Drama, 22 February 1949.
[95] BBC WAC: memo from Harman Grisewood to E. A. Harding, 24 March 1949.
[96] BBC WAC: memo from A. Watkin Jones to Harman Grisewood, 15 February 1950.
[97] BBC WAC: letter from Treece to Copyright Department, 12 September 1950.
[98] Henry Treece, 'The Tragedy of Tristram', in *The Exiles* (London: Faber & Faber, 1952), pp. 13–39 (p. 21).

close enough to normal speech patterns to retain idiomatic immediacy, and his syntax is sufficiently lucid for rapid comprehension by a listener, but the overall effect is heightened by a rich visual imagery that can vividly recreate past scenes, and illuminate the essential individuality of the three protagonists. All have hearts, but Mark's is 'a rotten walnut in / [his] body's shell' (p. 21); the only flower that Tristram's 'dry, sour heart' will sustain is 'bitter willow-herb' (p. 16); whereas Yseult Blanchemain 'fed the snow-starved birds, / And robins sat forever in her heart' (p. 18). Dejectedly aware of his histrionic role, Tristram fears that he 'must speak his words / Though no one listens, to eternity' (p. 39). His foreboding now conveys an additional irony, for Treece's drama has not received great attention, even though he created in this concentrated play not only the best Tristan play on air, but probably the finest of all the original Arthurian verse dramas broadcast.

Substantial interest was, however, aroused by R. C. Sherriff's *The Long Sunset* (HS 23 April 1955). Set in a Roman villa near Richborough in Kent, it dramatises the tragic fate of those Romans left behind when the legions sail away in AD 410. Threatened by Saxon invaders these abandoned settlers call in a tough West Country soldier of fortune to help them. Because the soldier is called Arthur (played by Joseph O'Conor), this makes it the first BBC play to attempt a realistic demythologised portrayal of the historical figure as a practical astute leader, who knows that if you want to impress your men, 'always talk to them at sunset, with your back to the sun. It makes you look bigger.'[99] Though the leading Roman settlers are killed at the end of the play, we are, of course, aware that the Arthurian resistance will historically triumph, not only by temporarily withstanding the Saxons but also (through a strange paradox) by creating the basis for the British Empire, the true successor to Rome. Ideas in Britain may have come from the south, but they are matured in the long twilights of the northern island (p. 87). At another level, the play has a determinedly modern application. Sherriff locates his work in the part of England he knows best – between London and the Channel – and the play's genesis lay in his own amateur archaeological excavations on the South Coast from about 1937, when he sensed a parallel between the collapse of Roman Britain and the current threat posed by Nazi Germany.[100] Such a focus is slightly broadened by his preview in *Radio Times* (15 April 1955), which speculates on what might have happened to the British in India if Britain had fallen in 1940. These analogies are heavily underscored by the fact that Sherriff's Romans think, speak, and act like twentieth-century Britons (or at least like those in London West End drawing room comedies). Nor do the parallels stop there, for, by the time that Sherriff's play was completed, the British Empire had started to unravel, with the result that modern Britons were increasingly aware of a new bond between their own sunset and that of Ancient Rome.

Although the play reads like a stage piece, and its pervasive sunset imagery demands the lighting effects available in a theatre performance, Sherriff made

99   R. C. Sherriff, *The Long Sunset: A Play in Three Acts* (London: Longmans, 1960), p. 75.
100  R. C. Sherriff, *No Leading Lady: An Autobiography* (London: Gollancz, 1968), pp. 309–16.

the bold and original decision to give it a radio première instead of putting it on a conventional stage, because he felt that a play that failed in the West End was 'dead and finished for' and, even if it later obtained a broadcast, listeners would not receive it with an open mind as it already bore the stigma of failure. Happily, what was, he claimed, 'a new departure' for the BBC seems to have come off very well for him in terms of publicity. Included in the *Saturday Night Theatre* slot on St George's Day, it drew an audience of five million.[101] Among reviewers, *The Times* believed it smoothly produced by Ayton Whitaker and well spoken (particularly by Brewster Mason as Julian, 'the noblest Anglo-Roman of them all'), but discovered little to applaud, disliking the hackneyed diction and characterisation; Trewin, sympathetic as always to an Arthurian theme, nevertheless thought the play 'unequal', its dialogue 'oddly slack at times', its characterisation often thin, 'and yet, all said, it takes the heart'.[102]

It certainly seems to have taken the public heart, as it was repeated twice that year (HS) and on another two occasions in the next, when it was broadcast even on the more popular Light Programme. The performances in 1955, 1956 and 1960 were all accompanied by various Douglas Relf illustrations in *Radio Times* **[plate 22]**. Theatre production soon followed, the Birmingham Repertory Theatre opening their season with it on 30 August 1955, and Bernard Miles later mounting a London production at the Mermaid. It also went rapidly into print, for Trewin included it in his *Plays of the Year* (1955); an acting edition followed in 1958, and a schools edition in 1960, when it was prescribed as a set book by an examination board.

Besides adopting such pieces from older established figures, the BBC continued to present work from a rising generation of playwrights. Among the best known of these was Giles Cooper, who wrote over thirty plays for radio, in one of which he takes up Sherriff's theme of a postcolonial Arthur. Structured around a Malorian subtext, *Without the Grail* (HS 13 January 1958) is set largely in modern Assam, where Felix, a patriarchal British tea-planter, regards himself as a latter-day Arthur, believing it his duty to preserve a stronghold of civilised values amid the chaos caused by the dissolution of Empire. He has a copy of Malory – he scorns Tennyson – from which he reads aloud to his family, and which he employs in a form of *sortes Vergilianae*. His opening the text at the account of the final combat between Arthur and Mordred has, indeed, great dramatic significance, for Felix will shortly kill his own son (who plans to escape from India to London), and will be beheaded in his turn by an adopted son (a Naga who dreams of restoring traditional ways). A daughter (a secret Communist) is drawn too into this Malorian pattern, taunting a visitor (who offers to help her escape) with being a Sir Lancelot rescuing 'a damsel in distress'.[103] Finally, the play's hostile critique of Felix is voiced by the visitor, who accuses him of taking only what he wants (the jousting and feasting) from the Arthurian story, but neglecting the idealism, the knightly aim of achieving the Holy Grail.

---

101 Sherriff, *No Leading Lady*, 348.
102 'Experimental Play Broadcast', *The Times* (25 April 1955), 17. J. C. Trewin, 'Drama', *Listener* 53 (28 April 1955), 767–8.
103 Giles Cooper, 'Without the Grail', in *Six Plays for Radio* (London: British Broadcasting Corporation, 1966), pp. 126–83 (p. 182).

(Just 'a fairy tale added on. Childish stuff,' Felix ripostes [p. 174].) Both Donald McWhinnie's production and the acting (Michael Hordern played Felix) were praised by Roy Walker, but he also placed his finger precisely on the play's weakness as a vehicle for ideas, for the characters remain too undeveloped and one-dimensional to be thought of as credible human beings.[104] Felix is, for example, caricatured far too grossly as preoccupied with the trivial question of the correct route around the table for port after dinner. Whereas Sherriff's play displayed some sympathy for colonial settlers and gave a certain vitality to them on air, Cooper's does not. His acute dislike leads him to belittle them to such an extent that he denies them artistic life. As a result the surface dazzle of his play's polished laconic style is not matched by sufficient psychological complexities beneath. Nonetheless, Cooper's work was appreciated enough within the BBC to be repeated in September that year, issued in book form and even adapted for television (BBC 13 September 1960).

Another leading contributor was the BBC staff-writer Frederick Bradnum, who wrote sixty plays and made numerous adaptations between 1954 and 1994. Among his earliest ventures was *The Cave and the Grail*, a highly original mix of Celtic folklore, Wolfram and/or Wagner, autobiography and social critique. BBC opinion was, however, strongly divided over its suitability. Although it enjoyed the support of Raymond Raikes and Leslie Stokes, it was for McWhinnie 'too ambitious', and for Gielgud 'a basic vulgarisation of one of the world's greatest legends'.[105] As a result, over three years elapsed before it was allowed to go on air (TP 7 July 1959). This verse drama was based, Bradnum declared, on a Norfolk legend about a magician who kept in a vast cave the souls of sailors drowned off the coast.[106] One sailor, however, survived to find his way into the cave, and release the imprisoned souls. Bradnum turns this into an Arthurian story by identifying the magician's cauldron ('wherein the secret of the world is contained') with the Grail, and naming the sailor Perceval.[107] He also makes it an allegory of religious development, because Celtic paganism, represented by the cauldron, has been transcended by Christ's sacrifice: the cauldron is now filled with His blood. Watched over by a Guardian Angel (Sian Phillips), Perceval (Ronald Fraser) uses his intelligence to outwit the giant, unicorn and witch that are sent to oppose him, before managing to set the sailors' souls free. The difficult part is then to free himself. First he has to withstand the scorn of figures from his own past, and become independent of his mother. Next, he must understand the sickness of modern civilisation, by experiencing the evils of industrialisation and war, and resist the materialist lures of Marxism, sensuality, and mass 'entertainment', all of which deride the Grail. As a revue chorus puts it:

---

104   Roy Walker, 'Drama', *Listener* 59 (23 January 1958), 173–4.
105   BBC WAC: Bradnum file.
106   Though Bradnum's familiarity with wartime Norwich is evident from his poem 'Norwich Revisited' (*Listener* 59 [5 June 1958], 943), the topography of Norfolk in his play seems more fanciful than realistic. The county has a coast but no sea caves.
107   BBC WAC: typed playscript of Frederick Bradnum, 'The Cave and the Grail'.

The Grail!
    Would you sail
With it in a ship
    To the Coconut Islands,
Or would you keep it
    In your favourite
Corner and invite blondes
    To see it!
The Grail!
    Would you hail
All your friends and give them
    A look at it,
Would you cook it in wine
    Or hang it
Like haggis or slap it down
    Or call it fine!   (p. 20)

Consumed with self-doubt, Perceval is on the verge of abandoning his quest, but some children beg him to continue so that they may have hope. He therefore perseveres, and succeeds: by gratefully kissing the hideous Grail Maiden (who promptly becomes beautiful), and asking the appropriate questions of the Maimed King. The latter is duly healed, and the land's fertility restored, but Perceval is now obliged to receive the wound himself, and on seeing the Grail is struck blind. Accompanied back to our world by the Grail Maiden, he must patiently await an unspecified time when he can communicate his secret vision to others. Thus the play, like Gracq's, rests tantalisingly and gnomically open-ended:

    Our strength must hold in knowing
    Bud, tree and soaring bird
    Are part of the design that flowing
    From the master hand desires
    Immediate perfection, outside of man
    Who strives to read the secret fires
    Or trace his vision in the sand.   (p. 29)

Leslie Stokes's prior assessment was that Bradnum's 'belief gives the writing an [impressive] integrity', though he had 'perhaps bitten off a theme which he is not strong enough to chew'.[108] Only performance could show 'whether or not the attempt succeeds or fails, and at the worst it will be a distinguished failure'. Writing in *The Listener*, Ian Rodger was undeterred by the 'fey beginning that frightens away all but the Third Programme's devotees', and his initial fear that the work would 'founder in an over-poetic fog'.[109] He considered that Bradnum's verse 'succeeded in saying something hard and clear'. The play was firmly produced by R. D. Smith, and 'was balanced remarkably by some very

---

108   BBC WAC: memo, 8 March 1956.
109   'Norfolk Orpheans', *Listener* 62 (16 July 1959), 111.

fine music by Mr Humphrey Searle, who provided both magic sensations and some music which wittily burlesqued popular music'. Unhappily, as Bradnum's play has never reached print or even been repeated, its reputation remains, like its hero, suspended in limbo.

# 3

## 1960–1979: 'The old order changeth, yielding place to new'

### Music

With the major reorganisation of networks in 1964, the time allocated to classical music was greatly increased and, with the advent of stereo and VHF, sound quality was appreciably enhanced. As radio reaped the beneficial side effects of technological advance and globalisation, these were golden decades for Wagnerian opera, *Parsifal* being broadcast fifteen times in its entirety, *Tristan* eighteen. *Parsifal* came mainly in the form of stage recordings from the Bayreuth Festival of the previous year, though these were interspersed with live broadcasts from Covent Garden (under Reginald Goodall and Georg Solti) or recordings of the Vienna Philharmonic conducted by Solti. Twice concert performances were mounted in the London Promenade season. In the first (Solti), only Acts 2 and 3 were performed (1966), but on the other occasion (Boulez) the whole work was broadcast over two evenings (1972).

Among *Tristan* broadcasts there was an even richer variety. Appropriately enough the greatest number (seven) came from Bayreuth because these years included the halcyon 1960s, when Karl Böhm conducted and Birgit Nilsson sang the role of Isolde, but four productions stemmed from Covent Garden (Furtwängler [2], Solti, Colin Davis), a couple from the Berlin Philharmonic at the Salzburg Easter Festival (Von Karajan), live performances from Scottish and Welsh Operas (1973, 1979), one from the Vienna Philharmonic under Solti, and two concert performances from the BBC SO and Chorus (Davis).

Not only were attractive *Radio Times* illustrations by Val Biro [plate 23], C. W. Bacon [plate 24] and Roy Ellsworth occasionally provided, but broadcasts were also complemented by the developing practice of incorporating interval talks by authorities on the music. In addition, Christopher Cook's one-hour feature, *Their Love Shall Drink Its Fill*, was especially noteworthy for its account of the composition of *Tristan* (R4 1974), while the regular *Record Review* programmes supplied an informed evaluation of the recordings made of key works, naturally including Wagner operas among these. The further extension of broadcasting hours for classical music from 1965 gave opportunity, too, for the more frequent airing of excerpts from these two works: *Tristan* especially benefited, and the number of 'Prelude and Liebestod' performances suddenly returned to 1920s levels.

Though there is no evidence of a comparable surge in excerpts from Dryden and Purcell's *King Arthur*, the whole work (or a sizeable chunk of it) was kept in public attention by six broadcast performances. Julian Herbage's arrangement seems to have been used for the concert version of seven scenes (only ninety-five minutes) by the BBC SO under David Willcocks (TP 4 November 1964), with MacNeice's linking text narrated by Marius Goring. It was claimed, though, that some of Dryden's text was included in the rather longer version (110 minutes) performed by Philomusica of London, conducted by Anthony Lewis (MP 3 March 1966, repeated 1974).[1] In contrast, the concert version (105 minutes) by the London Mozart Players conducted by Roger Norrington (MP 6 January 1970) was advertised as playing only the Purcell music for the drama.[2] A major change was instituted later that year, however, for a stage production premièred by English Opera under Philip Ledger at the Norwich Triennial Festival (R3 19 October 1970). For this Colin Graham had written a drastically new version, preserving the framework of Dryden's plot, but pruning episodes such as the human sacrifices to Woden, and most of the Pageant of Britain.[3] Boldly, too, he drafted a new Prologue for Merlin, created singing parts for Arthur and all the other principal characters, and in doing so introduced songs from other works by Purcell. In the view of *Musical Times* it was largely 'a tasteful pantomime with high class music, skilfully constructed'.[4] Acknowledging that the outcome is more Graham's *King Arthur* than Purcell's, *The Times* critic considered that the alterations had made the work 'a feasibility where it was previously a gigantic white elephant'.[5] The outcome was well received by the local audience,[6] for the singers performed well and, though the radio listeners could not see them, were 'richly and splendidly dressed'.[7] Listeners probably missed little on being denied a sight of the minimalist set – one that was designed for cheapness and portability, because this production did travel, to Edinburgh, Aldeburgh and Sadler's Wells, before presentation at a Promenade Concert over two separate evenings (R3 1, 14 September 1972), when it was supplemented by Michael Greenhalgh's interval talk on the collaboration between Dryden and Purcell. In Basil Lam's preview of this Prom, Ledger's severe reconstruction was cautiously approved for 'remedying the basic defect ... by which the principal characters are deprived of music'.[8] The fact that the set obscured the singers from many in the Albert Hall was of no concern to a radio audience for, according to *The Times* critic and a later brief note by Bayan Northcott, the musical performance was 'by all accounts ... exceptional'.[9]

1    Music Programme (MP) was a transitional daytime stage in the switchover from Third Programme to Radio 3.
2    At the original concert performance in Queen Elizabeth Hall on 17 October 1969, a narration written by Roger Norrington had been read ('somewhat too satirically') by George Roubicek: *The Times* (18 October 1969), III. Presumably this was omitted from the broadcast.
3.   *King Arthur: His Magical History. Based on an opera by John Dryden.* New version edited and adapted by Colin Graham. Set to music by Henry Purcell. Realised by Philip Ledger (London: Faber Music, 1970).
4.   Andrew Porter, 'King Arthur', *Musical Times* 111 (1970), 1250.
5.   William Mann, '*King Arthur*: Norwich', *The Times* (20 October 1970), 14.
6    See review by H. B., 'Triennial Festival: Première a Worthy Spectacular', *Eastern Daily Press* (20 October 1970), 7.
7    Porter, 'King Arthur', 1250.
8    Basil Lam, 'Purcell's *King Arthur*', *Listener* 88 (31 August 1972), 281.
9    Alan Blyth, 'King Arthur', *The Times* (2 September 1972), 11. Bayan Northcott, 'Last Week's Broadcast Music', *Listener* 88 (7 September 1972), 315.

Within two years of Boughton's death in 1960, Michael Hurd had published a biography, the first fruits of a lifelong dedication to his music, but Boughton was to disappear from popular recognition for many years.[10] His radio reputation would start to revive only in 1978 when, for the exact centenary of his birth, Carole Rosen compiled a forty-five-minute feature programme, *The Glastonbury Ring: A Study of Rutland Boughton* (R4 23 January 1978). Directed by John Cardy and narrated by Arthur Marshall, this memorial presented a blend of archival recordings (using the voice of Boughton, for example) while studio actors took the roles of leading musicians and critics (Harry Webster played the part of Boughton's 'staunchest champion', George Bernard Shaw). What emerged was a very sympathetic account of Boughton's early life and his attempt to stage an Arthurian cycle but, though the programme included a recorded excerpt from *The Queen of Cornwall*, none of the more specifically Arthurian operas was played, presumably because they are not contained in the BBC Music Library.[11] This omission was partly righted soon afterwards, when the BBC Concert Orchestra, conducted by Owain Arwel Hughes, gave a programme of 'Scenes from the Operas of Rutland Boughton', including among them not only items from *The Queen of Cornwall* but also from *The Lily Maid* (R3 11 February 1978, repeated October).

Meanwhile an important new English 'music drama' involving a quasi-Arthurian subject had come from another source. Gordon Crosse's *Potter Thompson*, a work for child-singers and actors, took up the folk legend of the Sleeping King at Richmond, and was provided with a libretto by Alan Garner.[12] Garner's earlier work had often presented Arthurian motifs without specific mention of Arthur, but reshaped them into a more general mythology that we sense is charged with deep personal significance. That is the case here. His Potter Thompson, isolated from other villagers by memories of an unhappy love affair, enters the subterranean world where the elemental powers of his craft (earth, water, air and fire) induce him to accept his personal loss (the past is past). He then accidentally starts to wake the Sleeping Hero, but takes the decision not to continue doing so (the future should not be summoned). Returning to the surface, reconciled to 'time-now, the only time in which a man can live', he joins with other villagers in celebration of the harvest. When Crosse's piece had opened at the Finchley Children's Music Group in January 1975 the running time was over two hours. This was, in Stanley Sadie's opinion, too long for children, though the music was 'beautifully written' for them, it being tuneful, delicately textured, and making good use of decorative patterns.[13] Cuts agreed by the composer, librettist and producer (Michael Elliott) were then made for a production at Blythburgh in Suffolk, which brought it down to ninety minutes,

---

10  Michael Hurd, *Immortal Hour: The Life and Period of Rutland Boughton* (London: Routledge & Kegan Paul, 1962). This was radically revised and enlarged as *Rutland Boughton and the Glastonbury Festivals* (Oxford: Clarendon Press, 1993).

11  BBC WAC: typed script of Carole Rosen, 'The Glastonbury Ring: A Study of Rutland Boughton'.

12  *Potter Thompson: A music drama in one act.* Music by Gordon Crosse. Libretto by Alan Garner (Oxford: Oxford University Press, 1977).

13  Stanley Sadie, 'Lively children's opera', *The Times* (10 January 1975), 11.

but the simultaneous broadcast later given on BBC television and radio (R3 17 May 1975) ran for only forty-five. Once again the curtailment had been made with the agreement of Crosse, Garner and Elliott for, as Hugo Cole argued persuasively, television time is essentially different from that in a theatre, and, since audience concentration is under greater threat at home, greater brevity is required by the home viewer.[14] John Winfield's performance as Potter Thompson was 'marvellous', even more effective 'scaled down for television.' The broadcast production had, in fact, benefited from the limitations of time and place 'by stimulating the ingenuity and imagination of the cameramen, very much as the limitations of child-singers and actors stimulated Crosse'.

In other music, the Tristan legend remained a powerful inspiration. While Bax's death in 1953 had, it is claimed, led to increasing neglect of much of his music, *Tintagel* continued to be played, and far more frequently so after 1967.[15] Denis Wright's *Tintagel Suite* for brass band received a lesser but steady performance, on one occasion being conducted by the composer himself, who enjoyed a long career with the BBC (1965). Frank Martin's *Le Vin herbé* was twice repeated (1970, 1974). Further afield (topographically), the Norwegian Ture Rangström's *Tristans Död* was sung by Jussi Björling (1965), and (historically) scholarly recovery of medieval music yielded up a pair of performances of what Richard Barber regards as probably the first surviving composition to be inspired by the legends, *Il Lamento di Tristan*.[16] The former, described as traditional thirteenth century, was performed by Archie Camden (bassoon) and Wilfred Parry (piano) (1966); the latter, when it was denoted as fourteenth century, performed by the Manitoba University Consort (1967). What is more, Messiaen's *Turangalîla Symphony* finally entered the standard repertoire. Although receiving landmark performances on the BBC in 1953 and 1954, it had not been heard on air since then. But this situation was to change radically during the mid-1960s. It was played by the Belgian Radio SO (1965) and the Belgrade Philharmonic (1966) and then given a well-publicised performance by the Royal Liverpool Philharmonic under Charles Groves in 1968 (TP 12 March). Prefaced by an explanatory article by Felix Aprahamian in *Radio Times*, in which the symphony was hailed as 'one of the great monuments of twentieth-century music', the performance was succeeded by a thirty-minute discussion involving Peter Maxwell Davies, Alexander Goehr, Charles Groves and members of the Liverpool Philharmonic Club.[17] Later that year the French Radio Philharmonic was heard (MP 9 September) in a recorded performance of a concert given in Oxford the previous year. At least another nine performances ensued in the next decade. Consequent upon this attention was an interest in the two other parts of Messiaen's Tristan triptych, of which *Turangalîla* was the second. The third part, *Cinq Rechants*, composed in 1949, had not been awarded its UK première until 9 February 1961, when it was sung by the BBC Chorus conducted by John Carewe. Thereafter it was occasionally heard again, and in a sudden flurry between 1969 and 1972, it featured at

[14]  Hugo Cole, 'Potter Thompson', *Listener* 93 (29 May 1975), 712.
[15]  Foreman, *Bax*, p. 375.
[16]  Richard Barber, ed., *King Arthur in Music* (Cambridge: Brewer, 2002), p. 1.
[17]  Felix Aprahamian, 'Musica Viva', *Radio Times* (12 March 1968), 41.

least six times (including a Promenade Concert performance). *Harawi*, the first part, was broadcast in 1965.

Complementing Tristan as a minor motif was the Lady of Shalott, through work that had been composed in earlier times. Phyllis Tate's *The Lady of Shalott* cantata was played twice (1961, 1979). The first of these occasions was a recording, made at the King's Lynn Festival in the summer of that year, of the work's *concert* première.[18] It was accompanied in *Radio Times* by an inventive vignette by Val Biro [**plate 25**].

There was also music for two ballets with the same subject. What was, however, misleadingly called Jean Sibelius's *The Lady of Shalott*, arranged by Gordon Jacob (1967), was in truth merely a selection of piano pieces by Sibelius (Op. 70, 75 and 85) that had been co-opted for use in Frederick Ashton's *The Lady of Shalott* (1931).[19] The other work was Sir Arthur Bliss's *The Lady of Shalott*, which had been performed in California by the San Francisco Ballet in 1958, but had not been heard by the composer until he conducted the BBC SO in its UK première, in a performance that used a narrator to describe the action (TP 30 December 1968).[20]

Elsewhere there are many other indications of the BBC's innovative approach. It awarded, for example, Benjamin Frankel's recently completed Eight Songs, Op. 32, their première (HS 8 January 1960), and played the piece again in 1968 (MP) and 1977 (R3). This qualifies as 'Arthurian' work because the second song is 'The Knight and the Grail', allegedly based on an anonymous sixteenth-century poem.[21] Broadcasts helped besides in the rehabilitation of older works by introducing new recordings when they were made: the New Philharmonia's 1970 recording (under Antonio de Almeida) of Ernest Chausson's *Viviane* was, for instance, featured in 1972 and 1975. Similarly, the BBC broadcast (1975) the new recording by the Bournemouth Sinfonietta (under George Hurst) of the long-neglected incidental music composed by Edward Elgar for Laurence Binyon's tragic drama, *King Arthur* (1923). More esoterically, it even broadcast Joseph Boismortier's *Don Quichotte chez la Duchesse*, an eighteenth-century musical play in which a character assumes a Merlin role (R3 9 February 1973).

Modern Arthurian pop music became institutionalised with Lerner and Loewe's *Camelot*, which, after its Broadway success, opened in London in 1964. Although *Radio Times* is, sadly, weak in providing lists in these years of what was played or sung, apart from items on the Third Programme, it is certain that lyrics from the musical were heard on the BBC very frequently indeed. Where they are cited in *Radio Times*, it is as 'Selections from *Camelot*', performed by Reginald Leopold and his Palm Court Orchestra for the Home Service or Radio 2. The only pop artiste that surfaces on Radio 3 is Rick Wakeman, who was topically interviewed (20 July 1975) about a recent album (*The Myths and Legends of King Arthur and the Knights of the Round Table*) that he had recorded with his regular rhythm group (plus a 45-piece session orchestra, a male voice choir and

18  See chapter 2, note 22.
19  David Vaughan, *Frederick Ashton and his Ballets* (London: Black, 1999), pp. 65–6, 476.
20  David Cox, 'Where was Bliss's "Lady"?', *Radio Times* (30 December 1968), 45. A stage performance was later given at the Haymarket Theatre, Leicester, on 13 May 1975.
21  Private communication from Frankel's stepson, Dmitri Kennaway.

the 48-piece English Chamber Choir), and about which he had ambitious plans for a live production that would be 'more a pageant than a rock show'.[22] In the event he settled for a performance on ice at the Wembley Empire Pool, though this ran for only three shows.

## The Historical Arthur

In the late 1960s the historical King Arthur became news. An archaeological excavation under the direction of Leslie Alcock at South Cadbury excited wide public interest for it seemed to confirm that an Iron Age settlement there had been refortified in the late fifth century. There were high expectations that Camelot would really be located and Arthur's historical existence verified. Some traces of this excitement may be detected on the more-listened-to channels on radio. Roger Laughton visited the dig and gave an account of it ('Digging up a Legend') on *Woman's Hour* (HS 15 August 1966). A month later the topic was treated very substantially when Laughton produced, as part of an archaeological series on the Dark Ages, a discussion between experts who were closely involved: Leslie Alcock, Philip Rahtz (an archaeologist who was currently excavating on Glastonbury Tor) and Geoffrey Ashe, who was Secretary of the Camelot Research Committee (HS 11 September 1966). Such media publicity was carefully designed as an extremely useful archaeological tool to obtain funding for the excavations.[23] It was successful in two ways: it elicited a grant from the BBC, and the wide media coverage encouraged many other donors. Perhaps this blaze of publicity was, however, finally counterproductive. So many coach-loads of tourists arrived at the village that they were deemed a nuisance to residents, and the ensuing problem was a contributory factor in the excavation's ending in 1970.[24] Two of the speakers from Laughton's panel would return to the air after writing their relevant studies. Ashe, who played an incalculable role in the popularisation of the Arthurian legend during this period, would appear on *Woman's Hour* (R4 17 May 1971) to discuss the 'Golden Age' of King Arthur, a theme that suggests he was being interviewed about his recent *Camelot and the Vision of Albion*, where he argues that the messianic myth of an Arthurian return offers a profoundly significant symbolic construct for the 'overcoming of darkness and death'.[25] Alcock, too, was invited to *Woman's Hour* in the following year to talk about his book, *Arthur's Britain*, wherein he concluded that Arthur *was* the leader of the combined forces of the small kingdoms into which sub-Roman Britain had dissolved, but that the long-term significance of his victory at Badon was very small, for the character of the English settlement had not

---

[22] Rick Wakeman, *The Myths and Legends of King Arthur and the Knights of the Round Table* (New York: Triangle Music Corporation, 1975), p. 4.

[23] The *Chronicle* series on BBC television broadcast *Arthur: The Peerless King*, a fifty-minute documentary that included an account of the South Cadbury excavation (BBC2 10 June 1967).

[24] Leslie Alcock, *'By South Cadbury is that Camelot …': The Excavation of Cadbury Castle* (London: Thames & Hudson, 1972), p. 205.

[25] Geoffrey Ashe, *Camelot and the Vision of Albion* (London: Heinemann, 1971), p. 220.

been changed in any way by that victory (R2 18 February 1972).[26] As he would later point out in 'By South Cadbury is that Camelot', he had not found Camelot, nor added anything directly to historical knowledge about Arthur as a person, but the quest had enriched 'our understanding of the historical Arthur, and of the situation in which he acted'.[27] I presume – justifiably, I hope – that Alcock's cautious approach would have fed into a later schools programme (History in Evidence: 4. The Last Romans) that examined the question 'Who was King Arthur?' (R4 16 October 1974).

## Reading and Adapting 1: Medieval Literature

The same question had been tackled, though from a different angle, by A. C. Gibbs, a lecturer in medieval literature at the new University of York, in his talk, King Arthur (TP 1 July 1965). As Gibbs shows, before Arthur achieved his 'romantic glory', he had served the medieval historian and poet as a symbol of political convictions. Gibbs therefore discussed the significance of Arthur in Geoffrey of Monmouth and Layamon. In a much lighter account of British folk heroes, an instalment of Dave Arthur's The Stuff of Legend would examine Arthur's continuing life through poetry, prose and song (R4 11 July 1977).

New adaptations of Malory continued to be made, though mainly for children. Remarkably, four different series were produced for schools: by Margaret J. Millar in four parts (1960), by Kenneth Cavender in six (1967), by Sam Langdon in four again (1971), and by a nameless hand in three (1977).[28] But alongside these a major series for adults was also created by Derek Brewer. His Morte Darthur was a copious undertaking, produced by Raymond Raikes, consisting of an introductory preview by Brewer, and twelve dramatised half-hour readings, with incidental music by Stephen Dodgson, and accompanied by a crisp Eric Fraser vignette [plate 26] in Radio Times (R3 January–April 1971, repeated September–December). Arthur was read by Robert Eddison, Launcelot by Robert Hardy, Guenevere by Maxine Audley, and Merlin/Mordred by Basil Langton. Francis Dillon was impressed by the 'fascinating' preview:

Unless they make an LP, I doubt whether we shall ever have another opportunity of hearing such a glittering cast reading Malory ... the casting seemed perfect.[29]

He was still impressed several episodes later:

The version of Malory now being serialised shies away from nothing: although newly ordered, as it were, it gives us all the fantasy, sex, violence, mysticism and sheer magic of the original. All the individual performances are jewels,

---

[26] Leslie Alcock, Arthur's Britain: History and Archaeology, AD 367–634 (Harmondsworth: Allen Lane The Penguin Press, 1971), pp. 359–64.

[27] Alcock, 'By South Cadbury', p. 212.

[28] Malory, King Arthur, adapted by Margaret J. Millar; Malory, Morte d'Arthur, adapted by Kenneth Cavender; The Tale of King Arthur, adapted by Sam Langdon.

[29] Francis Dillon, 'The BBC Voice', Listener 85 (21 January 1971), 91.

but perhaps Norman Shelley as narrator might be picked out for some delicate flicks of humour given entirely by nice timing and tiny stresses.[30]

This was probably the star 'medieval' production of the two decades (and arguably the greatest of all Malory broadcasts ever), but it received a fitting pendant in *Sir Gawain and the Green Knight*. Making 1971 truly an *annus mirabilis*, a version for adults was broadcast, and it arrived fittingly at Christmas. Written by Gwyn Jones, who most likely used his earlier prose version as basis, it was – as with Brewer's Malory – produced by Raymond Raikes with music by Stephen Dodgson and a *Radio Times* vignette by Eric Fraser **[plate 27]**.[31] An introductory talk by Jones was followed by three weekly episodes (R3 December 1971, repeated Christmas 1972). The poem also continued to attract significant attention at school level. Once again, it was Margaret Millar who produced a schools version in two parts (1960), which was twice repeated (1963, 1971) and probably in 1976 as well (no author is named). Her version was then replaced by David Self's new two-part adaptation (1978).[32]

With Chaucer's *The Wife of Bath's Tale* a different approach was tried. Instead of using Coghill's translation into modern English, the original text was read by Marjorie Westbury in a modern pronunciation (TP 1963, 1964).

In what seems a very remarkable innovation, Radio 4 moved into Continental Arthurian romance by mounting in its afternoon *Story Time* slot a retelling from Hartmann von Aue's *Iwein*. Translated and adapted from Middle High German by Susanne Flatauer, *The Adventures of Sir Iwein* consisted of five daily episodes of twenty-five minutes, read by David Ryall (R4 3–7 February 1975). Flatauer's text makes very pleasant reading. She handles the narrative appropriately for serial transmission by ending each of the first four episodes at a cliffhanging moment, and the ironically idiomatic tone that is adopted suits both fidelity to Hartmann's original and the needs of her modern medium. When, for example, Iwein is about to fight the Lord of the Forest the narrator intervenes:

> But wait – I am not going to give you a detailed description of their combat, and I'll tell you why: there were never any witnesses to their fight, so I should have to make up all the details myself; one knight perished, and the other was so well-bred and discreet that he certainly declined to give an account of the cut and thrust of their struggle.[33]

The levity masks, of course, an essential seriousness of theme, and despite the time of broadcast, there are flickering sexual nuances (Iwein notes that the widow's 'milk-white body gleam[s] through where she had rent her gown'), which suggest that it is addressed also to an adult audience.

Finally, and to underline the fact that programmes now provided some readier access to Arthurian scholarship, Roy Owen was invited to give a talk

---

[30] Francis Dillon, 'A Modern Malory', *Listener* 85 (25 February 1971), 253.

[31] Gwyn Jones, *Sir Gawain and the Green Knight: A Prose Translation*, illus. Dorothea Braby (London: Golden Cockerel Press, 1952).

[32] Self's version was later published as *Sir Gawain and the Green Knight* (London: Macmillan Education, 1979), and reprinted in 1981, 1982 and 1983.

[33] BBC WAC: typed script of Susanne Flatauer, 'The Adventures of Sir Iwein': Part 1, p. 12.

on *The Grail Legend* (R3 7 April 1971), surprisingly the first on this topic that can be traced.[34] This was aptly scheduled to precede a recording of the Bayreuth *Parsifal* on the following evening, but Owen, who had published his own study of the evolution of the Grail legend a few years previously, used the occasion to review Emma Jung's *The Grail Legend*, an English translation of which had recently appeared.[35]

### Reading and Adapting 2: Post-Medieval Literature

The ritual that is attendant upon festive royal occasions tended to attract Arthurian music. This was the case at a special concert to mark the Jubilee of Queen Elizabeth II (R3 2 June 1977), when scenes were included from William Davenant's *Britannia Triumphans*, a masque originally staged by Inigo Jones before Charles I in 1637, and in which Merlin plays an introductory role. The essence of such events was, of course, their rarity.

On a more recurrent note, one particular BBC producer, Terence Tiller, figured in several Arthurian programmes of this era, and played a key role in the reintroduction of neglected literary works. He was, for example, responsible for a long-overdue reading – it had been twenty-five years since the last substantial one – of Spenser's *Faerie Queene*, which was given in thirteen half-hour episodes in 1977 (R3). It was Tiller, too, whose name will recur prominently with regard to Tennyson's revival.

The revived reputation of Tennyson and the Pre-Raphaelites among academics in this period marked a significant shift in literary values, and the change was soon felt in BBC programmes. Although the more traditional taste of Home Service listeners and schools programmes had always kept faith with Tennyson, his name had appeared only very intermittently on Third Programme. Major change, though, stemmed from the United States, where the publication of Jerome Buckley's *Tennyson: The Growth of a Poet* (1960) may be regarded as a watershed, because it was particularly influential worldwide in shaping the critical opinion of scholars for the rest of the century towards *Idylls of the King* by praising the poem's symphonic coherence and its concern for modern social and moral problems.[36] In the same year, the poet was made the subject of a favourable interpretation in *Tennyson: A Personal Reassessment*, a pair of one-hour programmes on the Third by Patric Dickinson, a poet who worked regularly for the BBC (TP 23, 28 September 1960), and who had 'read and loved the poetry

34 See also Nina Epton's forty-minute programme *The Christmas Grail: The Story of a Miracle* in *The Way of Life* series (HS 1 January 1961). This programme, which was set in Galicia, may be linked to a sculptured calvary in the village of San Vincente, which she described in *Spain's Magic Coast: From the Miño to the Bidassoa; A Personal Guidebook* (London: Weidenfeld & Nicolson, 1965), p. 49.

35 D. D. R. Owen, *The Evolution of the Grail Legend* (London and Edinburgh: Oliver & Boyd, 1968). Emma Jung and Marie-Louise von Franz, *The Grail Legend*, tr. Andrea Dykes (London: Hodder & Stoughton, 1971).

36 See Laurence W. Mazzeno, *Alfred Tennyson: The Critical Legacy* (Rochester, NY: Camden House, 2004), p. 104.

of Tennyson for many years'.[37] Dickinson's programmes were given considerable publicity, for they were repeated twice within six months. To stoke the
controversy, Harold Nicolson, whose earlier book had done so much damage
to Tennyson's critical reputation between the wars, was then allowed a twenty-
minute slot in which to respond to the attack that Dickinson had made upon his
views (TP 2 April 1961).[38] Later that year, Charles Tennyson replied for the former
laureate in his *Tennyson, my grandfather* (HS 17 December 1961, repeated 1962).
As of old, readings continued, often by eminent actors: 'The Lady of Shalott' by
Peggy Ashcroft (1960, 1967), Marius Goring (1961), and one by Anon (1971); 'The
Passing of Arthur' by James McKechnie, and 'Morte d'Arthur' also by Anon.
More pertinently, the lesser known 'Pelleas and Ettarre' was read on Third by
Derek Hart, following an introduction by Patric Dickinson (1966). Third then
hosted a fine talk by D. J. Palmer in a series on the relationship between art and
literature. His *The Laureate in Lyonnesse* (31 May 1967) argued that in *Idylls of the
King* Tennyson's acutely observed descriptions created a landscape that was not
only visual but visionary, and, being charged with symbolic feeling, was parallel
to the 'preternatural intensity' of a Burne-Jones painting, for both men's work
was leading towards the symbolist movement of the late nineteenth century,
and was a precursor of surrealism. Palmer's talk gained fairly wide coverage, as
it was repeated a few months later and reprinted in *The Listener*, together with
three illustrations from Gustave Doré's edition of Tennyson's *Idylls*.[39] Though
these drawings are not mentioned in Palmer's talk, their symbolic landscapes
are congruent with his argument, and reveal the fascination that was now felt
with depictions of the *Idylls*. Within a year, Third mounted a major celebration
of the poem, in the form of a musico-dramatic adaptation by Hallam Tennyson,
a BBC producer who was also the poet's great-grandson (2 February 1968). It
was given the generous time allowance of an hour and three-quarters, and a
distinguished cast, with Carleton Hobbs as the narrator, Stephen Murray taking
the part of King Arthur, Irene Worth Queen Guinevere, and Anthony Jacobs Sir
Lancelot. Hallam Tennyson says that this adaptation dated from 1959, when
he and his father first compiled a dramatic version of *Idylls* taken mainly from
'The Coming of Arthur', 'Lancelot and Elaine', 'Guinevere' and 'The Passing of
Arthur', for performance under the auspices of The Tennyson Society.[40] To this
sequence he now added 'The Holy Grail' and music specially written by Elizabeth Poston, whose 'evocative use of thematic material greatly enhance[d] the
dramatic unity of the work'. In order to 'increase the flow of the story' he had
added some verse of his own, which, he hoped, did 'not too obviously stand
out from the rest'.

Though Paul Bailey's review in *The Listener* was scathingly hostile to Tennyson's poem ('as intellectually satisfying and dramatically rewarding as an
evening spent in polite admiration of Granny's petit-point'), Third was not

---

[37]  BBC WAC: Dickinson file, letter of 5 October 1960.
[38]  Harold Nicolson, *Tennyson: Aspects of his Life, Character and Poetry* (London: Constable, 1923).
[39]  David Palmer, 'The Laureate in Lyonnesse', *Listener* 77 (22 June 1967), 815–17.
[40]  Hallam Tennyson, 'The Idylls of the King', *Radio Times* (2 February 1968), 61.

discouraged.[41] Hallam Tennyson went ahead with a programme on *Tennyson and Music*, which included a reading by Carleton Hobbs from *Idylls of the King* (TP 19 July 1974), while Terence Tiller created three major programmes devoted to the origins and development of Arthurian mythology, and the literary and psychological sources of Tennyson's Arthurian poems: *The Road to Shalott*, *The Road to Astolat* and *The Road to Camelot* (TP 3 September 1971, 14 January 1972, 24 March 1972). For the second of these Eric Fraser contributed an evocative vignette [plate 28].

But it was not only Tennyson who was coming back into fashion: the Pre-Raphaelites, too, were being examined with new interest. Much of this interest was, however, merely biographical, and revolved around lurid perceptions of their bohemian lives and loves. In contrast, Bridson's *Man to Be Strong: A Profile of William Morris* (HS 16 June 1963) was exceptional in emphasis, for it was sedulously evasive over the Jane Morris and Rossetti love affair. It was unusual also in including Guenevere (played by Jill Balcon) among the historical figures in this forty-minute retrospective of Morris's career.[42] Surprisingly, however, her given role is not essentially Arthurian. She quotes a fifteen-line passage from 'The Defence of Guenevere' about choosing the cloths of heaven or hell, a passage that evidently meant much to Bridson as he had previously borrowed from it in his *King Arthur*. But in *Man to Be Strong* this quotation is torn from its original literary context, where it alludes to the Queen's difficult amatory dilemma, and is interpreted instead as an aesthetico-political choice between tyranny/vulgarity/ugliness and social justice/dignity/art. Neither of her later quotations (from 'Midway of a walled garden' and *The Earthly Paradise*) has any Arthurian source or reference whatever. The play is organised around a debate between Morris and The Sceptic, but the latter is only a fall guy: the *donnée* is that Morris's (and Bridson's) socialist views are always correct. Dramatic interest is soon extinguished. The only specifically Arthurian works by William Morris that were broadcast seem to be the two poems that were included in a series of Pre-Raphaelite verse, when Mary Wimbush gave a reading of 'The Defence of Guenevere' and Bruce Beeby, Godfrey Kenton and Mary Wimbush read 'King Arthur's Tomb' (TP 21 May, 8 June 1967). The title of J. H. B. Peel's forty-minute play, *The Rum 'Un: Hawker of Morwenstow*, suggests, too, that a focus on colourful biographical incident shaped the continuing interest in this poet (HS 1 December 1963). The theme was picked up by two talks: Michael Underhill, *Morwenstow Revisited* (HS 15 September 1967), and E. W. F. Tomlinson's *Hawker of Morwenstow* (R3 25 August 1975). According to a note in the index of *BBC Radio Drama*, Howard Barker suggested the writing of a play about Hawker in January 1977, though this suggestion does not appear to have been pursued.[43]

As for twentieth-century verse, the marked attention given to Eliot's *The Waste Land* in the early 1970s was probably stimulated by Valerie Eliot's edition of the facsimile and transcript of the original drafts. In the very week of publication she introduced extracts from the poem on air (R3 7 November 1971). Two

41 Paul Bailey, 'Woe', *Listener* 78 (8 February 1968), 187–8.
42 BBC WAC: typed playscript of D. G. Bridson, 'Man to be Strong'.
43 *BBC Radio Drama Catalogues, 1923–1975*. Microform (Cambridge: Chadwyck-Healey, 1977).

major programmes followed: a Terence Tiller production (R3 23 December 1972), and one by Hallam Tennyson for which Alec Guinness did the reading (R3 1 December 1975). David Jones's reputation was kept green largely through the efforts of two of his friends: Douglas Cleverdon by means of repeats of his 1950s productions of *In Parenthesis* (TP 1964, 1968) and *The Anathemata* (TP 1978); and Harman Grisewood by means of a St David's Day talk on *David Jones: Artist and Writer*, which was immediately published by the BBC in book form (HS [Wa] 1 March 1966).[44] Jones's death in 1974 prompted a Robert Nye talk on the poetry (R3 26 October 1975) and a special feature by Peter Orr on *David Jones: Maker of Signs*, for which Cleverdon acted as producer (R3 6 November 1975).

A few other poets were noticed. In *A Portrait of Charles Williams* (TP 13 September 1961), Ruth Spalding presented a sympathetic evaluation of the writer, who had for some years lodged with her family in Oxford, but her programme seemed 'stilted' and 'incomplete' to Michael Swan for it failed to present an analysis of Williams's involvements with Rudolf Steiner, the Rosicrucian Order or the Catholic Church.[45] In the same year the 'Tristram' section from Henry Reed's 'Tintagel' was read by Marius Goring in a programme dedicated to *Poems on Mediaeval Themes* (HS 14 June 1961). Martyn Skinner, the author of a fine Arthurian trilogy in ottava rima, tried but failed to get his poem read on the Third.[46] The only new Arthurian poem, and one that was startlingly so, was D. M. Thomas's 'The Strait', which he read in a *Poetry Now* programme (TP 22 November 1965).[47] Here Thomas brilliantly combines ancient myth with a science fiction fantasy taken from Ray Bradbury's *Marionettes Inc*. When forced to separate from Yseult of Cornwall, this Tristan buys a *de luxe* humanoid plastic duplicate of her to take on his exile into space. Yseult even toys with the idea of giving the android to Mark before decamping with her lover:

> Lulled by the pleasure-tapes tamped to his skull
> day and night-long, her loving dupe would get
> all that he needed on a marionette,
> and none the wiser!

But Tristan refuses and departs with the beautiful android, a companionship that is envied by other crew members, whose needs are cruder, and who would be less tortured than he is by the 'ticking at its heart'. Dying later from gangrene, he summons the Cornish Yseult for aid, but the android does not pass on the return message. On arriving too late she is confronted by the humanoid, which passionately defends its role:

---

44  Harman Grisewood, *David Jones: Artist and Writer* (London: BBC, 1966).
45  Michael Swan, 'The Spoken Word', *Listener* 66 (21 September 1961), 443.
46  Martyn Skinner's trilogy had appeared separately in 1951, 1955 and 1959, and was collected as *The Return of Arthur: A Poem of the Future* (London: Chapman & Hall, 1966). See Rupert Hart-Davis, *Two Men of Letters: Correspondence between R.C. Hutchinson, Novelist, and Martyn Skinner, Poet, 1957–1974* (London: Michael Joseph, 1979), p. 129.
47  The poem was later published in *Penguin Modern Poets 11* (Harmondsworth: Penguin, 1968), pp. 118–22.

            God! All the times
i've bathed his wounds from rockfalls, faced the wind
of plunging meteors with him, walked the rims
of craters – shared this world, such as it is!
Fought off their paws … i say what more could *you*
have given him? Beauty? yet i see now my
skin is fairest, features equal. No! –
when your morse threatened to help him, my knees
shook, i felt these walls we'd built here cry
out in protest, force me to invent
what made this plastic melt in fear – a lie.

So, the poem concludes, love makes the Cornish Yseult 'divine', the android 'human'.

Thomas was Cornish born, and would later edit an anthology of Cornish poetry, *Granite Kingdom*, for which he wrote an introduction that surveys the county's links with the Tristan and King Arthur legends.[48] His chosen texts for the anthology included several Arthurian items: excerpts from Gottfried's *Tristan*, Swinburne's *Tristram of Lyonesse* and Tennyson's 'The Passing of Arthur'. It is likely therefore that some of these were included in the radio programme he made about this selection (R3 31 May 1971). Paralleling this literary mapping of the landscape was Christopher Hogwood's *In Honour of Cornwall* (R3 1 March 1975), in which the orchestral conductor related musical interpretations of the Tristan legend to those Cornish scenes associated with it. Both of these programmes neatly complement the Somerset claims, evinced in Peter France's feature *Glastonbury Power* (R4 21 July 1974) and Alan Gibson's talk *Arthur, Avalon and Sedgemoor* (R3 22 July 1974), which allegedly traced the enduring influence of Arthur on English literature.

Critical attention to Arthurian drama and prose fiction was very sparse. Two tentative Grail associations may be noted: a tribute by Ian Rodger to Giles Cooper (*A Writer for Radio*), which may have included discussion of his *Without the Grail* (TP 6 April 1967), and a eulogistic talk by P. J. Kavanagh on John Cowper Powys's *A Glastonbury Romance* (R3 6 July 1976). In contrast, there was, however, an increasing readiness to dramatise or read novels on air. The two major Arthurian novelists (in terms of influence) were both given in new versions. Twain's *Connecticut Yankee* was abridged by Marvin Kane and read by him in eight weekly episodes (1970), with an accompanying *Radio Times* vignette by Barry Wilkinson [plate 29], whereas White's *The Sword in the Stone* was adapted twice: for schools by Sam Langdon in four instalments (1971) and for the general public in *Story Time* by Neville Teller in ten (1978). On the back of this success Teller suggested that White's *The Once and Future King* should also be dramatised.[49] This proposal won the support of the BBC producer Graham Gauld, but it was soon discovered that Warner Brothers, to whom White had

---

[48]  D. M. Thomas, ed., *The Granite Kingdom: Poems of Cornwall* (Truro: D. Bradford Barton, 1970).
[49]  BBC WAC: T. H. White file, memo from Graham Gauld to A/SER, 5 June 1978.

sold the rights, were unwilling to make the novel available for radio dramatisation.[50] There the matter ended.

With the notable exception of Masefield's *The Midnight Folk* (1961) little was repeated from previous recordings. Nor were older novels treated. Apart from the serialised reading (R4 1979) of H. T. Lowe-Porter's translation (originally published in 1928) of Thomas Mann's deeply ironic updating, *Tristan*, the work taken up for broadcasting was relatively recent. Alan Garner's *Elidor*, for example, which like White's *The Sword in the Stone*, bridges the gap between adult and juvenile fiction, was serialised in a reading by Geoffrey Banks (1972). But if the novel happened to be intended for children alone it was likely to be *dramatised*. Some of the greatest Arthurian literature of the period was broadcast in this way: Rosemary Sutcliff's *The Lantern Bearers* reached radio in a *Children's Hour* six-part adaptation by Felix Felton (1961) only a couple of years after first publication, with Artos played by Jean England and then (as an older man) by John Bentley. Alan Garner's quasi-Arthurian *The Weirdstone of Brisingamen* was given in another six-part adaptation, by Nan Macdonald (1963), only three years after the book appeared; though Susan Cooper's *The Dark is Rising* had to wait five (1978).

There was a much wider time-lag for two fine adult novels that were each serialised in ten parts: Alfred Duggan's historical *Conscience of the King*, abridged by John Samson (published 1951, R4 1974) and Sir Arthur Quiller-Couch and Daphne du Maurier's nineteenth-century resetting of the Tristan story, *Castle Dor* (published 1962, R4 1977). Three other modern novels, however, were transferred to radio, and two of them quite rapidly. All of them have much looser Arthurian associations and lie outside the acknowledged canon, but I claim them as sufficiently Arthurian to deserve inclusion. The first of these is Agatha Christie's detective mystery *The Mirror Crack'd from Side to Side* (1962), in which Tennyson's poem 'The Lady of Shalott' is not only frequently quoted but richly functions as structural leitmotif throughout. This popular novel was adopted for the *Book at Bedtime* series, and abridged by Neville Teller into fifteen instalments (R4 1965).[51] The second is Samuel Selvon's *The Lonely Londoners* (1956), a pioneering account of West Indian immigrant life in the 1950s.[52] When the central figure (Moses) meets a newcomer off the boat train at Waterloo Station, he nicknames him 'Sir Galahad'. This nickname sticks, for it is thought appropriate for the character's bold, individualist, cavalier, yet naïve personality as he sets off on a series of wittily narrated adventures in search of acceptance by native Londoners, the implicit Holy Grail of his quest. Selvon, a frequent writer for radio, made a seven-part adaptation of this novel, retitling it *Eldorado West One* for its appearance on air (R4 1969). The third, and greatly inferior, novel is Ronald Kirkbride's *Yuki* (1967), whose eponymous Japanese heroine is rescued by Johnny Galahad from a drunken GI in Tokyo.[53] Not only does Johnny, who has been raised on stories of the Round Table, *sing* an eleven-line

50  BBC WAC: memo from Kathryn Pratt to Jane Gleed, 7 June 1978.
51  Agatha Christie, *The Mirror Crack'd from Side to Side* (London: Collins, 1962).
52  Samuel Selvon, *The Lonely Londoners* (London: Wingate, 1956).
53  Ronald Kirkbride, *Yuki* (London: Barker, 1967).

extract from Tennyson's 'Sir Galahad', but a mass of allusions throughout the novel identify him with the Grail knight. In a reversal, though, of the conventional quest formula, the female pursues the male ('it's the women who're the knight-errants today' [p. 134]), only to be repelled by his chilling awareness that 'his business did depend on the image of a Galahad, and one couldn't imagine a Galahad married to an Oriental, however attractive she was' (p. 162). As Johnny Galahad is, of course, revealed to be a fake and a gigolo, Yuki is shown to be the pure-in-heart. She ends happily by marrying an older, but good-natured, suitor, and settles into a comfortable English country house. This stereotypically risible account of gender and race was abridged by Honor Wyatt and read in ten instalments (R4 1971).

## Reading and Adapting 3: Drama

The sole new stage adaptation of this period was *The Dragon: An Allegorical Fairy Tale*, a translation by Max Hayward and Harold Shukman of Yevgeny Schwartz's *Drakon* (HS 1 March 1965), preceded in *Radio Times* by Shukman's résumé and a fetching illustration by Will Nickless [plate 30]. Though written in 1943, Schwartz's work had been closed down after single performances in Leningrad and Moscow. Not published in the USSR until 1960, it had then been briefly revived, but soon taken off once more. As the English translation of the play did not reach print until 1966, Nicholas Bethell's radio adaptation thus gave the play its first UK appearance in any medium.[54] In the play a dragon has exacted tribute from a town for four hundred years. For the last two hundred the townsfolk have given up trying to resist, even when Sir Lancelot, 'a distant relative of the well-known knight errant', arrives. Lancelot is, however, accustomed to fighting for people against their own will, and has already been wounded three times in similar ventures.

He therefore overrides their fearfulness and narrow self-interest, and with the help of Cat and a few local craftsmen obtains the necessary weapons to defeat the Dragon and rescue Elsa, that year's sacrificial victim. Though victorious, he is wounded and vanishes. In his absence the rascally Mayor claims to be the Dragon-slayer, appoints himself President, imprisons the craftsmen, and resolves to have Elsa as bride. He is foiled by the eventual return of Lancelot, who not only marries Elsa and releases the innocent prisoners but undertakes to stay in the town to eradicate, by gentle means, the Dragon that lives on within every person. The application of Schwartz's political fable was evident, as Soviet authorities quickly recognised. The lightly humorous and good-natured tone makes for very effective satire, and the theme is perennially relevant. That was recognised by its publication by Penguin in the following year, and the BBC's giving it a repeat in 1969 (R4 21 December).

The only other piece was also Continental. Though not a new adaptation – because Peter Watts's radio version was retained – Jean Cocteau's *The Knights*

---

[54] Yevgeny Schwartz, 'The Dragon', tr. Max Hayward and Harold Shukman, in *Three Soviet Plays*, ed. Michael Glenny (Harmondsworth: Penguin, 1966), pp. 135–218.

*of the Round Table* was given a new production by Joe Burroughs (TP 24 August 1967), with Robert Harris as King Arthur, Stephen Murray as Lancelot, and Denys Hawthorne as Galahad. It was accompanied by an explanatory note in *Radio Times* by Carl Wildman, which reveals a marked shift in critical inter-pretation of the play.[55] Whereas C. N. had claimed in his 1951 preview that Cocteau expressed no opinion and drew no moral as to whether reality was to be preferred to illusion, for Wildman the play presents a much more committed dénouement: since Galahad, representing the poet, brings peace to Camelot with 'the freshness of his vision'. An amoral aestheticism has thus been rebranded as social engagement.

## Making it New

It may seem odd that the reawakened interest in Arthur (evinced through archaeology, the stage and screen versions of *Camelot*, a revival of interest in Malory and Tennyson's *Idylls of the King*, and the flowering of contemporary Arthurian poetry and children's fiction) should not be reflected in radio drama. But that is the case. The ending of *Children's Hour* in 1964 may have been a contributory factor in this dearth, with regard to new plays for juveniles, but post-war *Children's Hour* had only rarely shown an interest in Arthurian work.[56] At an adult level the great Arthurian ventures of the 1950s are not carried over into the 1960s.

It might so easily have been very different, for what could well have been three major dramas were aborted at different stages of their development. The first of these involved T. H. White. As early as November 1958 it had been agreed to commission White to write a sixty-minute play for radio on the subject of Sir Tristram.[57] By January of the following year, White had accepted the commis-sion, and a fee of £250 was agreed for two performances of the work. Half of the amount was then paid to White, the remainder was payable on completion.[58] A year later there are signs of the BBC's anxiety at White's lack of progress with the script. Barbara Bray approaches White's literary agent, and is reassured, so writes to White, saying that she is pleased to hear that he has completed about half the play.[59] In June she is writing to the agent again in enquiry.[60] Five months later the agent reports that White has not forgotten the play, but he is preoccu-pied with arrangements for the staging of *Camelot* in Boston, and until that is out of the way cannot settle down to writing.[61] Ten months later a further enquiry to the agent yields the reply:

55  Carl Wildman, 'With Cocteau in Camelot', *Radio Times* (24 August 1967), 42.
56  This lack of interest in Arthurian matter is evident in Wallace Grevatt, *BBC Children's Hour: A Celebration of Those Magical Years*, ed. Trevor Hill (Lewes: Book Guild, 1988), which mentions only a very few of the Arthurian programmes that were broadcast.
57  BBC WAC: T. H. White file, memo from Barbara Bray to Miss Dean, 3 November 1958.
58  BBC WAC: memo from Miss Dean to Script Editor, Drama (Sound).
59  BBC WAC: letter from Barbara Bray to T. H. White, 29 January 1960.
60  BBC WAC: letter from Barbara Bray to Jean Leroy, 9 June 1960.
61  BBC WAC: letter from Jean Leroy to Barbara Bray, 16 November 1960.

We have asked Mr White what the position is with regard to the play on Sir Tristram which you commissioned him to write and he replies that unfortunately he has been ill for some time and is still not quite well enough to concentrate on writing. He feels that he will not be able to write a really good play until he is fit again and hopes you understand the delay. But he asks me to tell you that he is longing to write it and will do so as soon as he possibly can.[62]

There the matter appeared to rest. White would die without completing the commission.

The second near thing concerned Louis MacNeice, who had long been interested in the Arthurian subject.[63] In the early 1920s he had revelled in reading Malory at his Sherborne Prep School; at Marlborough he had written an Arthurian story for a college magazine – whereas his friend Anthony Blunt (the future spy for the USSR) 'despised' Tennyson. At Oxford he edited a short-lived magazine, *Sir Galahad*, in 1929. Still an admirer of Malory's prose he published an essay on him in 1938. A journey with William Alwyn in 1953 took him to Glastonbury, 'with a halt at the George Inn to brood on beer and the *Morte d'Arthur*', a meditation that bore its poetic fruit in *Autumn Sequel* (1954).[64] So when in 1961 he proposed writing a play called 'The Remorse of Sir Gawayne' the result could have been a very significant production on an aspect of the Arthurian legends that has received little recent attention. But his suggestion was turned down by the Third, presumably by P. H. Newby, the novelist who was then its Head.[65]

In the following year, however, the Arthurian outlook seemed to have been improving, because Home Service accepted Frederick Bradnum's *For the Death of a Beast*, a play based on Malory's tale of Balin and Balan. Bradnum considered it some of the best work he had done for radio, and felt that *Morte Darthur* was 'full of radio narrative material'.[66] A letter to Michael Bakewell a few weeks later concedes the need for some alterations to his script, but defends his overall approach:

As you know I have stuck to Malory's storyline, such as it is, as much as possible. There are many inconsistencies and ambiguities in this story. Some of these I have tried to clarify, using contemporary psychological references or else making the symbols directly meaningful to our present condition. But Malory is often very dark and Book 2 is as dark as any in his whole story. To bring to it too much rational light would, I think, make a poem into a prose statement. I think poetry is a phenomenon: which is as good a way of describing the story of Balin and Balan as any.[67]

---

62  BBC WAC: letter from Josephine Harrison to Michael Bakewell, 26 September 1961.
63  See Jon Stallworthy, *Louis MacNeice* (London: Faber & Faber, 1995).
64  Barbara Coulton, *Louis MacNeice in the BBC* (London: Faber & Faber, 1980), p. 139. After publication in book form, *Autumn Sequel* was produced for broadcasting by Joe Burroughs, and read by Marius Goring and Robert Irwin in six parts (TP 1954).
65  Coulton, *Louis MacNeice*, p. 182.
66  BBC WAC: Bradnum file, memo to SED (S), 1 January 1961.
67  Bradnum to Michael Bakewell, 7 February 1962.

Cuts were, nonetheless, made and 'some necessary narration' added.[68] In Val Gielgud's view, it needed still more cutting to eradicate 'a certain amount of T. H. Whitery here and there which rather jars' and an occasional passage of 'diffuse verbiage', but he considered it greatly improved.[69] Bradnum, who was no longer in full-time BBC employment at this point, was accordingly paid his fee of 170 guineas, and the play was scheduled for Week 48. Unfortunately by September it had been found 'too difficult' by the Head of Home Service (E. R. Lewin), who recommended that it should first be done as an experimental production before either he or Third Programme decided to broadcast it.[70] Although Martin Esslin, who was then Assistant Head of Drama, apparently tried to get it an experimental production, this attempt seems to have come to nothing. Bradnum was left to reflect that his play 'was straight forward enough and would entertain. … Third is its proper place.'[71] He would go on to write very many other radio dramas that were broadcast, but this particular Arthurian venture seems, alas, to have foundered abjectly.

In these two instances it appears to have been the personal decisions taken by Newby and Lewin that prevented two Arthurian plays emerging. Their quelling of interest was remarkably thorough. No new Arthurian play would be broadcast until 1977.

During this Waste Land period for Arthurian drama, one may detect only Martin Jenkins's new production of R. C. Sherriff's *The Long Sunset* with Julian Glover as Arthur (R4 1971, 1976), and two short humorous programmes. The funnier is Ba Mason's talk in *Woman's Hour*, 'How I Met the Lady of Shalott' (LP 22 March 1966), which includes some clear-eyed comment on the poem, pointing out that the Lady had used her mirror as 'a kind of very early television set', and that if the knights could only cross 'themselves with fear' when they saw her corpse they must have been 'a rotten lot'.[72] How could they hope to find the Holy Grail if the sight of a dead girl in a boat made them tremble? Mason recalls, though, how she fell in love with the Lancelot of Tennyson's poem and consequently joined the school choir that was rehearsing a musical setting of it, before her own inability to sing in tune got her the sack. The second item was a burlesque sketch included in the *Round the Horne* comedy series (LP 17 March 1968). Topically inspired by the release of the film *Camelot*, it presented the team's usual fare of ponderously lewd *double-entendre*, though giving the camp actor Kenneth Williams an apt role as Sir Mincealot.[73]

The long overdue Arthurian drama eventually arrived in the shape of Gordon Honeycombe's *Lancelot and Guinevere* (R3 18 December 1977). After enjoying a successful career as a news announcer on independent television, Honeycombe resigned to become a full-time writer. This play is thus one of the first fruits of his change in career direction. Lasting two hours it tells the story of the final five

68  Memo, 30 April 1962.
69  Val Gielgud to SED (S), 16 May 1962.
70  Memo to AHD (S), 3 September 1962.
71  Letter from Bradnum to Martin Esslin, 17 September 1962.
72  BBC WAC: typed script of Ba Mason, 'How I Met the Lady of Shalott', p. 1.
73  The script has been published as Programme 4 of Series 4, in Barry Horne and Mat Coward, *The Best of Round the Horne* (London: Boxtree, 2000), pp. 183–93.

books of *Le Morte Darthur* in eight scenes: the poisoned apple, the Fair Maid of Astolat, the Melliagance incident, the arrest and rescue of Guinevere, the siege of Joyous Gard, the siege of Benwick, the Last Battle, and Lancelot and Guinevere at Amesbury.[74] The play was given special treatment by the BBC. Advertised in *Radio Times* by a very handsome Eric Fraser woodcut [**plate 31**], it was directed by Martin Jenkins; the cast included Anna Massey as Guinevere, Norman Rodway as Lancelot, Peter Jeffrey as Arthur and Timothy West as Malory; and the music specially composed by Derek Oldfield involved a lute, solo singing, drums for the combats and a choral for the Pope. This was clearly an ambitious effort, and deserving of a charitable reception, but despite these auspicious signs the text does not read well. It resembles a version for schools: the characters lack depth, complexity and credibility, while the vocabulary and syntax are so close to Malory's that it seems an abridgement rather than a reworking. For example:

> Then, as the French book sayeth, Sir Lancelot began to resort unto Queen Guinevere again, and forgot the promise and the perfection that he made in the Quest. For, as the book sayeth, had not Sir Lancelot been in his privy thoughts so set inwardly to the Queen as he was in seeming outward to God, there had no knight passed him in the Quest of the Holy Grail. And so they loved together more hotter than they did aforehand. Many in the court spake of it. And ever as Sir Lancelot might he withdrew him from the company of Queen Guinevere for to eschew the slander and noise.[75]

Six months afterwards a repeat was broadcast, and two years later the play was staged for six performances at the Old Vic, London, with the same producer but different music (by David Cain), where the event was promised to herald 'a new working arrangement' between radio and this theatre.[76] The stage version restructured the play around the imprisoned figure of Malory (again played by Timothy West), the action switching between Malory talking about his books and the enacted scenes for which Newgate prisoners took the roles of Arthurian personae.[77] In the first half, much new and disparate material (e.g. the Grail) was included and there was a sexing up of the action (we see the naked Elaine), whereas the second half reverted to the radio script. Though Sherriff's play had transferred smoothly to the stage, Honeycombe's did not, and critical reaction was very hostile. It was 'little more than an elaborated reading' (*Times*), Honeycombe 'had not been bold enough in distancing himself from the radio version' (*Sunday Telegraph*), its technique of 'linking short scenes with long passages of text belongs to radio' (*Evening News*), it was 'an arthritic attempt to excite new interest in the Arthurian legend' and not a 'persuasive advertisement for radio drama's contribution to our culture' (*Guardian*).[78]

---

74  *Radio Times* mistakenly announces that it is based on 'the last *two* books'.
75  Theatre Museum, London: typed playscript (for radio) of Gordon Honeycombe, 'Lancelot and Guinevere'.
76  Theatre Museum: programme for the performance at the Old Vic Theatre, 10 September 1980.
77  Theatre Museum: typed playscript (for stage).
78  Information on all reviews is taken from folder of press cuttings at Theatre Museum.

The only other relevant work was Lee Torrance's quasi-Arthurian *Half Sick of Shadows*, a fifty-five-minute play directed by Graham Gauld and presented in the *Afternoon Theatre* slot (R4 13 July 1979). Though 'The Lady of Shalott' is not directly named, Tennyson's poem forms the implicit foundation of the whole piece.[79] It is set in Edwardian times, in a village where an historical pageant is being rehearsed. Among the residents are Sir Edward and Lady Evergill, who live in a towered, Victorian Gothic, riverside mansion. Edward (George Baker), a famous London actor, is taking part in the pageant as a knight. His very young and beautiful wife, Donna (Jo Manning Wilson), who is 'like something out of a fairy tale', spends most of her time, however, in an upstairs room, reading poetry and weaving a tapestry. Into this she weaves such Tennysonian images as a knight, people going to market, a page, and a shepherd lad. While doing so she sings snatches of a song:

> As a knight went riding, riding by
> On the road to London Town.
> And he did love a fair lady,
> Whose heart was his entirely …
> She waited for him faithfully,
> While he rode to London Town …
> She waited in a tower of stone,
> She waited for him all alone,
> All dressed in a lily white gown
> As he rode to London Town, etc.   (pp. 4–5)

The tapestry has entered so deeply into her life that she also has vivid imaginings, unseen and unheard by others, that her knight is approaching. She has, we are told later, been married before: to a scoundrel who was killed when drunkenly falling off his horse. Perpetually fantasising about the event, and subconsciously reshaping it, she recurrently imagines that an attendant is climbing the stairs to bring the tragic news of her gallant knight's death. She has been cursed, she believes, and applies to her own predicament a quotation from John Donne's 'A Hymn to God the Father':

> I have a sin of fear that when I have spun
> My last thread I shall perish on the shore.   (p. 10)

Nor does she look outside except by means of a mirror, which she claims 'tells the truth' (p. 26). Dreaming fearfully of horses with tossing black plumes at a funeral, and of two young newly-weds swallowed by the shadows, she remarks, 'I am half sick of shadows' (p. 33). Although her present husband's kindness and the discreet help of a visiting doctor seem to be helping her, events reach a dramatic climax during the pageant, when Edward falls from his horse. Despite the fact that he is not seriously hurt, a messenger (wearing the medieval costume of the pageant) is sent to Donna. Prompted to look out of the window, she thinks she sees a 'knight' approaching. The mirror falls and is shattered, and she cries,

---

[79]  BBC WAC: typed playscript of Lee Torrance, 'Half Sick of Shadows'.

'The curse has come upon me' (p. 65). After taking some tablets, she wanders out into the garden, finds their small dinghy, and floats downstream to her death. 'She has a lovely face,' sighs the voice of her unseen knight (p. 73).

On the page, the material seems inert because of the clichéd sentiments expressed by most of the characters. Nonetheless, the story's legendary core has a residual power to attract. And, while the unfolding pattern of the narrative seems heavily determined by Tennyson's poem rather than by any inherent dramatic logic of its own, the plot is very ingeniously constructed. Moreover, perhaps the mysterious ambience was quite successfully rendered on air, for the disembodied presences and ghostly imaginings of the central character are eminently suitable for the medium of radio.

# 4

## 1980–2005: 'Wave after wave'

*Music*

Wagner continued to dominate the period, twenty entire performances apiece of *Tristan* and *Parsifal* being broadcast, live or recorded. The range of venues continued to widen. Though Bayreuth remained the main source, accounting for 27 per cent of productions, *Tristan* came from eleven different venues, *Parsifal* likewise. Notably, nine of the *Tristan* stemmed from UK productions, and not just from Covent Garden but also from Welsh National Opera (for whom Anne Evans sang a fine Isolde role), Scottish Opera, the BBC SO, Glyndebourne (the first Wagnerian opera to be performed there), and its first staging at English National Opera (1981), when Reginald Goodall conducted what is considered one of the finest of all musical interpretations of the work.[1] Two of these broadcast occasions were accorded attractive *Radio Times* colour illustrations: one by Bill Sanderson for a Bavarian State Opera performance while for a Covent Garden production John Storey produced an inventive variation on the Rubin Vase image so renowned among gestalt psychologists.

For *Parsifal*, in contrast, the BBC took four live productions from the New York Metropolitan under James Levine and a broad haul from Continental opera houses in France, Germany, Austria and Italy. Significant new ground was broken one Good Friday when for the first time a complete Bayreuth production was broadcast simultaneously with BBC television, Siegfried Jerusalem taking the role of Parsifal (R3/BBC2 9 April 1982). Additionally, the associated radio talks, features and record reviews continued to provide scholarly background.

From 1996 Radio 3 increased its coverage to 24 hours a day, and the playing of excerpts began to increase exponentially for *Tristan*, 'Isolde's Liebestod' becoming one of the most performed of all classical pieces on radio. It was sung or played orchestrally, and in various arrangements by Humperdinck, Crees or Kocsis. It appeared as a *Fantasy* by Stiegler, as a *Symphonic Synthesis* by Stokowski; it was arranged as a piano duet in Chabrier's *Souvenirs de Munich*, and in the shape of Liszt's transcription for a single piano it was played by at least sixteen different soloists.

Though much Purcell was broadcast, his *King Arthur* could not rival this blaze of Wagnerian popularity. Some attention was, at last, paid in talks by Roger Savage (R3 1981) and Peter Holman (R3 1983) as to how Purcell's work

---

[1]  Michael Kennedy considered that Anne Evans 'gave the performance of her life', *Sunday Telegraph* (21 February 1993). Jeremy Beadle, 'Discography', in programme for *Tristan und Isolde* (Welsh National Opera, 1993), 34–6.

had been performed in the Restoration playhouse but, even when a fine, though slightly shortened, stage version of the dramatic-opera was presented by the Manchester Camerata at the Buxton Festival in 1986, this was not broadcast, the BBC continuing to prefer concert versions, in particular that by the Monteverdi Choir conducted by John Eliot Gardiner (1983, 1986). Matters changed considerably, however, in 1995, the tercentenary year of Purcell's death. Under the umbrella title of 'Fairest Isle' it was declared a celebratory year of British music and culture, the BBC broadcast all Purcell's works, and non-broadcast performances were widespread. Radio 3 began the season promptly by presenting Steven Wyatt's *Fairest Isle\**, directed by Martin Jenkins (8 January 1995), a sensitive, intelligent, wide-ranging and well-acted documentary drama about the creation of *King Arthur*. Haunted by the sharply questioning ghost of Purcell (Ian Hughes), the aged Dryden (Benjamin Whitrow) recalls their difficult personal and artistic relationship, as their work developed amid the shifting quicksands of the dynastic background. Interspersed with extracts from the opera, the repeated aria 'Fairest Isle' serving as a unifying thread, the play was allowed the generous time limit of an hour and three-quarters. It was a deserving prelude to the flagship event of the year, Graham Vick's production of *King Arthur*, performed by Les Arts Florissants under William Christie. This unabridged version had opened in Paris earlier that season, been transferred to Caen, and was then staged at Covent Garden for only three performances. The first was watched by Humphrey Carpenter, who reviewed it later that night (R3 3 May 1995); on the final evening the whole work was broadcast live, when it was introduced as the first complete staging for a hundred years (R3 5 May 1995).

Lest listeners should fret over not seeing Vick's quirky costuming and décor, a radio compère supplied a commentary. Newspaper reviewers were not uniformly won over by the work: Paul Taylor admiring the 'charm and humour' of the spectacle, but bemoaning 'the anaemic non-Malory story', and his colleague Mark Pappenheim believing that Purcell 'almost perversely eschews every invitation to musical development of his plot' (*Independent*, 5 May 1995). Malcolm Hayes followed suit, liking the 'intelligently thought-out staging', but thinking that Dryden's 'ceaseless wordifying' should have been cut, and 'most of the music' sounded as if Purcell had been bored by the project (*Sunday Telegraph*, 7 May 1995). For Michael White, too, Dryden's 'acreage of spoken dialogue' did not live up to the 'epic intensity' that Vick had envisaged: 'it would have taken an Olivier … to fill out these roles'. Moreover, the musical direction by William Christie lacked the necessary rhythmic bite, making it far inferior to John Eliot Gardiner's recording (*Independent on Sunday*, 7 May 1995). Christie's own recording was soon to feature again, however, in the regular *Building a Library* series (R3 27 May 1995). At the Proms that year, a new concert version by the English Concert and Choir under Trevor Pinnock was unveiled, with Denis Quilley taking the role of narrator. Jeremy Beadle gave a preview of this (R3), and the work was broadcast the following night (R3 13 August). Before the year was out a third production went on air, when Classic FM broadcast a performance from The Hague by the Guildhall School of Music and Dance, combined with the Royal Conservatory, and conducted by Ton Koopman (CFM 28 December). From then on, though, *King Arthur* was given a long rest on air, resurfacing only when Lucie Skeaping gave a talk on Purcell's theatre work (R3 2003) and when the William Christie recording was played over five separate mornings in a special Arthurian week (R3 16–20 February 2004). Over the two decades more excerpts from *King Arthur* were played than had been the practice since the mid-1930s to the mid-1940s, but the stream never became a river.

These remained very lean years for Rutland Boughton's Arthurian works, none of which featured even during the British Year of Music. What did surface was a reading by Nigel Anthony (R3 1985, repeated 1987) of the poignantly ingenuous *Self-Advertisement for Rutland Boughton*, a privately printed pamphlet he had issued in 1909, setting out his aims for music. Twenty years would elapse before he received more attention. This occurred when, to coincide with a later pop festival at Glastonbury, the poet Ian McMillan paid a warm thirty-minute tribute to Boughton's lofty ambitions in *The First Glastonbury Festival: Summer 1914*\* (R4 21 June 2005). Among the contributing voices is that of Michael Hurd, but although reference is made to the Arthurian operas no music from them is, alas, performed; and despite some discussion of the town's evolution into a modern cultural centre no mention is made of Alice Buckton's key role therein.

The major operatic figure that does emerge in these years is, however, not British but French: Ernest Chausson. Chausson had spent ten years in composing both libretto and music for *Le Roi Arthus*, but the work had to wait until four years after his untimely death in 1899 before it reached the stage in Brussels. The work then fell largely into obscurity, though French radio had broadcast Act 3 in 1934 and a revival of the whole work in 1949.[2] A pre-war recording of excerpts from Act 3 with the baritone Arthur Endrèze in the role of Merlin eventually found its way over the Channel in 1981, when an excerpt was included in a *This Week's Composer* programme that was devoted to Chausson. This served as appetiser for the UK première broadcast of the entire work in a recording made in the previous year by the National Orchestra of France conducted by Lionel Friend (R3 28 September 1982). When a commercial recording later became available, with the same orchestra conducted by Armin Jordan, Paul Griffiths thought it 'the great operatic discovery of the year', and particularly admired the singing of Gino Quilico (Arthus) for his 'close sympathy for the noble frank-ness of Chausson's work' (*Times*, 11 October, 16 December 1986). Extracts from this were occasionally played on air but the most significant broadcasts were of other complete performances, all by different companies. These came from the Netherlands Radio Orchestra and Chorus under Edo de Waart (1994); and the Sofia and Russian Chamber Choir and Vienna PO under Marcello Viotti (1996), before a concert performance (the UK live première) was mounted by the Chorus of Scottish Opera and the Royal Scottish National Orchestra conducted by Frédéric Chaslin at the Edinburgh International Festival in 2000. A recording made there was broadcast a month later (R3 30 September). Critical reception was mixed. Raymond Monelle praised the singing of Simon Keenlyside (Arthus) and Christopher Maltman (Merlin), but did not like the other soloists or the conductor (too 'interested in thrust and impetus'), and considered that the

---

2   See Tony Hunt, 'Ernest Chausson's *Le Roi Arthus*', in *King Arthur in Music*, ed. Richard Barber (Cambridge: Brewer, 2002), pp. 61–89 (p. 64).

work lost greatly in its concert version because one was then more conscious of Chausson's overscoring, his heavy brass, and his 'inability to learn from Wagner's economy' (*Independent*, 20 August 2000). Confirming Monelle's assessment of the singers, Claire Wreathall, however, believed that the conductor 'drew magnificent playing' from the orchestra, and she maintained that Chausson's music may be 'unsubtle' and tremble on the borders of schmaltz, but is so 'fabulous', 'richly chromatic', and 'gorgeously lyrical' that she would like to see it fully staged (*Independent on Sunday*, 27 August 2000). That has not, alas, come about in Britain, but radio listeners could have tuned in to the live broadcast from La Monnaie, when a new production conducted by Daniele Callegari was mounted in the theatre where the opera had its 1903 première (R3 29 November 2003). On this occasion the audience was, according to Roderic Dunnett, 'treated to a miracle', for the big choruses were 'terrific', the cast 'unbeatable', and the 'orchestra served up a feast for the Round Table' (*Independent*, 6 November 2003). This newfound celebration of *Le Roi Arthus* was rounded off by a studio recording made by Apollo Voices and the BBC SO under Leon Botstein (R3 28 May 2005). With eight complete performances of the opera broadcast within this period Chausson has clearly moved back into critical and popular favour. Not only was he given a very sympathetic appreciation by the delightfully witty and learned Donald Macleod in the *Composer of the Week* series (R3 28 March–1 April 2005), but for the last twenty years his tone poem *Viviane* has made a regular appearance in the radio repertoire.

The 1980s proved a fruitful period for other Arthurian opera. Frank Martin's *Le Vin herbé* received three performances by the Park Lane Music Players conducted by Simon Joly (1982/3/4), while another by the Netherlands Radio Choir and Chamber Orchestra under Bernard Klee would follow in 1993. Adopting the same subject, Gillian Whitehead had composed her *Tristan and Iseult*, a chamber opera with libretto by Malcolm Crowther and Michael Hill, for performance in her native New Zealand in 1978. A studio recording of this short work (it lasted only an hour and three-quarters) was conducted by Lionel Friend and broadcast in 1980 (R3 15 April). Immediately before it was heard, in an inspired example of programme planning a record of Bax's *Tintagel* was played, to create a suitable atmosphere by evoking the 'castle-crowned cliff' and its Arthurian associations. *Radio Times* complemented this by printing a medieval illustration of the lovers.

Three very different British works were also given their first broadcast performances. Michael Tippett's *New Year* may be accounted 'Arthurian' because it features a modern Merlin, in this case a computer wizard of that name, who designs a spaceship that will cross Time and Space to bring us news of the future.[3] It had been co-commissioned by the BBC, Houston Grand Opera and Glyndebourne Festival Opera. The American production took place first, while the Glyndebourne production, with James Maddalena in the role of Merlin, was broadcast in the following year (R3 14 July 1990). A year later a new Glyndebourne version was even given the accolade of a simultaneous television broadcast on BBC2 (R3 21 September 1991). More substantially Arthurian was Richard

3   Michael Tippett, *New Year. Opera. Words and Music* (London: Schott, 1989).

Blackford's *Gawain and Ragnell*, a sixty-minute opera for children, with libretto by Ian Barnett, first performed in 1984. Two years later it was transmitted on a special day devoted to music written and performed for, by and about children. Treble voices sang the parts of Arthur, Guinevere, Gawain and Ragnell, while an adult baritone took the role of Gromer Somer Jour, accompanied by a children's chorus and members of the City of Birmingham SO conducted by Paul Herbert (R3 2 January 1986). This was a pleasantly fresh and light-hearted item. A far weightier work was Harrison Birtwistle's *Gawain*, with libretto by David Harsent, which was staged at Covent Garden in 1991. Only six performances were given, the last of these being chosen for radio broadcasting (R3 22 June 1991). Among music critics the consensual view was that the occasion was a triumph, perhaps even 'one of the most monumental achievements' in the Garden's history (*Financial Times*).[4] This was ascribed to Birtwistle's immensely original and dramatic music, and to the magnificent production in which Elgar Howarth (conductor), John Tomlinson (Green Knight) and Alison Chitty (set designer) were singled out for special praise. David Harsent's libretto came in for strictures, though, for being 'portentous' (*Times*) and 'self-consciously poetic' (*Sunday Telegraph*).[5] There were complaints, too, that the Turning of the Seasons masque was too long, and that the orchestra so overpowered some singers that surtitles would have been helpful. Critics might have added that Birtwistle's writing for the soprano voices makes it virtually impossible to understand what the latter are singing. (Why commission a special libretto if it can't be followed?) The radio listener's desire for visual access to this opera was later met by a television showing a year later (BBC2). Two years after that, a few cuts were made and the libretto was revised for a new production from Covent Garden (R3 1994), which was once again well received by critics, although it was noted that the low prices for seats indicated that 'the public was still making up its mind' (*Independent*, 15 April 1994). The difficulty of singing, playing and staging the opera has confined its performance to Covent Garden. And even when it was revived there in 2000 (when the technology famously failed), it was *not* awarded a broadcast. There are signs of critical opinion cooling. Though one critic wrote of it being among 'the greatest of all 20th century operas',[6] Michael Kennedy was steadily revising his opinions: 'I have seen *Gawain* three times and disliked it more each time.'[7] It has not since featured frequently on radio. Only one extract from the CD recording issued in 1996, for example, seems to have been broadcast (R3 1998). There has been a potentially significant offshoot in that Birtwistle assembled an orchestral fantasy from five sections of the opera, with vocal parts given to specific instruments. Named *Gawain's Journey*, this was given its first performance at the Huddersfield Contemporary Music Festival by English Northern Philharmonia conducted by Paul Daniel in 1991. In a recording of this event it thus received its radio première a year later (R3 5 June 1992). But neither has even this far more accessible work gained any considerable attention on air.

---

4   Max Leppert, *Financial Times* (1 June 1991).
5   Paul Griffiths, *The Times* (1 June 1991). Michael Kennedy, *Sunday Telegraph* (2 June 1991).
6   *The Times* (13 January 2000).
7   *Sunday Telegraph* (16 January 2000).

Plate 1. *There were no loud-speakers in Lyonesse*, Mervyn Wilson. *Radio Times* (1930)

Plate 2. Advertisement for Ediswan Valves, Anon. *Radio Times* (1926)

Plate 3. Advertisement for Polarphone, Fleet. *Radio Times* (1923)

THE
# RADIO TIMES
## THE JOURNAL OF THE BRITISH BROADCASTING CORPORATION

NATION SHALL SPEAK PEACE UNTO NATION

Vol. 39. No. 497. [ Registered at the G.P.O. as a Newspaper. ]  APRIL 7, 1933.  Every Friday. TWO PENCE.

A Concert Performance of extracts from Wagner's great work will be broadcast on Good Friday evening

Plate 4. *Parsifal*, Clixby Watson. *Radio Times* (1933)

Plate 5. *Tristan and Isolde*, Donia Nachshen. *Radio Times* (1931)

Plate 6. *Tristan and Isolde*, Anon. *Radio Times* (1932)

Plate 7. *Parsifal*, Elizabeth Rivers. *Radio Times* (1930).

Plate 8. *Tristan and Isolde*, Clixby Watson. *Radio Times* (1936)

Plate 9. *Merlin*, C. W. Bacon. *Radio Times* (1937). © The Bacon Estate

Plate 10. *The Sword in the Stone*, Robin Jacques. *Radio Times* (1939). © The Jacques Estate

Plate 11. *Sir Gareth the Fair*, Carmen. *Radio Times* (1938)

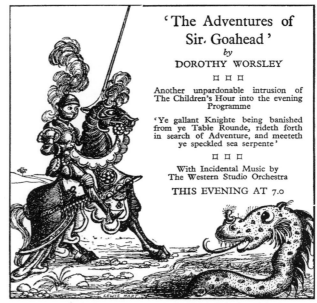

Plate 12. *The Adventures of Sir Goahead*, Lewis Hart. *Radio Times* (1934)

Plate 13. *King Arthur*, James R. Hart. *Radio Times* (1937)

Plate 14. *Parsifal*, Tom L. Poulton. *Radio Times* (1947)

Plate 15. *Parsifal*, Eric Fraser. *Radio Times* (1959). By kind permission of the Fraser family

‘A YANK AT THE COURT OF
KING ARTHUR’

A free adaptation of the extravagant story by
MARK TWAIN
in
SATURDAY-NIGHT THEATRE

Plate 16. *A Yank at the Court of King Arthur*, Norman Mansbridge. *Radio Times* (1954)

Plate 17. *The Sword in the Stone*, Bruce Angrave. *Radio Times* (1952)

‘THE SWORD IN THE STONE’
An Arthurian fantasy based on the book by T. H. White
at 2.30

Plate 18. *The Sword in the Stone*, Bruce Angrave. *Radio Times* (1952)

Plate 19. *Paolo and Francesca*, Laurence Scarfe. *Radio Times* (1952).
© The Scarfe Estate

Plate 20.
*The Unknown
Soldier*, Eric
Fraser. *Radio
Times* (1942).
By kind
permission
of the Fraser
family

Plate 21. *The Unknown Soldier*,
Dorothea Braby. *Radio Times*
(1953). © The Braby Estate

Plate 22. *The Long Sunset*, Douglas Relf. *Radio Times* (1955)

Plate 23. *Parsifal*, Val Biro. *Radio Times* (1972). © Val Biro

Plate 24. *Tristan and Isolde*, C. W. Bacon. *Radio Times* (1965). © The Bacon Estate

Plate 25. *The Lady of Shalott*, Val Biro. *Radio Times* (1961). © Val Biro

Plate 26. *The Morte Darthur*, Eric Fraser. *Radio Times* (1971). By kind permission of the Fraser family

Plate 27. *The Green Knight*, Eric Fraser. *Radio Times* (1971). By kind permission of the Fraser family

Plate 28. *The Road to Astolat*, Eric Fraser. *Radio Times* (1972). By kind permission of the Fraser family

Plate 29. *A Yankee at the Court of King Arthur*, Barry Wilkinson. *Radio Times* (1970)

Plate 30. *The Dragon,* Will Nickless. *Radio Times* (1965)

Plate 31. *Lancelot and Guinevere*, Eric Fraser. *Radio Times* (1977). By kind permission of the Fraser family

Plate 32. *The Sword in the Stone*,
Robin Jacques. *Radio Times* (1981).
© The Jacques Estate

Plate 33. *Trystan and Essyllt*, Mike Walker.
*Radio Times* (1986)

Plate 34. *Passings*, Ian Pollock. *Radio
Times* (1984). © Ian Pollock

Plate 35. *'Yes, Henry made
that to hide the wireless set'*,
L. Bowyer.
*Radio Times* (1936)

'Yes, Henry made that to hide the wireless set'

With regard to more purely instrumental music the mid-1980s saw a burst of interest in Hans Werner Henze's *Tristan: preludes for piano, tape and orchestra*, a composition that draws on a wide range of musical sources from the *Lamento di Tristan* to Wagner. Featured in the *Composer of the Week* series, his *Tristan* was played in a recording by the Cologne Radio Orchestra conducted by the composer (R3 9 March 1984). This seems to have provided the impetus for its being taken up by British orchestras. A performance in Southampton by the Bournemouth SO under Oliver Knussen was later broadcast (R3 24 November 1985), as was another in the following year by the BBC Philharmonic conducted by Edward Downes (R3 15 September 1986). The pianist on that occasion, Ian Brown, was shortly afterwards heard performing the work in Cologne (R3 10 December 1986). Apart from rare performances such as that by the BBC Philharmonic under Alexander Lazarer at a London Barbican festival of Henze's music (R3 15 January 1991) and a later rendition by the English Northern Philharmonic under Diego Masson (R3 27 November 1994), the piece seems, however, to have now fallen out of favour. For example, a recent edition of *Composer of the Week* devoted to Henze included no *Tristan*. By contrast, Bax's *Tintagel* soared in popularity and its performance is listed about ninety times during this period, a frequency second only to Wagner. His Cornish links, moreover, formed the subject of a radio feature by Tommy Pearson (R3 21 May 1996). Messiaen's *Turangalîla Symphony*, too, established an increasingly strong position with about forty listed performances, and attracted an illuminating talk by Paul Griffiths on *Messiaen and the Tristan Myth*, which discussed all three of his related works on the theme (R3 19 April 1988, repeated 1993). This consuming interest in Messiaen had already led to at least a couple of interpretations of his first Tristan piece, *Harawi*, for it was performed by Jane Manning (soprano) and Howard Shelley (piano) and then by Michele Command and Marie-Madeleine Petit (R3 1980, 1983). Other Tristan works were manifest. These ranged widely, from performances of a 'Sir Tristram' in Michael Oliver's *Music Weekly* (R3 1982) and a motet in the manuscript of the thirteenth-century *Prose Tristan* (R3 1993) to works composed very much in Wagner's shadow, like William Bergsma's *Fantastic Variations on a theme from [Wagner's] 'Tristan'* (R3 1985) and Franz Waxman's *Tristan and Isolde Fantasy* (1997, 2003). There were, besides, freshly written compositions such as two pieces by David Bedford: his *Toccata for Tristan*, originally commissioned by the BBC for performance during the Manchester Olympic Festival, was then played by the Britannia Building Society Band conducted by Howard Snell (R3 12 March 1991), while its very attractive companion piece, *Ronde for Isolde*, was given its broadcast première by the Royal Northern College of Music Wind Orchestra conducted by Timothy Reynish (R3 27 March 1992). Another intriguing BBC commission was William Mival's powerfully evocative *Tristan – Still*, a piece intended to complement Wagner's opera. Mival took a tiny moment from the start of the Love Duet in Act 2 as a point of departure for his own work and, playing with the legend that Wagner had composed a string quartet for his new love Cosima, Mival conjures up a ghost of what this string quartet might have been. The 'still' of the title is thus meant to suggest not only the stillness of water but also that Wagner is still an influence, and finally that the Wagnerian fragment is slowed down, stretched out in this modern version. Fittingly, the Mival piece received its world première

at a Wagner concert, immediately before the performance of Act 3 of *Tristan* by
the BBC SO conducted by Donald Runnicles (R3 19 February 2003).

If Tristan remained a potent source for musical inspiration, the Lady of
Shalott went into decline. Apart, that is, from a complete concert performance
of Bliss's *The Lady of Shalott* by the BBC Concert Orchestra conducted by Barry
Wordsworth (R3 10 September 1991), and a playing of Messiaen's *La Dame de
Shalott*, an impressionistic work for piano, which he had written at the age of
nine, and which had been recorded by Yvonne Loriod in 1981. A notable Tennys-
onian legacy was, though, evident in Patrick Piggott's single-movement Piano
Concerto, to which he gave the subtitle 'The Quest', as he treated the work as
an allegorical journey of his own creative soul and acknowledged its debt to
Tennyson's late poem 'Merlin and the Gleam'.[8] Piggott, who was Head of BBC
Music in Birmingham, had died before it was publicly performed, but Malcolm
Binns, the pianist for whom he had expressly composed the piece, would shortly
give it a world première (R3 7 April 1991). Elsewhere it is King Arthur, himself,
who is at the centre of works by two English composers that recur quite steadily.
Like Messiaen's both are archival revivals. Elgar's *Suite: King Arthur* figured
prominently throughout the 1980s because of a recording by the Bournemouth
Sinfonietta conducted by George Hurst, while two pieces by Benjamin Britten
were reconstructed from work he had originally done for the BBC. The first of
these, his incidental music for the serialisation of T. H. White's *The Sword in the
Stone* in 1939, had been adapted by Colin Matthews into a *Suite: The Sword in
the Stone*, which was performed by the Aldeburgh Festival Chamber Ensemble
conducted by Oliver Knussen in the première at the Aldeburgh Festival in 1983.
A recording of that occasion received its first broadcast performance in the
following year (R3 22 January 1984), and a similar live performance would be
broadcast in 1990. As for the second Britten piece, Paul Hindmarsh described
in the first programme of his series on *Britten's Radio Music*, how he had been
prompted by the current 'Fairest Isle' year to reconstruct an orchestral suite
from the incidental music Britten had written in 1937 for Bridson's *King Arthur*.
Taking some two-thirds of the original music, Hindmarsh shortened and made
necessary adjustments to produce a *Suite: King Arthur*, which he then proceeded
to play in a recording by the BBC Philharmonic Orchestra conducted by Richard
Hickox, its first broadcast performance (R3 6 December 1995).

In the same year an even more heroic task of British Music reconstruction was
undertaken by Jeremy Dibble on Hubert Parry's unperformed and unpublished
opera, *Guenever*, when he consulted the manuscript in order to create what he
called 'Guenever's Soliloquy', by scoring Act I scene iv together with a concert
ending, for a world première by the BBC Concert Orchestra conducted by Barry
Wordsworth with the soprano Shelley Everall as Guenever (R3 26 September
1995).

As long-neglected nineteenth-century music was revived by new commercial recordings these, too, began to find a place on air. In this way two works
by Arthur Sullivan have been made more widely available. A recording of the

---

[8]   Colin Scott-Sutherland, 'Patrick Piggott (1915–1990), an introduction', *British Music* 23
      (2001), 17.

*King Arthur Suite*, based on the incidental music he provided for J. Comyns Carr's verse drama at the Lyceum Theatre in 1895, has been played at least a couple of times on air, as has the music written for *The Masque at Kenilworth* (1864). The latter includes Sullivan's setting of Henry Chorley's Arthurian lyric, 'The Lady of the Lake', wherein the Lady rises from the water, under which she has slept since the times of King Arthur, to salute the new golden days of Queen Elizabeth.[9] A major work still awaiting full coverage on radio, though, is Isaac Albéniz's *Merlin*. Of the concert version premièred in Madrid in 1998, only excerpts have been heard in Britain (R3 2000, 2004). Remarkably, when the opera was finally staged in 2003, this world première would be shown the following year on BBC digital television (and is now available on DVD), but without a simultaneous transmission on radio. (Was this a BBC ploy to encourage us to buy digital boxes?)

Despite its fine quality, Elinor Remick Warren's *The Legend of King Arthur*, a setting of Tennyson's 'The Passing of Arthur', reached a British audience very late. Although performed in America in 1940, it seems not to have been known in Britain even though Warren had once hoped for a performance at the Three Choirs Festival. In a programme previewing the 1995 Festival, Tony Staveley told how an American friend had sent him a tape of the work, and how his own pleasure in it led to its performance at that year's event. Lewis Foreman then provided an analysis of Warren's work, and played extracts from the 1990 recording by the Polish Radio SO and Chorus of Cracow, conducted by Szymon Kawalla. It is probable therefore that this was the first time her work had been heard on the BBC (R2 25 August 1995). Occasionally the BBC set up a special Arthurian music programme that would assemble key works. In 1988, for example, one such programme gathered Chausson's *Viviane*, Elgar's *Suite: King Arthur* and Bax's *Tintagel* (R3 30 March 1988). Most memorably, Penny Gore devoted her daily two-hour programme to an Arthurian theme for a week, during which she drew deeply on the BBC's vast store of material. In this extraordinary week she included not only the standard fare but also Ron Goodwin's film theme *Launcelot and Guinevere*, Ropartz's *La Chasse du Prince Arthur*, Billy Mayerl's *The Legend of King Arthur*, MacDowell's *Lancelot and Elaine* and even Richard Addinsell's *The Isle of Apples*, performed by the BBC Concert Orchestra conducted by Kenneth Alwyn, which must have formed part of the original incidental music for Clemence Dane's *The Unknown Soldier* (R3 16–20 February 2004).

The inclusion of Ron Goodwin indicates how what was once regarded dismissively as light music is now treated more respectfully and slowly being co-opted into the Radio 3 canon. This has meant that Franz Waxman's *Suite: Prince Valiant* (R3 1993) and excerpts from Rodgers and Hart's *A Connecticut Yankee* are thought suitable for listing in the *Radio Times* and even for inclusion in the Proms (2002). When a major new production of Lerner and Loewe's *Camelot* was mounted in Edinburgh with the Scottish SO under Gareth Hudson, and featuring Jason Donovan as Mordred, the whole piece was broadcast (R2 21

---

[9]  *Kenilworth, A Masque of the days of Queen Elizabeth as performed at the Birmingham Festival.* Words by Henry F. Chorley. Music by Arthur S. Sullivan (London: Chappell, 1865).

March 1998); while Robert Cushman's survey of this musical area entitled *From Connecticut to Camelot* (R3 15 August 1994) managed to turn up a delightful lyric by P. G. Wodehouse and Jerome Kern, 'Sir Galahad', from the musical *Leave it to Jane* (1917), of which the chorus runs:

> It makes me sore and sad
> To read about Sir Galahad
> And all the knights of that romantic day.
> To amuse a girl and charm her
> They would get into their armour
> And pop into the fray.
> They called her lady-love,
> They used to wear her little glove
> And everything she said went.
> Oh, them was the days
> When a lady was a lady
> And a gent was a perfect gent.

Yet, just as the BBC has unearthed such intriguing curiosities, it has also continued to perform work that is not commercially available, like Stephen Dodgson's *Merlin*, a piece for unaccompanied guitar, recorded at the Paris International Guitar Week in 1990, and borrowed from French Radio (R3 6 August 1991); or David Matthews's *The Sleeping Lord*, an impressive setting of David Jones's poem, given its UK première by the Nash Ensemble with Patrizia Kwella as vocalist at the Bath Festival (R3 1992). It has also continued to promote the invigorating new American music of John Adams by broadcasting, for example, the City of Birmingham SO under Simon Rattle performing *Harmonielehre*, whose central section is based on the notion of King Anfortas's wound (R3 22 October 2004).

## The Historical Arthur

Few programmes were devoted to the question of Arthur's historicity despite the fact this was probably the main Arthurian concern among the general public. The reasons for this dearth may be that the academic radio talk by a single speaker was a genre that was falling out of fashion and, besides, broadcasters were switching archaeological topics from radio to the more suitable medium of television. Even when there was an important excavation at Tintagel in 1998, leading to the discovery of the intriguing 'Artognou' inscription, and when these findings were given wide coverage in both quality and popular newspapers, they do not seem to have made an impact on national radio. As will be seen in a later section, several notable historians were brought into radio programmes, but only to give cameo performances within features whose emphases lay elsewhere than on historical fact. Apart then from a stray schools programme (*Who was Merlin?* 1982), Tom Salmon's investigation of the Arthurian legend at Tintagel in *Around the Coast of Cornwall* (1985), and an archaeological survey of Glastonbury by Julian Richards (2002) – exploring how Arthur, Guinevere and a young Jesus Christ all 'played a part in the ecclesiastical spin' that contributed to the success of the medieval town – what historical enquiry there was existed within the setting of introductions to the modern way of life in Glastonbury.

Three programmes are symptomatic. A feature* by Radio Norfolk – sited a long way (in English terms) from Glastonbury – uses the ploy of Norfolk people's very vague ideas about Glastonbury as a strategy for treating the town in hushed reverent tones as a very holy place, indeed 'the most holy ground on earth'. A brief account is given of Arthur's exhumation and the burial of the Grail, but this is soon replaced by 'more interesting' matter: the boyhood visit there by Jesus, who later returns to spend His Lost Years in contact with the Druids; the arrival of the Virgin Mary, Mary Magdalene and (on a short visit) Lazarus. As the presenter comments: 'Why would this lovely story persist through the ages if it were not true?' And despite a faint disapproval expressed about modern commercialisation and 'fake gurus', we are swiftly swept up again into the pagan mysteries of ley lines, the Glastonbury Zodiac, the interlocking circles and triangles of the town plan, and the temple of the stars (RN 1990). A slightly more sophisticated feature by Bel Mooney, *Somerset Winter: Glastonbury** (R4 2 January 1994), also chooses to explore the Glastonbury of pagan and Christian 'old belief' rather than history. Her interviews with local residents touch lightly on local legend that the Grail is concealed under the waters of Chalice Well, and soon move off into allegorical interpretations of the Arthur myth (it allegedly provides an allegory for people's own lives, whereas the Grail allegorises a universal quest), for the real focus of her account is not the Arthurian story but a sympathetic dip into the warm ambience of yoga exercises, meditation, therapy, homeopathy and flower remedies wherein the flowers are gathered at points where ley lines cross, of a guesthouse owner whose musical compositions make listeners weep, or of the speaker from the University of Avalon who insists that the earth energy is very powerful there.

The most intelligent history programme came from an unlikely source: Leslie Forbes's *History of Britain in Six Menus*, Part Two of which consists of *A Feast for King Arthur** (R4 16 June 1996). Located within the Abbot's Kitchen at Glastonbury Abbey, well away from the Dutch hippies outside who are intent upon esoteric energies and vortices, Forbes invites two well-read cooks to prepare what their research claims to be authentic Dark Age food: hog's pudding, chitterlings, smoked eels, minced chicken with plum and cherry, lardy cake, all washed down with mead, cider and wine. Discussion of the social role of food in the Dark Ages moves on to a brief allusion to the role of food in the Arthurian tales. Her guests at this Round Table are each allotted their vignette viewpoint. Background music on the psaltery is to be provided by Bob Stewart. John Matthews recounts the story of Arthur's exhumation and the present whereabouts of the glass bowl found in Chalice Well. An archaeologist from Alabama speculates on the significance of the circle in Celtic culture (for tables and dwellings, etc.); Bryn Roberts (from the National Library of Wales) reads from the Welsh manuscript of *Culhwch and Olwen*; the Celtic folklorist Juliette Wood (from Oxford University) brings a mirror backed by an erotic scene of a lovers' hunt. Graham Phillips arrives with a sword resembling Excalibur and his theory that he has traced the historical King Arthur. His assertion provides the spark to light the veritable fire of scholarly debate. Phillips is shot down: etymologically by Roberts and historically by Wood. With an admirably light touch Forbes has thus recreated a lively academic symposium, a latter-day version of Thomas Love Peacock's wittily and learnedly disputatious, social gourmandising.

In fact the historical Arthur was not found – he announced himself:

> For years I had burning questions on my mind … life, the universe, philosophy, and I couldn't sleep at night, but now it's really easy. I just go to bed and think who I am – King Arthur. Why are you here? To reunite the Celts, bring them back together, save them. No problem. Straight to sleep.

These are the words of Arthur Uther Pendragon, the star subject of a radio feature* (R4 30 December 1993). Dressed if the occasion demands in flowing robes and wielding Excalibur, he claims to be a reincarnation of the spirit of King Arthur, regarding himself as fully employed in this role, and therefore not drawing unemployment benefit. Declaring that he is 'king of the people who want him to be king', he is 'fighting for truth, honour and justice' at the head of his Warband of eco-warriors. At the time of the broadcast this particular fight was focused on the question of access to Stonehenge at the solstices. The custodians of the monument, English Heritage, had rescinded public access after damage done there by previous hippy invasions. In resisting this ban, he was exciting considerable media attention for arguing that he, as a Druid, should be given access to 'the Stones' since they form a holy site for his religion. To make his point about religious freedom, he encourages a couple of protesters to claim squatters' rights in a peaceful sit-in at Christmas in Winchester Cathedral. They leave having secured the offer of future help from the Canon. Although arrested at Stonehenge in earlier years for breaching the ban, he is successful this time in touching the Heel Stone. The programme fleshes out his New Age context with recordings of solemn rituals among Druids at Primrose Hill and the more Dionysian festivities during Beltane. It also conveys his jocular badinage with police officers, and details with deadpan humour his courteous solicitor's judicious advice. From all of this the personality of Arthur comes across very forcefully and engagingly: original, shrewd, quick-witted, fluent of tongue, firmly locked on to his driving purposes. He is a powerful statement of the Arthurian legend's ability to survive and invent new forms.

## Reading and Adapting 1: Medieval Literature

Important new adaptations were made of medieval literature, but not always from the usual sources. No new retelling of Malory, for instance, surfaced until *The Death of Arthur* was given in a series of ten half-hour readings by Philip Madoc, a work which was taken from a previously published commercial recording of an abridgement by Perry Keenlyside (OW 2005). Of *The Mabinogion* likewise there is little trace, except for a reading by Gwyn A. Williams from the Merthyr diaries of Lady Charlotte Guest, the work's first translator into English (R3 5 October 1983).

Of Chaucer rather more was heard. David Wright's verse translation of *The Canterbury Tales*, first published in 1985, was later broadcast with Prunella Scales starring in *The Wife of Bath's Tale* (R3 29 July 1987). When Mike Poulton's adaptation of *The Canterbury Tales* was premièred by the Royal Shakespeare Company at Stratford, Nigel Swain reported on it for *Night Waves* (R3 9 December 2005). More ambitiously, Colin Haydn Evans's four-part adaptation of the *Tales*, in which *The Wife of Bath's Tale*\* formed the second part, was produced by Nigel Bryant (R4 20 March 1991). Verbally, Evans's version is so freely inventive that it may almost be deemed a new creation rather than an adaptation, but he firmly retains the characters, plot and spirit of the Chaucerian original. After a Prologue involving much lively chaffing between the pilgrims, the Wife (Rosemary Leach) tells her story, which is enlivened by some attractive music (composed and played by Sue Harris) and by a dramatisation of the key scenes (featuring William Chubb as the Knight, Tina Gray as the Queen and Mary Wimbush as the Old Woman). What marks this as a pioneering production, however, is the realism of the love-making between the Knight and the Old Woman. Not only is he obliged to watch her undress, but he is also induced to have full sexual intercourse with her, before achieving a protracted climax. This is therefore probably the Arthurian legend's first on-air orgasm. As a consequence the rapist Knight is finally brought to realise that the ugliness he had seen in the Old Woman was merely a reflection of his own corrupt heart. Having learned to love her, she now appears beautiful: her beauty is his awakening. Evans's treatment has great power: it is vigorous, spellbinding and very moving.

Chaucer may not have cited Sir Gawain as the knight in question, but elsewhere he was so named, and his deeds continued to attract significant and original attention. An early example of this is a twenty-minute talk given by W. M. S. Russell, *Sir Gawain in Reading* (R3 9 January 1982).[10] In the ruins of Reading Abbey, Russell had happened upon a play being performed by Reading Street Theatre, in which a sinister Black Knight was threatening to do dire things to King Arthur and his court unless they could solve the riddle of what women want most. Suggestions from the audience included a husband and a washing machine. He had stumbled on a performance of *Lady Ragnell, or The Loathly Lady*. This little play was, he thought, 'performed with great verve and enthusiasm' and, considering the 'lack of a fixed script and a rather impromptu proceeding, it was surprisingly coherent and well coordinated'. His pleasurable experience led him to ponder on comparable legends of the Loathly Lady (which his talk examines in detail) and the relationship between spoken tradition and written source. Wondering whether this production owed anything to the folklore of spoken tradition, he later wrote to the director of Reading Street Theatre, Chris Bertrand, who explained that he had told the story to the cast, who had then improvised it scene by scene. His own source had been a book he had read in childhood, a paperback of Roger Lancelyn Green's retelling of the Arthurian legends.[11] Consulting Green's introduction, Russell reads that the relevant

---

10 BBC WAC: typed script of talk.
11 Roger Lancelyn Green, *King Arthur and his Knights of the Round Table. Newly Retold out of the Old Romances* (Harmondsworth: Penguin, 1953).

chapter was based on 'a Middle-English poem and a ballad, and seems never to have been retold' (p. 5). As Russell amusedly observes, Green's retelling has been transmitted by Bertrand to the Street Theatre and thence to their audiences (not to mention Radio 3): in 'a fascinating new kind of transmission process', it must be becoming part of the folklore of Berkshire.

For schools the BBC continued to present different versions of *Sir Gawain and the Green Knight*: the two-part series commissioned from David Self in 1978 was repeated in 1982, but was then replaced in 1990 by a three-part series written by Fiz Coleman. At an adult level there were a number of major reconstructions and assessments of the poem. The lead in this was seemingly taken by Rosemary Hartill in her *Immortal Diamonds** series, which investigated the ways in which various poets have dealt with the idea of God. Her first half-hour programme chose *Sir Gawain* as text (R4 3 June 1990). With Marie Denley (lecturer in medieval literature at King's College London) on hand for specialist advice, Hartill presents an intelligent résumé of the poem, using an occasional quotation from the Middle English before switching to a modern verse translation read by Nigel Forde (though uncredited it is by Brian Stone) and bursts of medieval music. Hartill and Denley concur in stressing throughout the deceptive ambiguities of the original, are unhappy with the Green Knight's apportioning blame to Morgan le Fay, and they conclude that the ending is left deliberately open: as we are all fallibly human, we cannot judge the inwardness of another man's conduct – only God can. Some indication of the widening appreciation of the poem is that it was soon presented wholly through Brian Stone's verse translation in five fifteen-minute episodes (1991). Read once again by Nigel Forde, it too reached the larger audience of Radio 4 rather than Radio 3. Moreover, a side effect of Birtwistle's opera was its success in arousing interest in the literary version. At the première, for example, an interval talk on the Gawain legend was given by Charlotte Brewer. Similarly, at the 1994 revival of the opera, Graham Fawcett and A. S. Byatt joined a studio discussion of the medieval poem. The most sensitive and scholarly retelling was given by Christopher Page in two sixty-minute programmes appositely placed just before Christmas, *Sir Gawain and the Green Knight** and *Camelot One Christmastide** (R3 7 and 14 December 1997). Page, a Cambridge University lecturer in Middle English, provides an academically authoritative account, quoting key terms in Middle English, and for certain highlights in the story employs an abridgement of William Vantuono's translation, read by Bob Peck, that preserves the alliteration and tail rhymes of the original poem. A reminder that Page is also an expert on medieval music, and founder of Gothic Voices, is the fact that fine examples of medieval songs and dances are interspersed throughout. A worthy successor to the programmes was Jeremy Noel-Tod's *From Camelot to Birkenhead** (R4 9 August 2004), which varied the approach by focusing rather on the poem's origins and landscape. He takes as his cue the recently published or forthcoming translations by three modern poets (W. S. Merwin, Bernard O'Donoghue and Simon Armitage), quoting from all of these as the programme develops.[12] Adopting the journalistic

---

[12] W. S. Merwin's version had already appeared in the USA (Knopf, 2002) and Britain

genre of on-the-spot reporting of a treasure hunt, he describes the poem's manuscript history, and its present appearance, by means of an interview with Chris
Fletcher, curator of literary manuscripts in the British Library. He learns from
Derek Brewer of the post-war pleasure of lying on one's sofa at Oxford reading
the Tolkien and Gordon edition, identifying with Gawain's predicament and
remaining baffled by the absence of any critical article whatever on the poem
in those days. From David Harsent, librettist for Birtwistle's opera, he hears of
the knight's journey into self-discovery. With Simon Armitage he energetically
explores possible settings for the poem in the Peak District, listening politely to
Armitage's continued emphasis on the poem's regional qualities and ecological
message, before having these views placed in a sounder, and more universal-
ised, context by Jocelyn Wogan-Browne, an academic medievalist. It is a lively,
intelligent and informative programme, admirably attentive to the verbal detail
and quiddity of the poem.

Armitage's translation is taken up briefly, too, in *A Map of Britain**, a series of
poems chosen by the poet laureate, Andrew Motion, on the theme of place. In
the twelfth and last of the series, 'Off the Map', he uses an extract from the poem
to illustrate how even celebrations of definite places, such as the Gawain-poet's
Wirral, may also convey the sense of being lost (R4 14 May 2005).

This fascination with English landscape is carried over into radio treatments
of the Tristan story. Malcolm Billings's twenty-minute talk *In Search of Tristan*
takes him to Cornwall in quest of legendary origins (R4 20 January 1982), a
quest that is greatly expanded in Christopher Page's forty-five-minute feature *In
Search of Tristan** (R3 28 March 1999), for which Oliver Padel acted as consultant.
On location in Cornwall, with a copy of Béroul's French text in his hand, Page
uses atmospheric sound effects and his own visual descriptions to evoke the
winds, waves and sea mists of the Atlantic coast setting for his presentation of
the French version, and he links the medieval poet's narrative with appropriate
glosses on places alluded to in the text (St Michael's Mount, Tintagel, St Samp-
son's Church, Malpas), historical venues that he ironically counterpoints with
modern actuality: the Forest of Morois, for instance, is long gone, and Lantyan,
a palace in Béroul, is only a small farmhouse surrounded by rusty barbed wire.
Page's narrative proceeds on three levels: a résumé and commentary given by
Page, interspersed by Christopher Wright's readings of an English translation,
and a wonderful series of musical interludes that includes songs from a thirteenth-century source (presumably Bibliothèque Nationale MS Fr.776). Béroul's
toughness is not shirked; as Page points out, this is often a 'cruel and cynical
poem', revealing 'almost a diseased love-triangle', from which the complex
character of Mark emerges as the most interesting protagonist. Wrapped in mist
at the standing stone outside Fowey, Page brings his programme full circle and
returns the myth to historical reality and modern topography by reading the
fifth/sixth-century inscription: Drustanus.

No such topographical prop had been required, however, for a signal occasion: *Tristan and Iseult**, a ninety-minute recording from that summer's York Early

(Bloodaxe, 2003). O'Donoghue's would be published by Penguin in 2006, Armitage's by
Faber in 2007.

Music Festival (R3 9 October 1991). For the text of this, Joël Cohen combined English versions of Gottfried von Strassburg and Thomas de Bretagne. The music he reconstructed from twelfth-, thirteenth- and fourteenth-century sources, his most important being a French manuscript of the *Prose Tristan* in Vienna (MS 2542) that contains seventeen strophic lays. In all, half of his score came from music originally associated with the story, the other half being closely related in mood and content. Cohen not only narrated the story and directed the musicians of the Boston Camerata, but also played the lute himself. In this splendid form, Gottfried's version finally reached a British radio audience.

Significantly augmenting this introduction of Continental romance was the adoption for the *Book at Bedtime* series of Pauline Matarosso's translation of the thirteenth-century *The Quest of the Holy Grail* (R4 May–June 1998). Abridged into ten fifteen-minute parts by David Hartley, it was very ably read by Sir Derek Jacobi. As with other readings in this popular series, the work had to stand alone without dramatisation or ancillary sound effects, though Clifford Harper produced a striking colour illustration for *Radio Times*. That the medieval story was thought suitable in this stark format for Radio 4 makes this a small Arthurian breakthrough. Although Matarosso's translation had appeared in Penguin Books almost thirty years before, this was a long-overdue landmark broadcast.[13]

## Reading and Adapting 2: Post-Medieval Literature

When versions of Gascoigne's *The Princely Pleasures* masque at Kenilworth had previously been broadcast, they had been intended for juveniles. Derek Wilson's programme (R4 26 August 1984) was, however, addressed to older listeners and focused on the Earl of Leicester's unsuccessful attempt to win the love of Elizabeth I.[14] In the course of the masque he puts on to impress the Queen, the Lady of the Lake lands from a floating island to announce that she has awakened from her long post-Arthurian sleep to attend the new sovereign. When the evil Sir Bruce sans Pité takes the Lady prisoner, Arion and 'all the gods' beg her to yield to the knight's matrimonial advances. In Wilson's witty handling the masque is not only reported admiringly by Robert Laneham (its traditional recorder) but regarded ironically by various other speakers, who comment on the wasteful extravagance of Leicester's ostentation, and maintain that his motives are absurdly transparent. Enraged by all this talk of knightly wooing, Elizabeth storms off. As Katherine divulges: 'At the end of it my lady consented to stay but, I warrant, she told our host plain that there was to be no more talk of marriages' (p. 27).

Spenser's *Faerie Queene* continued to be neglected and, even when 'dramatised' by Philip Palmer in two sixty-minute episodes, was traduced rather than translated* (R4 30 September, 7 October 2001). Palmer is overly intent on giving the material a wholly alternative slant. As Spenser's value system is turned

---

13  *The Quest for the Holy Grail*, tr. Pauline Matarosso (Harmondsworth: Penguin, 1969).
14  BBC WAC: typed playscript of Derek Wilson, 'The Princely Pleasures at Kenilworth'.

upside down, the Bower of Bliss is represented as a paradise of free love. Arthur and his knights are pompous and vainglorious. George is the descendant not of Saxon kings but of a thief and a whore. Una is sexually abused by her father. After Guyon crosses a sword bridge to rescue Gloriana he rapes her, for which he is banished the court. He then blinds George in one eye. The knights' viewpoints are shattered by those of the Dwarf, who represents the atheist man-in-the-street, while Spenser's narrative is constantly interrupted by Stella, who claims to see the 'whole picture' in contrast to his limiting moralism. Eventually Spenser is obliged to accept her position, and to show greater sympathy. … Although this is all designed to be lively and provocative, it does not work. Palmer's vision is so modishly and gratuitously dark, so predictably naughty at the expense of some conventional safe targets, that it becomes stultifying.

Throughout these years *Radio Times* gives fewer details of individual poems that were read on air, but the centenary of Tennyson's death prompted two appearances of 'The Lady of Shalott': a reading by Peggy Ashcroft with an introduction by John Betjeman (R3 21 September 1992) and a special feature, *Tirra Lirra by the River**, on what was termed 'his best-loved poem' (R4 25 July 1992). In Beaty Rubens's production of this thirty-minute feature, the entire poem is read very dramatically by Frances Tomelty, while a demotic touch is added by the inclusion of some disarmingly frank views of the poem from young Lincolnshire schoolchildren. At several pauses in the reading, time is found for expert opinion from, for example, Christopher Ricks, Marion Shaw, Angela Leighton, Michael Thorne and Claire Tomalin, who offer close readings of textual detail, and voice their very diverse interpretations of the poem's meaning – interpretations that are so diverse as to lend credence to Marion Shaw's sensible view that 'mystery' is the key to the poem's attraction. Jeremy Maas provides a linkage with associated paintings and drawings, categorically stating – quite wrongly – that Elizabeth Siddal was the poem's first illustrator. A novel feature of Tomelty's reading is that both the 1832 and 1842 endings of the poem are recited. Responses to these differed, some feminist critics preferring the conventional affirmations of the earlier version, while Ricks, with greater justification, regarded it as much less moving than Lancelot's closing prayer for the Lady that was included in 1842.

In a rare mention of nineteenth-century Arthurian drama, *Radio Times* carried a photograph of Ellen Terry in the role of Guinevere. Though it did not acknowledge that this was taken from J. Comyns Carr's *King Arthur* (1895), it served as preview for a programme presented by John Gielgud (R4 7 December 1980) in which he read extracts from *A Victorian Playgoer*. This was a recently published collection of play reviews that his mother (Kate Terry Gielgud) had written privately for a friend.[15] As *King Arthur* is one of the plays she described, and as Ellen Terry was her aunt, it is quite possible that her perceptive review of this production was included in the broadcast.

The literary fortunes of David Jones were significantly revived again in 1981 to coincide with a major exhibition of his paintings at the Tate. Peter Orr's talk on

---

15 Kate Terry Gielgud, *A Victorian Playgoer*, ed. Muriel St Clare Byrne (London: Heinemann, 1980).

*The Poetry of David Jones* (R3 13 March) was followed by a reading of *The Sleeping Lord*, arranged by Orr (R3 21 July), and then a repeat of the 1955 production of *In Parenthesis* (R3 30 August). Another milestone would lead to another notable feature programme. The centenary of David Jones's birth prompted Jeremy Hooker's *A Map of David Jones*\*, produced by Michael Roberts (R3 5 November 1995). This was an admirable feature, placed under the complete control of a scholar-poet, who draws on his own first-hand knowledge of Jones, and on recordings made by the poet, to elicit with scrupulous exactness the individual quality of Jones's mind and writings. Very usefully, he plays excerpts from the former BBC productions of *In Parenthesis* and *The Anathemata*, which affords a modern listener the opportunity to hear Dylan Thomas and Richard Burton in their original roles. Hooker's account was repeated a year later, and was succeeded by a sixty-minute programme in which Nest Cleverdon introduced scenes from her husband's productions of *In Parenthesis* (R4 7 November 1998). His pioneering adaptation was also retained for a new production\* directed by Alison Hindell to mark the ninetieth anniversary of the outbreak of the First World War (R3 14 November 2004). For this broadcast new, and very effective, music was commissioned by John Hardy to replace Elizabeth Poston's. For speakers, Hindell turned markedly towards a female presentation, and broke with Cleverdon's previous productions by handing over almost all the narrative to female voices: Sian Phillips as Action, Sara McGaughey as Thought, and Marion Edwards as Memory. Although Sian Phillips reads excellently (and the other two very well), to apportion so much of the narrative to female voices seriously compromises the timbre of Jones's poetic utterance: though women are highly important in Jones's work, they are not the dominant voice of his trench warfare. Disappointingly, the male voices in the parts of the main soldiers in Hindell's production are barely adequate, and those in the lesser roles decidedly amateur. The greatness of Jones's theme carries the production through but, when compared with the recordings included in Hooker's feature, it is largely an echo of distant thunder.

Of other mid-twentieth-century Arthurian verse little was heard, but the *Behind the Book* series selected Eliot's *The Waste Land* for exploration (R4 2005) while *Dear Martyn Skinner* (R4 29 April 1992) featured the ten-year correspondence between Roger Ellis (a poet from London) and Martyn Skinner, the unduly neglected author of an Arthurian epic. It is quite likely that Skinner's letters would have mentioned his difficulties in obtaining publication and radio publicity for his work.

One contemporary poet did, however, create a radiantly memorable programme. For the first in a new series of *The Spirit of Place*, Brian Patten was commissioned to examine myth-making in *Tintagel on Trial*\* (R4 14 October 1995). Not all of this forty-five-minute feature is given over to Arthur, but he forms the main focus. Conversation with two local experts (the author Michael Williams and the polymath Charles Thomas) provides a scholarly frame for the question of Arthur's legendary connection with the area, before Patten moves on to explore the tacky souvenir shops. Shown a plastic Excalibur he sensibly asks how it could ever sink into a lake. At King Arthur's Café the ingredients of various baked potato fillings are explained to him. The 'Sir Lancelot' has sausage and baked beans, 'Sir Tristram' cheese and onion, 'Guinevere' coleslaw, and the speciality 'Merlin' prawns in mayonnaise. As Charles Thomas had already remarked, the locals do not like to cheapen the legend in these ways, but they have no economic alternative. And whereas Williams sees the funny side of the commercial adaptations, Patten protests overmuch. On the question of tourism, too, it is a little disappointing to hear him repeat the old fallacy about Tennyson being the first tourist to visit Tintagel. Nonetheless, Patten is splendidly inventive on this topic. He produces a spoof recording (with all the antique crackles) of 'Tennyson' histrionically reciting an excerpt from 'The Coming of Arthur' about the babe washed ashore at Tintagel, then creates a witty poem, 'Why, Mr Tennyson, welcome to Tintagel', delivered in the vigorously brash style of a Cornish fairground showman, who connives in baiting the tourist trap:

> Your deeply held conviction
> That Arthur's not a fiction
> At first we found irrational
> But now we find it's quotable
> And as it helps the gullible
> To whom nothing is implausible,
> Welcome, Mr Tennyson, welcome down.

Patten is himself caught between two worlds: between the seedy modernity he is so good at conveying, and a wistfully elusive romanticism that he finds, for example, in St Nectan's Glen, whose 'haunted' atmosphere he evokes as the 'real' vale of Avalon. These two worlds come together in another poem he writes for the programme, 'Where are they now, those medieval heroes?' The answer he gives is that they still live in Tintagel, though in degraded roles:

> Sir Lancelot's old and wheezy,
> He sits in the backroom of the King Arthur Tavern.
> His mind half-gone; he mistakes the glass of wine
> Shaking in his arthritic hands
> For the Holy Grail.
> Sir Percival's a write-off.
> Released under the care-in-the-community scheme
> He's back in Tintagel embarrassing the day trippers …
> Spectral creatures glimpsed in Tintagel High Street
> Late at night by a few solitary believers.

Among the true believers are a group of young children whom Patten questions, and who unhesitatingly aver that King Arthur was 'real'. 'More real than Superman?' he asks. 'Yes!' they chorus immediately. This leads him to make a much more serious (and highly successful) poem, 'Arthur and Superman', which he recites to a fine musical accompaniment composed by Nick Sargent. Here Arthur speculates on whether bullets, 'if they'd been invented', would have bounced off him too. But he cannot imagine himself wearing 'those iridescent blue tights' or 'shiny black boots':

> No, my cloak was of a different hue,
> Threaded with ancestral dreams

And a longing for order ...
There was a need of me
For kings came and went ...
They were like mayflies
And their thrones like ice on a summer sea.

But Patten's theme is the creation of modern myths, and so he allows Arthur to wonder what will happen to the Superman myth:

His story is as giant as my own.
His war against Evil the same as mine.
Years hence, after the new Dark Ages,
When the new plagues have receded
Which of us will be remembered?
Perhaps we'll become one,
Myth melting into myth
As the stars grow older.
Camelot and Metropolis,
Avalon and Krypton,
The once and future story.

Michael Williams had earlier voiced the need for an 'heroic concept' to replace the current fashion for an anti-hero. Patten has obliged with a very attractive synthesis of ancient and modern myth.

But if poetry was elsewhere permitted to languish, twentieth-century fiction received increasing attention. In the 1980s the chief focus still dwelt on T. H. White. A four-part serialisation (presumably a repeat of Langdon's 1971 series) for schools of *The Sword in the Stone* (1981) was shortly followed by Neville Teller's adaptation of it for a *Saturday Night Theatre* production by Graham Gauld in which Britten's music was retained, Michael Hordern took the part of Merlyn, and Toby Robertson was Wart (R4 26 December 1981), while Robin Jacques produced a new (and superior) design for *Radio Times* [plate 32].

The fullest critical treatment that White has so far received on air came in Gillian Thomas's stylish feature, *The Matter of Britain: An Impression of the writer T. H. White\** (R4 17 December 1986), produced by Piers Plowright. Resisting the temptation to cover too much biographical and literary ground, Thomas presents a finely dramatised portrait of White that is largely drawn from his own writings, with Jack May giving a virtuoso performance as White himself. Against a dominant theme of White's concern for the history, landscape and culture of Britain, this account centres on White's unhappy relationship with his mother, his inspired teaching, manic pride in acquiring new technical skills, and his complex feelings about a self-imposed Irish exile during the war. Among the experts who comment on how these themes informed White's Arthurian books are Richard Barber and François Gallix. For Barber, White's lack of deep personal knowledge of women led to his weak portrayal of Guenever and Elaine in contrast to his masterly re-creation of Lancelot. Gallix detected a sadistic trait in White that led to his concern with ways of harnessing people's bad natures: King Arthur's attempted (and only partially successful) solution is therefore to set up chivalric institutions that compel Might to serve Right. What the best solution would be is left engagingly open, the programme ending with a reading from *The Book of Merlyn* that voices White's hope that some Arthur of the future will return to give us happiness once more and chivalry 'and the old mediaeval blessing of certain simple people – who tried in their own small way, to still the ancient brutal dream of Attila the Hun'. From the late 1980s interest in White seemed then to flag, though *The Sword in the Stone* was read in a ten-part abridgement by Chris Barlas (R5 1994).

Except for schools programmes the BBC did not commission new work for children on radio. It did, however, foster major contemporary writers in a number of other ways. There were interviews with Alan Garner (1984), Roger Lancelyn Green (1984), Rosemary Sutcliff (in 1984, 1988) and Susan Cooper (1993), while Kevin Crossley-Holland talked about his Arthurian trilogy in the *Work in Progress* series (2001). Novels were given in serialised readings: Cooper's *Greenwitch* (1981) and *The Dark is Rising* (1985); Sutcliff's *The Road to Camlann* (1982) and *The Lantern Bearers* (1984). Traditional legends were retold in Crossley-Holland's *The Slumber King*, presented as *The Morning Story* (1990) and later as *Book at Bedtime* (1992); or in an anonymous *Jack the Giant Killer* (2003). Dramatisations were also made of key novels: Jan Mark adapted Peter Dickinson's *The Weathermonger* (1982); Olwen Wymark did Rosemary Sutcliff's *The Sword and the Circle* (1987), and David Calcutt adapted Susan Cooper's *Over Sea, Under Stone* (1995) and *The Dark is Rising* (1997) for productions by Nigel Bryant. More recently, the inauguration of the digital Oneword station has provided a channel dedicated to reading books on air. It has already included Bernard Flynn's audiobook, *King Arthur and the Knights of the Round Table* (2003), and a serialisation of the first two books in Crossley-Holland's splendid *Arthur* trilogy (2003): *The Seeing Stone* and *At the Crossing Places*.

A similar pattern may be detected in adult fiction. Increasingly interviews were arranged with the authors of key recent Arthurian novels: with, for example, Robertson Davies about *The Lyre of Orpheus* (R3 1988), Anthony Burgess on *Any Old Iron* (R4 1989), Paul Griffiths on *The Lay of Tristram* (R3 1991) and Iris Murdoch on *The Green Knight* (R4 1993). Daphne du Maurier's Cornwall provided the topic of a programme presented by Angela Rippon (R2 1997).

Very occasionally a modern novel was fully dramatised. J. B. Priestley's banal satire on modern advertising, *The Thirty-First of June*, was adapted by Brian Sibley for *Afternoon Theatre\** (R4 3 January 1983); Agatha Christie's *The Mirror Crack'd from Side to Side* was dramatised by Michael Bakewell (R4 29 August 1998, repeated 2005); and the brilliant intellectual firework display of Robertson Davies's *The Lyre of Orpheus* was dramatised by Roger Danes with music by David Dorward (R4 11 February 2001), and with John Guerrasio playing the role of the modern Arthur. The fullest adaptation (and fittingly so because the novel has become a very influential interpretation) was accorded to C. S. Lewis's *That Hideous Strength\**. Responsibility for this selection was due to the producer Nigel Bryant, who felt sure that the story had 'enormous radio potential' and so commissioned a dramatisation by Stephen Mallatratt in four hourly parts (R4 2–23 February 1990). Lewis's portrayal of a country divided against itself, between a fascist scientific bureaucracy and an Arturo-Christian traditionalism, is so densely written that some splendid scenes, such as the college meeting that is adroitly manoeuvred into acceptance of the machiavellian planning proposal to acquire Merlin's Well for the technocrats, were inevitably discarded from the radio adaptation, and comic minor characters like Mrs Maggs subsumed into others. Though some changes were inappropriate – it was confusedly ineffective to present the destruction of the villains at the Belbury banquet solely through Jane's vision – other innovations worked well. The music written and performed by Vic Gammon, for instance, evoked the heightened atmosphere of the intro-duction of the Fisher King rather better than Lewis's text does. Among the strong cast, Jane (Kathryn Hurlbutt), Mark (Andrew Wincott), Wither (Geoffrey Banks) and Merlin (Robert Eddison) all shone. Reviewing it after hearing the first episode, Nigel Andrew thought it all made 'terrific radio, exciting, colourful and uninhibited'. It was 'hokum, no doubt, but hokum of a very high order, and immensely enjoyable'.[16]

Occasional serialised readings continued: Twain's *Connecticut Yankee at the Court of King Arthur* was revived (OW 2004), Victor Canning's popular (and deservedly so) *The Crimson Chalice* was given in *Woman's Hour* (R4 1981), and both Samuel Selvon's *Lonely Londoners* (R4 1997) and J. B. Priestley's *The Thirty-First of June* returned to the air as *Book at Bedtime* (R4 2005).

Most significantly of all, Dennis Potter's short story *Excalibur*\* was read by Martin Jarvis to mark the fourth anniversary of Potter's death (R4 8 June 1998). Potter and his elder daughter had read it aloud at the opening of the new Ross-on-Wye Public Library in March 1988, and it had shortly afterwards been published in a small American magazine but, although Potter has achieved great renown as a television dramatist, this story is not widely known in Britain.[17] The narrative is disturbingly original. On a summer evening Sir Ronald Moreston, man-of-letters and retired Chairman of the Arts Council, sits on the lawn of the former Manor House, listening to his daughter Clarissa reading from what he likes to call 'Lawn' Tennyson. She is reading 'The Coming of Arthur' idyll. The scene may appear conventionally 'idyllic' but these two people are locked into private and unshared angsts. She is middle-aged, plump, unattractive, and reads very lamely. He is conceited, morose and petulant. Tennyson's text divides rather than unites them, as each is troubled by particular phrases in the reading. Like Arthur, Clarissa 'yet had done no deed of arms', and 'vext with waste dreams' she longs for a lover's eyes to 'smite' her. Mention of the light in Guinevere's eyes, however, triggers in Sir Ronald a deep inner anxiety caused by a recent dream of a woman pointing at him on a crumbling cliff top, and his awaking to receive a letter from a literary researcher ('some nosy bitch') who might discover the secret extramarital sex he had once enjoyed. Though his daughter feels sympathy for him ('Poor old devil'), he regards her with venom, rudely telling her to match the 'clarions shrilling into blood' in the text with a more zestful delivery. Suddenly she snaps, hurls the book at him and shouts, 'Bastard!' Bleeding from the nose, and cursing, he rushes into the house to wash his face. She resumes her reading, but her delivery grows in power and

16  'Classic Serial', *Listener* 123 (8 February 1990), 47.
17  Humphrey Carpenter, *Dennis Potter: A Biography* (London: Faber & Faber, 1998), pp. 475–6. Dennis Potter, 'Excalibur', *Bomb* 27 (Spring 1989), 54–7.

confidence as she narrates how the Lady of the Lake bestows Excalibur upon Arthur: 'Take thou and strike!' While her baffled father watches from the house as she reads 'with such grace, such feeling', she continues to the end, closes the book and looks calmly at her father, who is, she now realises, 'not long for this world'. Thus transformed she knows she will sleep well, and looks forward to the next day's reading. 'There was much to be said for "Lawn" Tennyson,' she realised. Though deceptively simple, and economical in form, Potter's pungent reworking of the Tennysonian narrative has a rich texture, worthy of being regarded as a minor modern Arthurian classic.

The modern literary haul was overwhelmingly focused on the English-speaking world, even America being largely ignored, and only a token programme was related to Continental writing. This was the pianist Stephen Pruslin's talk *On Acquiring Thomas Mann's 'Tristan'*, which describes his attempt, while visiting Manhattan, to buy a copy of the novella in the original German (R3 1989).

Radio reviews of contemporary Arthurian theatre productions were also scarce, but two were of particular interest. In her *Welsh Arts Week** programme, Jane Dauncey described how *Trystan and Essyllt* was staged by Theatr Taliesin Wales in Cardiff as a community project involving both local Welsh people and Hindus of Indian origin (R4 August 1986). The story was chosen by the director, Stewart Cox, because it is a 'universal love story', akin to that of Krishna and Radha, and he claims to have selected a version that has recently been neglected by Celts, who have followed Franco-German forms instead. It was also chosen for highlighting certain parallels (arranged marriages and journeys to distant lands) between the ancient Celtic world and that of modern Hindus. Both Welsh and Indian traditions were therefore fused within the production. A core of profes-sional actors was supplemented by a large cast of young local amateurs, while specialist teachers were brought in to train the performers in classical Indian and Welsh folk dances. Anut Biswas composed a score (it sounds very attractive in the extracts played) combining jazz, classical western music, and traditional Celtic and Indian melodies. There was not only a mixture of costumes but also a variety of instruments (harp, cello, tabla …) and of languages (Welsh, English and Hindi). In *Radio Times*, Mike Walker's drawing delightfully evoked the occa-sion [plate 33].

A comparably exciting event came from Lancaster, according to a report by Brian Sibley on John Chambers's *Tales of King Arthur**, presented by The Dukes Theatre, and directed by Ian Forrest (R3 5 July 1990). Though Sibley felt the 'simplistic' script failed to make Arthur a credible person, this deficiency was compensated for by the spectacular setting of the work, for this was an outdoor 'promenade' performance in Williamson Park, with the audience expected to walk around and view scenes set at different spots in the picturesque landscape. As darkness falls, Sibley is entranced by the magical atmosphere of the torch-light and the bonfires, a dragon leaping from the trees, the barge disappearing across the lake to Avalon. …

Another item that is of some interest because of the time allotted to it on a popular wavelength was *Broadway Babes*, a two-hour *Arts Programme* in which Gloria Hunniford followed the fortunes of Britain's Youth Music Theatre. Thanks to the sponsorship of Andrew Lloyd Webber, they had taken their production of *Pendragon* (together with Brecht's *The Threepenny Opera*) across to America, to stage it on Broadway for eight days (R2 18 February 1996). Meanwhile the appeal of Monty Python is unabated. The Broadway opening of the musical *Monty Python's Spamalot* was saluted by two notices in quick succession on the BBC's most widely listened-to channel: by Michael Ball (R2 3 June 2005) and Elaine Page (R2 5 June 2005).

Since popular interest in the Arthurian legends is increasingly driven by cinema, it is surprising that *Radio Times* names so few programmes that reflect this phenomenon. Rare exceptions are a preview of Boorman's *Excalibur* (R4 1981); a report on the re-release of Disney's *The Sword in the Stone*, coupled with a current exhibition of Arthurian film, mounted at the London Museum of the Moving Image, to coincide with the release of Warner Brothers' *The Magic Sword: Quest for Camelot* (R3 1998); and a preview of Bruckheimer's *King Arthur* (R4 2004). The only major programme has been Gerry Northam's lively *Monty Python and The Holy Grail\**, a feature that marked the re-release of the original film (R4 27 October 2001). Occasional brief clips from it are used throughout the programme to underline a point or raise a laugh while Northam interviews Terry Jones, the film's co-director. Jones narrates how the work evolved from a sketch using coconuts to simulate hoof beats, and explains that he did not want the film to switch too much between the Middle Ages and the twentieth century (he was instrumental in securing this change of plan). On reflection he considers that his portrait of thirteenth-century England was often historically accurate with regard to taunting and the military hurling of dead animals, but that he probably exaggerated the dark, muddy, rotten-tooth aspects. To discuss the wider questions about Arthur's role, Northam turns to Nicholas Higham (from Manchester University), who presents the sceptical case against there being a sixth-century Arthur of any historical significance in any known location. With a slight change of emphasis, Ronald Hutton (of Bristol University) concedes that there may well have been an Arthur, and if there was he would almost certainly have been Christian. After Hutton's explanation of the political use made of the Arthurian myth by Geoffrey of Monmouth and Edward III, Northam contributes to a discussion on the perpetually changing interpretation of Arthur by quoting from a book he was given as a Sunday School prize in 1956 (Alice Hadfield is the unnamed author) that presented Arthur as an evangelical Christian hero.[18] Not averse to a sweeping generalisation, Hutton then argues that Arthur, the 'only' hero who can unite the British, reaching 'everyone' through literary and visual sources, was the Victorian role model for the Empire's dominant ethic: 'Bible and brutality'. Higham suggests that Arthur's present popularity owes much to anti-German feelings arising from the two World Wars, as a consequence of which the nineteenth-century concept of a continuity between the Anglo-Saxons and our modern democratic state has been replaced by the British figure of Arthur as symbol of national identity. For Hutton, Arthur's shadowy historicity and his interpretative plasticity enhance his appeal.

---

[18]   Alice M. Hadfield, *King Arthur and the Round Table*, illus. Donald Seton Cammell (London: Dent, 1953).

As should be becoming clear, the chief preoccupation of these programmes has been fiction rather than fact: Arthur is now valued more highly as a mythical hero than as an historical one. This was signalled by the title of a programme involving listeners' questions put to Jennifer Westwood and W. R. J. Barron, *Myths, Legends and Romance* (R4 11 February 1986), and echoed in words later used by Barron on a television programme *The Real King Arthur* (Channel 4, 2000): 'the key to romance is the projection of what we would like to believe but know in our hearts is not true'.[19] Moreover, there is a growing fascination with the evolution of the myth, and celebration of its continuous development through different media. Two talks by David Huckvale, given during the intervals of a broadcast of Wagner's *Lohengrin* (R3 2 July 1994), illustrate this tendency. The first, *Who is the Grail?\**, uses Lohengrin's question as starting point for a wide-ranging analysis of the many forms taken by the Grail. Whether it is identified with an inanimate stone, as in Wolfram's *Parzival*, or with Mary Magdalene's womb, as in Baigent, Leigh and Lincoln's *Holy Blood, Holy Grail*, Huckvale ingeniously contrives to link both traditions through citing the belief of some medieval alchemists that their long-sought philosopher's stone was not an external object but something to be found within man himself.[20] Huckvale then relates how Wagner's own quest for a woman's unconditional love was reflected in Lohengrin's finding in Elsa the complementary half of his own nature: representing his Jungian anima, a creative union within himself, she is for him the real Holy Grail. In his *Parsifal*, Wagner takes this psychic integration a stage further: through suffering one may achieve a higher form of knowledge about the reality of existence, for the Grail lies within us if only we can find it. As Huckvale demonstrates, Wagner's handling of the myth is much closer to modern psychology than to the original sources. The second talk, *Avalon\**, shows how Wagner's desire for Art to breathe fresh life into religious symbols in order to reveal deep truths was matched by poets and painters in nineteenth-century England, the rediscovery of Malory leading to Burne-Jones's lifelong fascination with the Arthurian legend, and to Tennyson's perception of the Grail story as the spiritual centre of the *Idylls*, whereas William Morris would view the Grail as the necessary fusion of Art and Socialism that would heal a sick and unjust society. The Arthurian tradition was, however, deflated by Beardsley's playful aestheticism and, despite Rutland Boughton's sustained attempts to revive it, the quest would never be the same again because, in Tennyson's words, 'the times /Grew to such evil that the holy cup /Was caught away to Heaven and disappeared'.[21] That may have been an apt way of rounding off a short and lively talk, but there was, of course, very much more to be said. And it was said in three notable feature programmes.

The earliest, *The Matter of Arthur\**, was part of the popular *Kaleidoscope* series. Presented by Paul Vaughan, and produced by John Powell, it ran for forty-five

---

[19] Quoted in Sue Powell's obituary notice of W. R. J. Barron, *Independent* (15 May 2004).
[20] Michael Baigent, Richard Leigh and Henry Lincoln, *Holy Blood, Holy Grail* (London: Jonathan Cape, 1982).
[21] 'The Holy Grail', ll. 56–8, in *Tennyson: A Selected Edition*, ed. Christopher Ricks (London: Longman, 1989).

minutes, was tightly organised in theme, and included a range of fresh material (1979/1994).[22] It begins with the first three stanzas of Francis Brett Young's poem 'Hic jacet Arthurus Rex', read superbly by David March against a soft accompaniment from the Prelude to Wagner's *Tristan*, and pausing on:

> where do those tragic
> Lovers and all their bright-eyed ladies rot?
> We cannot tell – for lost is Merlin's magic.[23]

That is the cue for Vaughan to question whether this knowledge is really lost, for Arthur still haunts the imagination of the West. To investigate the elusive origins of the legend, he turns to Geoffrey Ashe, who describes the impressive scenery at Tintagel, and to a reading from Tennyson's 'The Coming of Arthur' (with heavenly chorus) about the babe arriving on the ninth wave. Moving to South Cadbury, Ashe claims this 'as the nearest we can get to ground walked on by Arthur', and at Glastonbury he supplies an account of the area's religious significance, the twelfth-century exhumation and Ralegh Radford's later dig. On the question whether Arthur's grave was found, Ashe prefers to leave the matter 'open' until the missing leaden cross can be recovered. An overview of Arthur as 'shape-changer' is then given by Richard Barber, tracing the hero's long evolution from Welsh commander to great feudal king to Victorian idealist and then back again to basics with a touch of mysticism now incorporated. For confirmation that this is still a living legend, attention then switches to John Steinbeck, whose profound interest in it is detailed by Steinbeck's wife (Elaine) and Robert Wallsten, a family friend.[24] The chivalric legend was not only a literary subject for Steinbeck: it was 'a code to live by', we are told. As the novelist identified personally with Lancelot, an appropriate excerpt is then read from his retelling of 'The Noble Tale of Sir Lancelot of the Lake'. Skilful use of music within the programme leads to Barber's assessment of Wagner's major reshaping of the material, a reshaping of equal artistic stature with Tennyson's, for Wagner restores the primeval passion, the 'magical and superhuman' quality of the early Tristan story, which had been lost in courtly retellings. Complementing this musical treatment, Powell draws the listener's attention to Arthurian art, and briefly cites the medieval manuscript illuminations and Pre-Raphaelite paintings that are illustrated in Barber's anthology *The Arthurian Legends*.[25] Returning to Young's poem, the final two stanzas are read, which end with the phrase: 'Arthur is gone.' To rebut that pessimistic closure, John Matthews is on hand to outline the concept of 'Albion, the mythical state of Britain', that signifies a belief in another and better country (he cites Charles Williams on Logres) as represented by the Grail sites of Glastonbury or Nanteos. He moves on to the abiding

---

22  This was first broadcast on R4 in late November 1979. For the repeat (8 January 1980) *Radio Times* names Peter Vansittart, John Boorman and Andrew Davies among the participants. But in the version I listened to (British Forces Broadcasting Service, April 1994) they were replaced by John Matthews.

23  Francis Brett Young, *The Island* (London: Heinemann, 1944), p. 16.

24  Elaine Steinbeck and Robert Wallsten were joint editors of *Steinbeck: A Life in Letters* (New York: Viking, 1975).

25  Richard Barber, *The Arthurian Legends: An Illustrated Anthology* (Woodbridge: Boydell Press, 1979).

core faith in Arthur's messianic role, and the feeling that a return is imminent. Upon which, Vaughan glides smoothly into Malory's statement (from 'Yet some men say' to 'Hic jacet Arthurus Rex, quondam Rex que futurus'), accompanied by a splendid burst of orchestral brass from Wagner's *Parsifal*, to round off his programme very neatly.

The second feature was Terry Jones's *The Once and Future King\**, another in the *Arts Programme* series, which ran for two hours (R2 1 September 1996). This lavish allocation allowed Jones to give above average time for his invited experts to express their views fully, and to include a substantial number of readings by Duncan Alexander, and diverse musical excerpts. Jones, who wears his considerable learning very lightly, starts by recalling that his own first enduring image of Arthur was drawn from Tennyson's 'Morte d'Arthur' (which is then read to the accompaniment of Wagner's *Götterdammerung*), but now accepts that Old Welsh writings such as the encounter with the gatekeeper in *Culhwch and Olwen* (also read, in translation) come 'closer to reality'. To assess the evidence for an historical Arthur he turns to Michael Wood, who talks us through the extant sources, concluding that there is 'no early testimony' for Arthur's existence, though this absence did not prevent the growth of vigorous Celtic folk legend by the late twelfth century. It is then Richard Barber's turn to explain how every later age has viewed Arthur from a contemporary standpoint, and to trace the literary transformation of the legend from Geoffrey of Monmouth via Chrétien, Malory and Tennyson to twentieth-century fiction. To historical novelists, Barber claims, Arthur is 'a gift' because his lack of historicity means that he can be perpetually reinvented. Of these writers, T. H. White is the finest, for he has an 'unparalleled' ability to take the framework of the traditional Malorian story and yet breathe into it a completely new life, both comic and tragic. For the views of a living novelist, Jones then contacts Bernard Cornwell, another writer who confesses to having loved the stories since meeting them in picture books as a child. In fact, Cornwell asserts his belief in a real Arthur, a 'great, great British hero' who gave pride to later Celts. Though Arthur is seen as a great and good man in Cornwell's fiction, he is also placed within a realistic sixth-century setting, in which he is primarily a fighting man, a hard character, a pagan, and akin to the 'ravager of Britain' mentioned in *The Welsh Triads*. In other parts of his programme Jones ranges quite widely through other art forms. At the Birmingham City Museum and Art Gallery, the curator, Stephen Wildman, guides a reporter around the Pre-Raphaelite section, pausing to comment on Arthur Hughes's cartoon for *The Birth of Tristram*, Frederick Sandys's *Morgan le Fay*, and three Dante Gabriel Rossettis: *Sir Galahad at the Ruined Chapel*, *Sir Launcelot in the Queen's Chamber*, and *King Arthur and the Weeping Queens*. Wildman's commentary is pleasantly designed to relate the underlying story of the knights to its place within a Victorian context. Turning then to popular music, Jones plays two songs from the Broadway production of *Camelot* (sung by Richard Burton and Robert Goulet), and Ella Fitzgerald's rendition of a Rodgers and Hart lyric from their musical *A Connecticut Yankee*, before settling into an extended conversation with Rick Wakeman. Like Cornwell, Wakeman is a lifelong enthusiast for Arthur, constant exposure to Tintagel as a child having encouraged him to play at being King Arthur in childhood games in the spirit of Just William, Richmal

Crompton's hero. Intrigued by the uncertainty of Arthur's existence and location, he regards the legend as attractively colourful, optimistic, and retaining the
ability to appeal across a wide spectrum of interests, from love to masculinity. As
for why his rock opera, *Myths and Legends of King Arthur*, was famously staged
on *ice*, he explains that was the only state in which he could book his venue,
the Empire Pool at Wembley. Moving on to cinema, Jones plays the Bing Crosby
song of 'Busy Doing Nothing' from the 1949 *A Connecticut Yankee*, a hit song
that both Jones and his next guest, Jeffrey Richards (of Lancaster University),
recall hearing played every week on *Children's Favourites* in the 1950s.[26] In the
discussion on films, Jones confides the information that in the first draft of his
*Monty Python and The Holy Grail*, the Grail was to have been found at Harrods,
because 'you can get anything there'. Richards picks out a few films to substan-
tiate his view that artefacts reflect the ethos of the eras in which they are created.
*Prince Valiant*, a product of the 1950s, 'the last chivalric age', epitomises Arthur
as a Christian king resisting barbarian usurpers. Cornel Wilde's *Lancelot and
Guinevere*, by contrast, foregrounds the 1960s fascination with sex and violence.
The 1970s revival of paganism is embodied in Stephen Weeks's *Sir Gawain and
the Green Knight*, while *Excalibur* reflects the ecological concerns of the 1980s
– Boorman even shot through green filters. As *First Knight* represents a 1990s
conflict between Round Table Blairite communitarianism and Sir Malagant's
individualist Thatcherite ethic, the eventual enthronement of Lancelot (here
born a commoner) indicates Britain's yielding of world authority to the United
States. For a summary of Arthur's enduring appeal, Jones reverts to his earlier
consultants, Wood stating that myth has a greater power than history, and that
Arthur 'is at the centre of our culture'. For Barber, the appeal is threefold. Arthur
is heroic; he is a mystery; and he is a deeply tragic figure, a classic victim of
the Wheel of Fortune. Maintaining the seriousness of this tone while veering
towards the more upbeat hope of a new Arthurian beginning, Jones arranges for
a reading from the noble closing paragraphs of White's *The Candle in the Wind*,
before announcing the programme credits, and concluding with the Malorian
'Hic jacet' against another triumphant crescendo of Wagnerian brass.

The final programme of this type, Julian May's attractive *The Story of the
Story\**, is much shorter and more narrowly focused. This was necessarily so, as
it was sandwiched between the première of Mival's *Tristan – Still* and an evening
performance of Act 3 of Wagner's *Tristan* (R3 19 February 2003). May starts on
location near Fowey in Cornwall, next to the granite standing-stone that bears
the inscription 'Drustanus hic jacet Connemori filius', the earliest occurrence
of these two names according to Charles Thomas. May then seeks to establish
a connection between Cornish landscape and Béroul's version of the legend.
Oliver Padel (Reader in Cornish Studies at Cambridge University) assures him
that there is no historical truth in the legend, but that Béroul had local knowledge of Cornish legends. Thomas confirms that it is a Cornish story, 'Cornwall's
greatest contribution to the romantic literature of medieval Europe', and he

---

[26] I can also vouch for the frequency with which this song was broadcast. Although I dislike
the number, I know the tune, and many of the words, by heart – a knowledge that must
have come to me through radio.

provides a résumé of the story's spread across Europe and into the German poem by Gottfried. After Charles Thomas, who is the real star of the show, gives a reading in the Old French of Béroul, he tells us of the pioneering task of translating the work back into Cornish, begun by A. S. T. Smith in the early 1950s, and completed by D. H. Watkins in the 1970s. Thomas then gives a reading of this, too, before moving on to some consideration of later literary works concerned with this living legend. The best of these is, he claims, Arthur Quiller-Couch's novel that was completed by Daphne du Maurier, *Castle Dor*, but he also awards praise to a novel set at King Arthur's Hotel in Tintagel by the American Mary Ellen Chase, *Dawn in Lyonesse*, which 'ought to be better known'.[27] Readings from both novels are given by Charlie Norfolk and Tom Durren. A theme raised earlier by Treeve Crago, a Cornish oral historian, had been Cornwall's quest for its own identity. This issue is taken up by Emma Rice, director of Kneehigh Theatre's new version of the legend, *Tristan and Yseult*, for she argues that the play is a very 'political' story, placing 'Cornwall at the centre of things', midway between London and Spain.[28] This is code for pressing her case for a separate Cornish identity to be achieved through weakening UK ties while increasing links with the European Union. Having shown in this way that the legend is continuously able to inspire new interpretations, a very smooth lead-in has been engineered by May for a return to the Tristan concert.

[27] Sir Arthur Quiller-Couch and Daphne du Maurier, *Castle Dor* (London: Dent, 1962). Mary Ellen Chase, *Dawn in Lyonesse* (New York: Macmillan, 1938).
[28] In addition to its West Country tour, *Tristan and Yseult* was later performed at The National Theatre (Cottesloe) from April to June 2005. See Paul Taylor's review, in which he claims the play is 'one of the best evenings in the theatre you could hope to find', in *Independent* (18 April 2005), 54.

# 5

## 1980–2005: 'Arthur is come again ... he cannot die'

### Making it New

Arthurian short stories do not seem to have been specially written for radio until this period. Two now made their appearance. Though their scripts cannot be located, *Radio Times* affords brief descriptions of these modern tales with Arthurian dimensions. In Donald Bancroft's *A Knight in Shining Armour* (R4 23 July 1982) 'Jennifer married Lancelot because of his nice old-fashioned ideas about chivalry'; while in Raymond Dixon's *Excalibur* (R3 20 February 1983) a man travelling on the London underground 'discovers he is locked up with the living dead'.

More substantially, in this quarter-century Arthurian drama bloomed and, for the first time since Bridson's 1937 play, Arthur himself was restored to a central position in a series of new works. The first of these was an early play by Ian Weir, written before he switched to television: *Passings** (R3 15 March 1984). It was directed by Glyn Dearman, and supplied with a striking illustration by Ian Pollock in *Radio Times* [plate 34].

Like Bridson, Weir takes the traditional story outline from Malory, but instead of following a chronological sequence he radically reshapes the temporal narrative, and does so with a skilful use of the radio medium. By starting at the end, with the approaching death of the hero, Weir makes Arthur emphatically the centre of focus, for the latter's story is presented through flashbacks of his own memory or through reminders by his companions. As he is old, weary, wounded, amnesiac and blinded, it appears quite credible that his present location, and immediately preceding events, should be described to him by Sir Bedwere (Trevor Martin) and the boy, Alan. In this way the radio audience, too, gains the background information it needs. Elsewhere the narrative jumps back and forth in time, as memories are prompted by a key phrase. Scenes are kaleidoscopic, with brief snatches of dialogue, punctuated by the evocative music composed and conducted by Philip Pickett. This internalisation and looseness of structure works well because the play is comparatively short (only seventy minutes) and concentrates on a few major incidents. The verbal tone is often playfully ironic, allusive and parodic. To describe Lancelot's arrival, Weir quotes the famous lines from Tennyson's 'The Lady of Shalott' ('"Tirra lirra," by the river', etc.); as the newly married Arthur leaves the church with his bride a watching woman sighs the clichéd 'Don't they make a lovely pair!'; a later onlooker at the scene of Guinevere's burning describes her as 'pale as a stick of rhubarb', on which the crowd murmur, 'Rhubarb, rhubarb.' Weir is adroit also in handing over most of the ensuing narration to two minstrels: one is young, good-natured and idealist, the other elderly, honest and cynical. The Young Minstrel stumbles verbally and rephrases, forcing himself to create the upbeat glamour of the young king:

> Dawn, gold sun on the king's castle.
> Arthur, best of Briton kings,
> Grey-eyed, gay-eyed, greets the morning.

But the more practised Older Minstrel smoothly and snidely records the rescue of Guinevere by a Lancelot who is

> not quite so swift perhaps or spry as he had been in days gone by. ... His helmet shines like silver in the sun and hides the bald spot on his head. ... A wondering page cries, 'Isn't that splendidly done for a knight his age!'

This twin narrative device not only gives variety of tone (from grave to gay) and a constant dramatic tension, but it firmly underpins the main themes: the ambivalence of Arthur's Camelot, the transience of man's creations, and the difficulty of relating the truth of events. Raised and instructed by a Scottish Merlin (Douglas Storm), the first words Arthur learns to say are 'benevolent dictatorship'. Though he later builds roads and drains for all, his policy is, in Merlin's opinion, over-reliant on aristocratic virtue. He can also be horrifyingly vindictive, as when he consigns all the rebel soldiers to death. Moreover, his personal life is deeply flawed. Here Malory's version is modified by Weir so that Arthur selfishly and knowingly seduces his half-sister Morgawse, before cold-bloodedly marrying her off to King Lot. Believing a prophecy that a newborn child could prove a threat, Arthur hypocritically claims that his sending all the newborn babes out to sea is not murdering them but placing them at God's mercy. Ironically he exempts the real threat, his own son Mordred, from this 'extirpatory action within a limited demographic category'. Yet by the close the aged king has acquired dignity, pathos and grandeur. The reality of Arthur's dual nature is, in fact, well conveyed by the use of two actors: Mick Ford as the fatuously conceited young king, and Paul Daneman (in a superbly poignant performance) as the anguished older man. Despite the fact that in earlier parts of the play the jokes are sometimes facile, and too many of the actors are given Mummerset accents, the ending is deeply impressive. When Bedwere is finally prevailed on to throw Excalibur into the lake, nothing supernatural occurs, but he readily subscribes to the more theatrical version (of grasping hand) that Arthur had dreamed. Though the latter also dreams of being taken off in a bark by three queens, he is in fact buried in a shallow grave marked by a handmade cross. But when Bedwere vows to restore the kingdom, and recounts the tale to a later audience, he has already falsified his own memories. He assures the Young Minstrel that he was an eyewitness of Arthur's passage to Avalon, and had overheard the dark queen promise that Arthur would return one day to help Britain. Urging the minstrel to recite this version of the end of Camelot, Bedwere declaims with great passion, 'We'll rebuild it. Just the way it was!' To which the alehouse audience euphorically responds. It is Weir's considerable achievement that we, too, are swept along by this golden promise. Knowing in our hearts that it is not true, we are nonetheless, as Barron noted above, in love with the romance.

That promised return of Arthur is effected in Dennis Ashton's *The Peril*\* (R4 9 December 1987), directed by Ian Cotterell as the third of five 'magical plays' in the *High Fantastical* series. Though lasting only forty-five minutes, it compresses a plot extending over half a century into eighteen scenes, in which Ashton gives the Alderley Edge legend an additional historical application.[1] One day in 1890, Albert Yardley (Manning Wilson) sets off to sell a white horse at market. On top of the Edge, a Stranger (Kim Wall) tries to buy the horse for an old coin bearing the image of a bearded man, but Albert refuses the offer. At market, however, he fails to find a buyer. On the way back the Stranger tells him that the horse is needed 'for when the peril comes', and leads Albert through an iron gate into a cave where King Arthur, his warriors and their white horses lie sleeping. 'They're short of one horse,' the Stranger says, and warns him not to wake them. The 'peril' will occur when 'George, son of George, is king.' In that reign they will ride out with Arthur at their head to save England. In terror, Albert runs off leaving his horse behind. His wife refuses to believe his story – he must have been drunk, she thinks – and he fails to find the gate again. Ten years later, while blackberrying with his sons, he tells them the story as he again searches vainly for the cave, but they don't believe him either. The play then traces the family's fortunes throughout the First World War and up to 1936, when the death of King George V is quickly followed by the abdication of his eldest son. Albert is startled to hear that the new king will assume the name of George VI on acceding to the throne. Realising that this will make him 'George, the son of George', Albert mutters to himself about the prophetic peril, but the family attribute this outburst to senile decay. Nonetheless, a few years later, when a German invasion of Britain is thought likely, the family recall Albert's rambling memories of King Arthur. This prompts his daughter-in-law to say that she believes Arthur's spirit could still be a source of inspiration. During the Battle of Britain her son is a Spitfire pilot in the Royal Air Force. When he comes home on leave he tells them that one very successful flying squadron had insignia showing a white horse holding a sword. Their leader was called Arthur, but they had all mysteriously disappeared, and no one knew who they were. Albert is very affected by this talk, and his words end the play:

> Like that man said, all those years ago, King Arthur has risen to save England from mortal danger and – my grandson was there helping him. That's something to be proud of, aye? Oh I'm glad I've lived to see it. We'll win the war, no doubt about that. Everything's going to be all right now.   (p. 47)

Summarily dismissing the play in *The Listener*, Nigel Andrew thought it very silly.[2] It is admittedly banal in characterisation, the dialogue is lifeless and the plot wooden, but the work has some interest on two counts. Not only is it original in grafting the Alderley Edge legend on to the messianic heroism of Second World War figures, but it very effectively exploits within its structure the archival resources of radio, for recordings of celebrated broadcasts are used at key points in the drama: Edward on his abdication, George VI at the outbreak

---

[1]   BBC WAC: typed playscript of Dennis Ashton, 'The Peril'.
[2]   Nigel Andrew, 'Thou art translated', *Listener* 118 (10 December 1987), 43.

of war, Churchill on the Battle of Britain. It consequently has the odd distinction
of being perhaps the first Arthurian play to incorporate historically significant
radio itself within the legend.

The next radio drama, *Arthur – The King** (R4 11 November–23 December
1990) had incomparably greater substance. John Powell, its producer, had long
wanted to do an Arthurian drama, and one which would not be 'a life-and-
times-of' nor a 'baroque pageant', but one in which the people were 'as real
as possible'.[3] He hoped that Graham Buck would write this but, when Buck
suddenly died, he turned to Graeme Fife. The lavish outcome was a series of
seven forty-five-minute episodes, each nominally organised around a single character: Merlin (Paul Scofield), Tristram (Rupert Frazer), Gareth (Crawford Logan),
Lancelot (Nicholas Farrell), Galahad (Henry Young), Guenever (Jill Balcon) and
Arthur (Keith Baxter). It was Fife's good fortune to be blessed with such a cast
of first-class actors. They even volunteered to wear chain mail and fight with
real broadswords and shields so that the battle scenes would appear as authentic
as possible. Their acting quality is matched by the skill of the producer. Powell
creates a multi-layered Arthurian world that compels extraordinary belief. The
majesty of Arthur the King is evoked by the series of calls and constant trumpet
flourishes, the lofty splendour of his palace by the sound of beating on the
giant doors and the resonant echoes of voices within. We sense that this is a
populous court. Welsh accents pervade. We hear the noise of feasting, dicing
and minstrelsy inside. Outside there is the world of hunting and battle. Horses
neigh, trot, canter and gallop, their bridles jingling. Bells toll, crowds cheer,
birds sing, winds whistle, wolves howl, seas roar, cocks crow, ravens croak.
And inside once more, the Queen bathes, while in the corners of the palace
the ladies-in-waiting gossip cattily. When violent thunderbolts rip through the
skies, and dragons belch fire, we believe in the magic and enchantment that the
play continually demands. All these sound effects are greatly enhanced by the
specially commissioned music of Steven Faux. This is a very extensive score,
lasting for two and a half hours, which combines traditional instruments (such
as lutes and citerns) with singers and electronics to create sounds that are haunt-
ingly beautiful in themselves and yet remain always wonderfully apt across the
whole range of scenes and emotions.

It was accompanied by a learned and wide-ranging book (that was also a
rambling, repetitive hotchpotch) in which Fife set out his vision of an Arthur 'as
he was originally intended: a mediaeval king', closely associated with the ethos
of the Crusades, whose continuing appeal is his fight against some form of Evil.[4]
In his play Fife presents Arthur's regality through courtly ceremony, for the latter
seems to have no significant civil or military role, and there is no evidence of a
national theme. The significant contests are moral, and involve choice. Asked to
choose between Excalibur and its sheath, Arthur mistakenly chooses the sword
(attack) rather than its covering (defence). Driven by lust he fathers a child on
his half-sister Margause, and then besottedly pursues Guenever.

---

3   Gillian Reynolds, 'Unearthing Arthur', *Daily Telegraph* (10 November 1990).
4   Graeme Fife, *Arthur the King* (London: BBC, 1990), pp. 7, 193.

In this world of ostensibly exclusive opposites, Arthur's essential struggle is with his half-sister, Morgan le Fay, who plays a pivotal role throughout the series, as adversary, manipulator and narrator. Because she cannot forgive Merlin for 'stealing' her brother, or Arthur for killing her lover Accolon, she uses Nimue to allure the magician (Arthur's benevolent adviser) into perpetual imprisonment. Fife ingeniously invents for her a campaign that is protracted and ubiquitous. She thwarts Arthur's attempted murder of the infant Mordred, and grooms him to wreak her vengeance. In giving the love-potion to Tristram and Isolde, she intends that their eternally misplaced love will destabilise the courts of Mark and Arthur. Jealous of Lancelot's love for Guenever, she tricks the crazed Tristram into attacking him. Having the Dame of Lyonesse in thrall, she arranges that the Dame's captivity by the Red Knight should be a pretext for sending Lynet to test Gareth's fortitude and chastity. Jealous also of Elaine's beauty she creates a dragon to turn King Pelles' kingdom into a Waste Land, and when the dragon is slain by Lancelot she contrives to lure the hero into Elaine's bed by drugging him with a pretended 'Grail' drink ostensibly provided by Guenever. On bringing Mordred (Tom Hunsinger) to court, she asks for reconciliation with Arthur, but her offer of 'forgiveness' is brusquely rejected by the King. Throughout the real Grail quest, she has no active role, but she gloats sarcastically over Lancelot's tribulations and the forlorn Guenever. When Lancelot runs mad, however, she intervenes more directly by lodging him at her castle. During his stay she records his deranged expressions of love for Guenever, and sends details of these to Mordred. In sleep she seductively appears to Arthur, inviting him into her arms to heal all his ills. As Arthur's kingdom falls apart, Morgan not only takes on the role of gleeful main narrator but drives on the action by foiling Mordred's cowardly attempt to make peace with Arthur: the viper at the Stonehenge parley is her creation. Finally she arrives, gently and mercifully, in the boat that will take Arthur to his long rest. Fife has thus given her a credible psychology, a coherent career, and made her ultimately a complex and not unsympathetic figure. By making her so complementary to the King's fortunes, Fife has dexterously rounded the narrative, which proceeds from initial unity through separation to an ultimate reunion.

Though the source material is broadly Malorian, Fife often reshapes it by simplifying it into a form more suitable for dramatic presentation. The telescoping of events traditionally leading to the final catastrophe is a case in point. In Fife's version there is no slaying of Gareth when Lancelot arrives to snatch Guenever from the stake, and thus no war sparked by thirst for vengeance on his killer. Instead it is Lancelot's previous killing of Agravain outside the Queen's chamber that prompts Gawain to seek redress, and he rapidly finds opportunity when Lancelot returns to challenge the would-be burners of Guenever. Gawain is slain by Lancelot on that occasion, but Guenever, however, refuses to accompany Lancelot into exile: 'I will not have my honour paid for. My honour is my own.' Civil war then breaks out between Arthur and Lancelot. The action has thus been quite intelligently streamlined.

Fife's reordering of plot is manifested by a brilliantly diverse array of narrative styles and viewpoints. Two examples may suffice. The first is Tristram's arrival at Camelot. When he repeats the Round Table oath, we listen to a dramatic ritual expression of the chivalric code that Arthur has formulated: any need for a great chunk of narrative explanation has thus been avoided. The second instance occurs when the civil war is presented not by an endless series of grunts and clashing steel but is instead evoked by Morgan in an ornate prose-poem. Though this may suffer on the printed page, it succeeded admirably on air by virtue of Anna Massey's menacing delivery and the background music by Faux:

> Now England is a chequered board,
> white squares the snow-drifting fields,
> ghostly in white mist, adazzle in watery sunshine,
> messèd into muddy black acres
> by ponderous knights churning the earth,
> and footslogging armies the pawns in their train.
> King, Arthur the King in Camelot.
> Rebel, Lancelot du Lac, blackened name, Lancelot in Joyous Gard.
> Castles between and Queen.
> Queen still, Queen Guenever in icy silence,
> her eyes blinkless like bell stones.
> And dark Queen by, Morgan le Fay.
> Queens rule the game where slow-legged Kings
> lurch square by cumbrous square.
> Queens rule the game from end to end the chequered board,
> the battle fought for Queens across the wide kingdom
> from Joyous Gard to Camelot.

Fife's fondness for wordplay (hart/heart; knight/night; venery/venison, etc., etc.) may occasionally be over-indulged, but it continually points up the story's parallelisms and ironies. The verbal inventiveness helps also to present Camelot as a highly ceremonious, cultured, literate court, appreciative of bards and musicians. Books are valued there. In a very original scene (it is to the best of my knowledge the first time Chrétien's tale had been heard on air), Guenever wakes from sleep with Lancelot to read the romance of *Erec and Enide*, and ruefully reflect on how that great love, too, had destroyed a hero's reputation. Significantly, Mordred hates books and poems. (Fife's years in the classroom had evidently taught him much about the bravado of insolent youth.[5])

That this is a past time is clearly marked by the many incidental details of horsemanship, swordplay and beautifully intoned Latin prayers, but Fife's characters seem timeless rather than medieval. They spring to life because their emotions are rendered so vividly. Galahad, described by Guenever as a 'noble icicle', is the sole exception, and he arouses little sympathy. Otherwise, human passions (anger, lust, love) abound. But the most dominant feeling is sorrow, and Fife's greatest quality is his embodiment of the many forms this takes. In an original handling of the myth, Fife reveals an aged Tristram, alone and half-mad, reminiscing over his love for the now-dead Isolde (Sarah Badel). Half-raped (and very audibly so) by Mordred, Guenever suffers acutely. And beside the pains of erotic love (as with Mark, Lancelot, Guenever, Morgan ...) there is also

---

[5]  Fife had previously been Head of Classics at Gresham's School: see Derek James, 'Lost in a legend!', *Eastern Evening News* (28 November 1990), 12.

the grief over the absence of children (Merlin, Guenever, Morgan) and the final sundering of companionship (Arthur).

The series was given above-average publicity and critical attention. For *Radio Times* Sven Arnstein created a stunning photographic image of a crowned Keith Baxter posed with a half-submerged Excalibur behind him. This was accompanied by an informative preview by Susanna Frayn.[6] In *The Listener*'s preview, David Self warned that 'some of the prose' was 'distinctly purple, and the acting even more so', but considered the whole work 'apt' and 'memorable', 'something that could not exist in any other medium', and likened it to Louis MacNeice's poetic features of the 1940s.[7] Later critics offered mixed responses. In *The Times* Martin Cropper initially recommended it for being 'gamey' and 'inventive', but tired of further episodes, which had 'lapsed into a rather awkward Dark Ages soap opera'.[8] A crushing review by the *Independent*'s Robert Hanks derided Paul Scofield's pronunciation, Fife's bad puns, Faux's music and Powell's sound effects.[9] Only Anne Karpf of *The Listener* was wholly enthusiastic, finding it 'wonderful', a 'pure pleasure', and believing that Fife had written something far more poetic than the mere transliteration of myth.[10] It was repeated a year later, but has otherwise dropped out of sight. Listening to it again, some fifteen years after hearing the first broadcast, I still rate it very highly, and rank it among the greatest of all Arthurian radio plays.

The nature of Arthur's return was given a strange twist in a play by Nigel Baldwin, an actor-writer at the Royal Court Theatre and author of many other radio dramas. His *Merlin and Arthur on the Way to Glastonbury from Deptford High Street (Not Forgetting Whatserface)*\*, directed by Richard Wortley, was presented in *Saturday Night Theatre* (R4 11 December 1993), preceded by a large colour photograph in *Radio Times* of Nicholas Le Provost wearing wizard's robes and conical hat.

The play opens in AD 490-odd with an environmentally responsible Merlin (Le Provost) aiming to save the planet from economic growth and future ecological disaster. He hopes to do this with the help of King Arthur, who will 'point mankind in a different direction' by symbolising an 'internal change in humanity'. The problem is that Arthur lives in the late twentieth century: he never appeared in the fifth to pull the sword from the stone, and so on. This was merely a story cooked up by medieval chroniclers to please their audience by giving the public what it wanted to hear. Merlin therefore attempts to transfer Arthur from the twentieth to the fifth century by casting a spell ('O great spirit of Atlantis / Listen to your praying mantis ...'). But as Merlin has apparently confused King Arthur with Arthur Daley (a wide boy in a popular TV series), his bungled spell succeeds only in bringing back Tony Daley (Dexter Fletcher), a market trader from Deptford in east London, who sells Excalibur Knives on his stall. He also inadvertently brings along Tony's half-sister, Faynia Morgan (Lesley Sharpe). Trying to put matters right next day, Merlin makes

<hr />

6   Susanna Frayn, 'The Magic of Arthur', *Radio Times* (10 November 1990), 4.
7   David Self, 'Listen Out', *Listener* 122 (8 November 1990), 34.
8   Martin Cropper, 'Dangerous ride for a disc-jockey', *The Times* (27 November 1990), 23.
9   Robert Hanks, 'Hit and myth', *Independent* (13 November 1990), 19.
10  Anne Karpf, 'Then and now', *Listener* 122 (29 November 1990), 47.

another mistaken capture: a radio journalist called Geoff Monmouth (Christopher Godwin), an Oxford graduate. Nevertheless, Merlin proceeds with his plan for this new Arthur to draw the sword from the stone, and inaugurate a new beginning for the human race. Tony is unpromising material, for he is a New Briton, interested only, he protests, in 'booze, birds and football – working-class culture'. But Merlin manages to persuade this ugly duckling that he will become a kingly swan. His sharp-tongued half-sister is, by contrast, a cut above him. The daughter of an actor, she readily quotes Shakespeare, attends séances, is into Wimmin and the New Age, and has a working knowledge of the Arthurian stories. She is astute enough, therefore, to realise that if she has a child by 'Arthur' she will be entitled to a Civil List pension and a life of ease. With the help of Geoff, who takes drugs, Tony is then doped with LSD. In the hallucinations that ensue, Faynia pretends to be the Lady of the Lake and manages to seduce her half-brother. As the misogynist Merlin had dreaded and long foreseen, a child is conceived. Convinced now that he is Arthur, Tony plans to rule tyrannically: he will get rich, spend wildly on luxury items, and behead his opponents. But these schemes come to nothing, because on arrival at Glastonbury he is unable to pull the sword from the stone. Desperately anxious to help him, Faynia pulls it out herself. She is, of course, immediately hailed as monarch herself, and history takes its course with the development of an alternative version. The action suddenly switches to the resulting modern matriarchal society. Geoff is despatched by his domineering female boss to cover a breaking story at nearby Chislehurst, where an elderly man is trapped in the caves. He learns from Tony and Faynia that when queuing with their friend Evelyn for the new *Caliburn* film about Queen Morgan and her Knights of the Round Table, in which Arthur has a minor role as 'the archetypal symbol of the weak male', they had met Merlin again. Merlin was much taken with the fact that Evelyn's name was almost 'Nyneve' backwards. He used his magic to produce a £50 note out of the air, and promised to show her how to do the trick if she would offer him her body prior to fulfilling a prophecy by confining him within a cave. When they all drove off to the caves, however, the roof immediately collapsed on to Merlin. To the echoing voices of the approaching rescuers, Merlin then awakes. It is the fifth century again, and we realise that the entire play has been a dream. In reality Lancelot has just arrived at Arthur's court, and the normal Round Table history will now unfold at Camelot. The play fades out to the sound of Mick Jagger and the Rolling Stones singing the truism 'You can't always get what you want'.

Le Provost makes a splendid Merlin, learnedly and irascibly obsessed, while Godwin is very good as the knowing reporter. The play's core 'environmental' message is trenchantly delivered and there is a lively burlesque of journalistic styles as the narrative is presented in the clichés of modern radio and television news or with the fake breeziness of the old-time cinema Pathé News. This ironic witty tone is maintained, besides, by interspersing the narrative with musical snippets and allusions, modulating from Richard Strauss to pop songs. And despite the fact that the facile sexual innuendo is too often louche and lewd, the play does give a (chilling) picture of many aspects of contemporary manners.

Within only three years of Fife's major Arthurian series, another was commissioned, and this was, like Fife's and Baldwin's, scheduled for the run-up to

Christmas. The ambitious new venture, a series of six hour-long programmes, *Arthur's Knight*\*, was written by the well-established poet and broadcaster Kevin Crossley-Holland, and was produced by Nigel Bryant (who has excellent Arthurian credentials as translator, playwright and director), while Richard Barber acted as series consultant (R3 21–30 December 1993). Crossley-Holland's main innovation was to take as focus Sir Thomas Malory himself, recalling how he had come to hear six key Arthurian stories. In the first episode ('Sir Gawain') the scene opens in Newgate where an elderly Malory, 'an old sagging man with ten teeth', is imprisoned. With ample time on his hands he reflects on his own adventurous life and the calamitous period he has experienced. Watching snowflakes fall he recollects a snowy Christmas at Ashbourne, when he was only thirteen and a squire in the service of Sir Nicholas Midwinter (Norman Rodway). According to family tradition, tales were told, and Sir Nicholas chose to tell a winter's tale that he had learnt from a fellow soldier at Agincourt, Ruby Repton, who had in turn learnt it from his father, Sir Robert Repton of Wirral, who had made a written record of it. The tale is of Sir Gawain and the Green Knight, which Sir Nicholas recounts with splendid verve to a rapt household audience. When he reaches the scenes of attempted seduction, though, he is helped out by his wife, Lady Anne (Heather Barrett), who speaks the part of Sir Bertilak's wife. Listening to his first Arthurian story has a tremendous impact on the young Malory, who is desperate to achieve knighthood and to see action. He senses for the first time, too, that he has outgrown his childish belief in the existence of mutually exclusive opposites. Maturer now, he realises that each apparent opposite contains the other. For him the significance of the Gawain story is that ideals such as honour, courage and courtesy are necessary for knights to aim at, but men are necessarily fallible as 'no man can be quite perfect'.

In the second episode ('Sir Bedivere'), when the persistently anti-clerical Malory hears the Greyfriars chanting he concedes that even monks share a form of ghostly fellowship – and he is grateful to the abbot for letting him use their library – but he affirms his preference for the warm interdependent fellowship of knighthood. He remembers how at the age of nineteen he was blooded. With the English forces, he had crossed the Channel with Sir William Ashton, to fight against the Burgundians. In the tense moments before launching a dawn attack, the English commander, Sir Mortmain (John Nettles), calms his men's nerves and raises patriotic fervour by graphically recounting an exemplary Arthurian tale. He narrates, as authentic history, the traditional episode from Geoffrey of Monmouth regarding Arthur's Continental expedition against the Emperor of Rome, when Arthur and Bedivere had fought the Giant of Mont-Saint-Michel. The blood-drenched story he tells has evident parallels with the war Malory was engaged in. It links contemporary Burgundian atrocities with the ancient rape of Helena of Brittany, though it also signals an occasional chivalrous contrast with them by noting Arthur's noble refusal to attack a sleeping foe, even when that foe is a giant. The ultimate lesson taught is that slaying the giant requires the co-operation of two men: 'what neither of us could have done alone we did together'. Battles are won, moreover, by leadership, careful planning, alertness to changed circumstances and high morale. Thematically linked to this need for common fellowship is the fact that a good commander takes care of his troops, tries to minimise his own side's casualties, and is able to resolve differences between his men. Like Arthur, the heavily outnumbered English are victorious in France, and Calais is secured, but Malory is made aware of the tragic loss of life when his childhood friend, Hugh the archer, is killed. He is also deeply conscious of human fallibility: even the heroic Arthur himself had behaved badly by looting Italy. Our nature, Malory realises, is to trespass; we therefore have to learn the difficult task of behaving otherwise. Remembering all these matters years later, Malory is still consumed with guilt for a major loss of companionship in his own life: that he had failed to resolve his lifelong dispute with his father, even when the latter was on his deathbed.

The problematic relationships with his family are probed more deeply in the following episode ('Sir Erec'). The smell of juniper, brought in to offset the stench of his prison room, revives tender thoughts of how his home had once been fragrant with the scent of juniper wood, blossoms and boughs. He had a wife and seven children. Memories of these lead him to reflect on the damage done to his marriage by his eight years of lawlessness, absence, imprisonment, and the two charges of raping Joan Smythe. The focus of this third episode is his memory of how his young wife, Elizabeth (Sandra Berkin), once told him a new Arthurian story she had learned from her father. While they lay in bed during their honeymoon the story she told was, like Fife's Guenever, that of *Erec and Enide*. As the narrative slowly unfolds – for it is interrupted by the entry of prurient servants, and Malory's importunate lovemaking – we note the parallels the French story provides with the life of the English married couple. Malory resembles Erec not only physically but also in his quickness to take decisions. He relishes the physical violence of the tale, and is interested in Erec's public world of duties and responsibilities, while the modest, gentle and obedient Elizabeth, who has never been to court, is painfully aware of her own resemblance to Enide. Because Chrétien's tale ends in blissful marital reconciliation, Malory professes himself dissatisfied with such a pat conclusion, for he senses that the roles of husband and knight are mutually exclusive, and he knows that he can never settle down so peacefully. Nor does he. For the next twelve years he is like a 'cannon', unreliable and prone to dangerous explosions.

How his life reached a turning point is told in the next episode ('Sir Accolon'). Malory was on trial at Nuneaton for killing a monk at Combe Abbey, but escaped to Bury St Edmunds, where he watched a trouvère performance of *Sir Gawaine and the Two Bitches* – poorly rhymed and too coarse, in Malory's opinion. But the troupe also featured a versatile conjuror and ventriloquist named Oliver Croo (Edward Petherbridge), whose passing references to Merlin and the supernatural intrigued Malory. Sensing his interest, Croo helps Malory evade arrest, and tells him his life story. He had trained as a schoolman at Oxford, although his deepest concern had been for magic. But, as he had allowed personal problems (an unhappy love affair) and family responsibilities (an ailing mother) to divert him from his esoteric quest into the natural laws that govern the dark forces of magic, Croo was now gnawed by regret over his wasted life. He then tells Malory a series of Arthurian tales, which are shaped by the power of magic to work for good or for ill. These show how Accolon tricks Arthur by an image of a False Guinevere into condemning the True Queen; how Morgan le Fay's attempt to rob Arthur of Excalibur is foiled by the magic of Merlin and Nineve; how Morgan secures the sheath of Excalibur; and how a love-infatuated Merlin lets Nineve imprison him within a rock. The early successes of Round Table chivalry are thus undermined by malign magic and by human fallibility. What Croo achieves is to jolt Malory into recognising that his own life is also being wasted, that he needs to transform himself, lest he be diverted from his life's true passion, the quest for King Arthur.

Nonetheless, Malory continues his violently unsettled career for another ten years until a second key moment, which is described in the episode that follows ('Sir Perceval'). He recalls how he had been wounded by a Lancastrian in the battle of Towton, and taken to a nunnery on the Yorkshire moors, where he is carefully nursed back to health. Over Easter he is visited by the abbess, Mother Anne (Diana Quick). The topic of the Holy Grail is introduced, because Mother Anne mentions that the version of the story she had noticed in the French book Malory had brought with him (the *Quest*) was very different from the one she had heard at Glastonbury. With hushed reverence she then recounts her version (*Perlesvaus*). Though relations between Malory and the abbess are very friendly, important differences emerge initially in the interpretations they place on the story: she is concerned with the hereafter, he with the here and now. Her condemnation of Gawain's worldliness, we learn, is coloured by her own experience of an unhappy marriage. His sympathy lies with Gawain and Lancelot, and he laments that impossible and unnatural demands were made on them by hermits, who insisted on chastity as a condition of success. Nonetheless, Malory wins her approval with his sudden perception that the Virgin Mary is the living Grail, and that the Grail could be both male and female. To which, in delighted agreement, she quotes Julian of Norwich's dictum, 'Jesus Christ is our real mother.' Everyone, she concludes, must seek their own grail. During his stay in the nunnery, Malory has undergone a great personal adventure, and his outlook is transformed. Like the Fisher King, his body is healed of its wound. And like Perceval, the Grail finder, he has learnt from his mistakes. From now on he vows to undertake his own quest, and King Arthur is going with him.

In the final episode ('Sir Mordred'), Malory describes the poisonous civil wars that had ruined England and landed him in Newgate for a second lengthy term. The chief villain and traitor in this affair was 'that creep', the Duke of Clarence, brother to King Edward IV. In order to entice Malory, Clarence (Michael Maloney) had paid an uninvited visit to him at Newbold Revel, claiming to be hatching a conspiracy that would oust his brother from the throne because of the Queen's undue influence over the kingdom. Malory is invited to participate, but remains coldly non-committal. In an attempt to win him over, Clarence then tells what is meant to be an exemplary tale: of how Mordred acted successfully against Queen Guinevere. Enacting the role of a later Mordred, Clarence hints that he, too, could reward his followers with new estates or take revenge on those who did not back him. Incensed by Clarence's treachery and his mocking attitude towards Lancelot and Arthur, Malory vigorously defends his heroes against these slurs, and he is tempted to drown the speaker in a nearby butt of malmsey (an ironic augury of Clarence's later fate at the hands of Richard III). The story of the Last Battle is then narrated by Clarence, with a sadistic delight in the gory details of wounds and the robbing of corpses. He goes on to describe the passing of Arthur and the eventual discovery of his tomb at Glastonbury. Malory, however, rejects this as a false account, and attributes it to monkish greed. Asked for his own opinion about Arthur's present location, Malory mentions the traditional possibilities, but, as his wife clearly favours the story of the Sleeping King, he is prevailed on to deliver his own tale of a journey he had made to South Wales. At Craig y Dinas he had met Gweno (Susan Mansell), a crazy old woman who suspected him of trying to find buried gold. She agrees to tell him the real story of Arthur's cave on condition that he has sex with her. After he carries out this obligation she tells him that her father had once entered a cave there, and found Arthur and his warriors lying among heaps of gold and silver. Though he had taken some of this, the knights had awoken, beaten him, and driven him out. When she prophesies that Arthur will come again to expel the English, Malory retorts that Arthur belongs now not only to Wales but to England, France and Germany: 'we need him wherever he is'.

Despite (or because of) his coolness towards Clarence's scheming, Clarence had contrived to have Malory arrested for plotting treason. Without a trial he is therefore back in Newgate again. He is grateful, however, for all that the stories had taught him. From them he has learnt how a man should behave in the face of adversity. Culpable though he may be of murder, rape, robbery and castration of a prison-officer, Malory determines to succeed at the second chance offered him – by recreating himself as a writer. The deeds of Arthur and his Knights of the Round Table provide a great model of behaviour that is decent, brave and honourable. Intending thus to raise Arthur's fame once more, Malory takes a personal oath of allegiance to the once and future king: 'I am his Bedivere. This is the redeeming of Thomas Malory.'

Compared with the lavish sound effects and music that were bestowed on Fife's series, Nigel Bryant's production of the Crossley-Holland is quite low-key. There are snatches of music and an occasional battle, but the many different locations are evoked mainly through purely verbal means: Crossley-Holland makes good use of significant sensory images that yield symbolic resonance – reeking pond, fragrant garden flowers, aged oak. The play's emphasis is determinedly internalised, and very successful for being so, because the significant action occurs within Malory's brain. On one level the play is akin to Honeycombe's *Lancelot and Guinevere* and John Barton's television version of *Le Morte Darthur* (BBC2 1984) in making the imprisoned Malory a frame for dramatisation of the Arthurian legend. But in both those works, the stories that were enacted were from Malory's own writings. What makes Crossley-Holland's treatment so original is that he presents stories that were supposedly a part of Malory's raw material. These stories may have inspired the medieval author to write, or he may have discarded them, or adapted them in minor or major ways. They are now assembled in a manner that is much fresher than a mere adaptation of the *Morte* would have been, and they reveal the development of a great creative artist. Moreover, Crossley-Holland's insistence – however tendentious that may be – on the primacy of the oral versions of these stories is a very effective device for radio. In a style that is 'contemporary colloquial', the tales are (paradoxically) very well *written* by Crossley-Holland, and they are superbly delivered by the radio actors to their cluster of intent listeners. In an adroit production ploy, two youthful speakers (Richard Pearce/Peter Meakin) are used to portray Malory as boy and then young man, before Richard Griffiths, as the old prisoner, assumes the play's dominant role of protagonist/interpreter. In this way his total character is heard gradually to grow and mature. Moreover, each occasion for the Arthurian retelling is artfully designed. The teller of each has a precisely defined motive for doing so; there is a subtly ironic interplay between the speaker and the tale's protagonists; while each tale serves not only to advance Malory's knowledge but also to reveal the development of his life, and to place it within an historical context. What emerges may be a very speculative biographical construct, but – with the notable exception of Malory's theory of the Virgin Mary as the Holy Grail (which seems far more Crossley-Hollandish than Malorian) – it triumphantly compels belief. On account of its originality of conception, high seriousness of theme, depth of perception, assured organisation and the rightness of its language, Crossley-Holland's play is the finest of all Arthurian radio dramas.

In great contrast came a minor work, with a playful interest in the historicity of Arthur, the light-hearted *Crosswords – Arthur in Bournemouth or Many Arrived Around (7 Letters)*\*. This was a sixty-minute piece by the prolific scriptwriter Jim Eldridge, and directed by Marilyn Imrie for the *Afternoon Play* slot (R4 18 November 2000). Stephen Cross (Geoffrey Palmer), a widower who sets cryptic crosswords for the local paper, meets Penny Harrison (Wendy Craig), an attractive, arty widow who is co-founder of a small Arthurian Preservation Society. In a Victorian travel book named *In the Steps of King Arthur*, she has read that, according to folktales, an old industrial area to the west of Bournemouth was once the site of Arthur's court. As she is convinced that plans by a superstore to redevelop this site will threaten any remaining archaeological evidence, she is anxious for the development to be halted. Although Stephen is very sceptical about the existence of an historical Arthur, and his putative connection with Bournemouth, he is persuaded to help her cause. His suggestion is to create an Arthurian crossword, which will heighten awareness of the issue; she adopts more direct tactics to stop the developers. Using metal detectors she visits the site with Stephen, and there she discovers a buried sword-hilt, and he a ring. While he is waiting for expert authentification of their finds, she secretly contrives to get a local free newspaper to run a lead story on the discovery: 'Is this Excalibur?' Her scheme is temporarily confounded by the revelation that she had planted the sword-hilt herself from a previous dig at Poole, but expert advice will reveal that the ring had once belonged to King Henry VIII. All thus ends happily in this well-acted piece: work on the superstore is halted for an archaeological rescue dig, while Stephen, who does not want his own life 'just to be history', makes up for lost opportunities by finding a present-day connubial bliss with Penny. To complement the broadcast, his 'Arthur in Bournemouth' crossword was published on the Radio 4 website.

A decade after Crossley-Holland's major work, the BBC commissioned another Arthurian series, *Arthur*\*, a set of six forty-five-minute dramas for the *Afternoon Play* slot (R4 22 October–26 November 2004), for which Kevin Hauff supplied a *Radio Times* colour illustration. The first three episodes were written by Sebastian Baczkiewicz, the second three by Steve Maye. Direction also changed hands: Gordon House doing the first two, Jeremy Mortimer the remainder. There was much doubling too among the cast, for there are young and old actors for Arthur (Ben Whishaw/Philip Glenister), Gwenfar (Alice Ford/Eve Myles) and Morgan (Eve Best/Jane Lapotaire). Though magic is much in evidence, the setting is, for the first time since Sherriff's *The Long Sunset*, ostensibly Early Post-Roman. The controlling voice is that of the older Morgan, a benevolent sorceress who drily narrates the shortcomings of a man's world. Although the main characters and the plot are broadly based on the traditional corpus, substantial modifications are made. Vortigern and Yvaine are named as the parents of Morgan and Margause, but when King Uther slays Vortigern and fathers Arthur on Yvaine, he orders that her daughters be put to death. This cruel intent is, however, foiled. Merlin (Ian McDiarmid) escapes with Arthur and Morgan to a sacred apple grove, while, instead of executing Margause, a kindly Lot (Clive Russell) raises her, renames her Rhyannon, and eventually marries her. Unaware of their blood relationship, Arthur and Rhyannon (Emily Wachter) will later fall in love and have a child. When she discovers the incestuous truth, however, Rhyannon loses her mind and commits suicide. Morgan then nurtures the child: her nephew Mordred.

The young Arthur has the customary rearing in rural obscurity by Sir Ector, before being guided by Merlin to establish his claim to kingship through drawing the Sword of Justice. He then turns into a bloodthirsty tyrant who slaughters half the population. It takes a visit from a mysterious Black Dog to prise him out of this murderous mode. Excalibur shatters, and its holder is wounded by an adversary. On the verge of death he slips into the Underworld of Annwn, whence Merlin retrieves him.

The drama's major conflict develops between Merlin and Morgan. His aim is to foster a powerful and intensely pagan kingdom, hers to practise religious toleration and to serve peaceful family values. He provides a new sword, wants Mordred dead, plots Arthur's marriage to Gwenfar, helps to preside over the establishment of a prosperous Camlot [sic], instigates an imperialist attack on Pellyn's Christian kingdom of Northumbria and, in the hope of securing a legitimate son for Arthur, secures from this attack a suitable Christian (the religiose Maura) as sacrificial victim for the gods. In contrast, a pacific Morgan cares for the war wounded, and secretly shows affection for Mordred (Stuart McLoughlin).

The attack on Pellyn, and the associated kidnapping of Maura, is a crucial event for it brings her brother Lanslot (Andrew Scarborough) to Arthur's court in search of vengeance. Failing to defeat Arthur in combat, he is nonetheless pardoned and becomes a trusted liegeman, but is pursued by Gwenfar's ardent love. The attack also prompts Arthur to lead a conciliatory mission to Pellyn, where he learns two secrets from the King's daughter, Elaine: that she has borne a son to Lanslot (unknown to him), and that Rhyannon is dead.

Fifteen years later, the kingdom is afflicted by drought and pestilence. Galhot (Liam Garrigan), who had travelled to Camlot hoping to kill his father (Lanslot) for 'godlessness', is persuaded by Arthur to undertake instead a quest for the Holy Grail, the finding of which will restore the land's health. Meanwhile

Mordred eludes Morgan's tutelage, and arrives at Camlot in search of fame and fortune, where he becomes a favourite of the King. Because Merlin fears that achievement of the Christian Grail will lead to the marginalisation of his own pagan culture, he induces Morgan to prevent Galhot's success by tempting him sexually. Merlin also urges Mordred to reveal the Gwenfar–Lanslot affair to the King. Both plans succeed. As Merlin wishes, the Christian Lanslot is condemned to death, but a rift emerges with Mordred, who desires also the Queen's death. In the event, Arthur covertly releases both prisoners. After Gwenfar stoutly resists Lanslot's proposal to place her in a nunnery, they separate, and he is reconciled with his son. Heavily outnumbered, Arthur fights a victorious battle against Ossa's Saxon immigrants, and on this occasion mercifully refrains from pursuing the vanquished. Nevertheless, he is later treacherously betrayed to the Saxons by Mordred. As they fall at each other's hands, Arthur is finally aware that Mordred is his son. In despair at the loss of Camlot, Merlin seeks to achieve union with the goddess Nimue by drowning himself, while Morgan takes Arthur on the barge to Avalon. In a surprise coda she reveals that she has the Grail.

All this might have made for a very powerful reinterpretation. That it failed to do so is due to the weakness of its intellectual basis. Though religious differences are said to underpin the action, investigation of them is wholly superficial. The Christians, we are told, worship the Cross, pagans the Snake: there the matter rests. Characterisation is similarly one-dimensional. Some effective acting may bring flickers of life to the roles of Lot, Rhyannon and Mordred, but only the older Morgan's character attracts a constant interest. Language seldom rises above the hackneyed. The following passage, where Arthur meets a cook who knew him before he became King, is representative:

GAURA:     Hold up, Arran, will you!
ARTHUR:   Arthur, Gaura. My name is Arthur.
GAURA:     Arran, Arthur. Can't be expected to keep up with all these names. Can we slow down please?
ARTHUR:   I am your king, and you would do well to remember that.
GAURA:     A proper bully, aren't we?
ARTHUR:   I could have you killed for saying so.
GAURA:     At this rate I'll be dead before I reach the hilltop.
ARTHUR:   On my way here, I was really looking forward to seeing you, Gaura.
GAURA:     Honoured, I'm sure!
ARTHUR:   Better days are coming.
GAURA:     But our Lord Ector's not coming back, is he?
ARTHUR:   I know you blame me for his death.
GAURA:     Not me, Arran. ...

The banality is numbing.

Fortunately a much more rewarding re-examination of the Grail legend was provided by the prize-winning novelist, Lindsay Clarke. His two novels had treated the Gawain stories within a modern setting, but this work would address a medieval subject more directly. Titled *A Stone from Heaven**, it was broadcast in two ninety-minute parts in the *Saturday Playhouse* and *Saturday Night Theatre* slots one Easter Saturday (R4 15 April 1995). Directed by Nigel Bryant, and with music composed and performed by Martin Allcock, it was based primarily on Wolfram von Eschenbach's *Parzival*. Indeed, it seems to have been the first radio adaptation of Wolfram and the first to incorporate Gawain within a Grail context. For *Radio Times*, Kim Marsland contributed a colour illustration of delicate sensitivity.

In form it combines the genre of romance with moral fable. Clarke creates a taut structure embodying a clear theme: since man has a complex nature, one must accept his apparently fundamental contradictions as essentially complementary. The theme is evocatively stated at the outset by Wolfram:

> There was a war in heaven once. The powers of darkness ranged against the Lord of Light; the bright angels and their darker brothers tearing the starry firmament apart. There was a war in Heaven once. We, my lords and ladies, lovers, contemporaries, friends, we, who are neither wholly good nor wholly bad, we, who consist both of shadow and of light, we sad, magpie creatures striving to be whole, we, who are only human, are the wounds.

While a strong narrative control is gained by foregrounding the role of Wolfram as humane, witty and perceptive teller of the tale (and Kim Wall performs the role consummately), great variety is given by the interspersed dramatic interludes, and the verbal symbolism is enriched by Allcock's magically mysterious score. The whole provides an admirable conversion of Wolfram's more densely constructed poem into a simple but shapely form more suitable for radio. In the first section ('The Wounding'), Wolfram traces the story of Parsifal (Ian Jeffs): his lineage, upbringing, combats, misadventures, marriage, and failure to pose the right question at the Grail Castle of Montsauvage. Then, at the hub of the play, Cundrie (Eleanor Bron) enters Arthur's court to deliver a searing indictment of the two main figures. Parsifal's sins of omission and commission are laid bare, whereas Gawain (Michael Lumsden) is scorned for being a false lover: both are traitors to the heart.

The second section ('The Healing') traces the endeavour of both knights to eradicate their shame. Gawain sets off in rescue of the four queens whom the enchanter Klingsor has in thrall. As the quest proceeds, it becomes evident that the tests involve not only Gawain's bravery but also his moral character. The dangerous Bed of Marvels he has to lie on is a fitting ordeal for such a faithless lover; the lion that attacks him is a symbol of his own passionate heart, while the proud lady (Diana Quick) who scorns his love is paying him back in his own coin. The eventual harmonisation in wedded bliss of this disparate pair of lovers foreshadows the later achievements of Parsifal. Schooled by painful experience, he learns that the wisdom of the heart cannot be acquired through blind obedience to another's teaching, but must stem from one's own heart; that the Grail is less an object than a presence. By a crucial reconciliation between Parsifal and his half-brother, the two sons redeem the earlier faults of their warring father. In a triumphant apotheosis, the Grail King is healed, the land's fertility restored, and Parsifal reunited with his wife.

Besides shortening and clarifying Wolfram's narrative, Clarke provides a distinctive personal reading of the legend by modifying its emphases. A strong anti-war message is encoded, as are concerns for a renegotiation of the balance of power between the masculine and feminine principles, for the rediscovery of the role of the unconscious, and for the evolution of a cosmic myth. In communicating these concepts he gives, for example, a Frazerian treatment to the Gramoflanz episode by transforming him into an axe-wielding Green Knight who defends his role as King of the Wood by fighting off challengers for the oak tree branch in the sacred grove. Cundrie, too, is similarly realigned: when she upholds the 'sovereignty of Britain' she melds into a Loathly Lady role. Elsewhere specifically Christian concepts are played down. Masses and priests – never very prominent in Wolfram – are airbrushed out. As are the virtues of chastity. Clarke's Grail bearer is not described as a virgin, nor is Anfortas condemned, as in Wolfram, for breaching the restraints of wedlock. More significantly, the religion of Fierefiz, Parsifal's half-brother, is clearly identified as Islam. Whereas at the end of Wolfram's story Fierefiz is baptised as a Christian this conversion does not occur here: thus even a non-Christian can witness the Grail mystery. As to the origin of the Grail, Clarke is more definite than Wolfram. The hermit Trevrizent (Edward Petherbridge) informs Parsifal that during the war in heaven the 'neutral angels' brought the stone to earth, where it remains under the protection of the Grail guardians as 'the stone of healing'. The substance of this stone therefore combines the 'virtues both of darkness and of light'. When the Grail appears in the closing scenes Clarke describes it in a series of analogies, likening it successively to the earth, 'which is mother and father to us all'; to the human heart; to a womb bearing twins (one male, one female); and to a final image of two lovers. Six years later he published an augmented version accompanied by an afterword, in which he set out his views more fully.[11] Nonetheless, by evading such laborious expositions, the broadcast drama seems the more attractive work. At the very least it offers a stimulating introduction to the great medieval German poem. In addition, it is a remarkable achievement in its own right. However baffled or sceptical we may remain about what Clarke intends by the nature and the value of 'those courageous neutral angels', he has created an elegant, moving and compelling work. As a Grail drama it rivals Gracq's, and is among the finest of all Arthurian radio plays.

The same year witnessed a Grail play by Alison Joseph that is very different in style but whose message is not wholly dissimilar. It has some affinity too with Baldwin's *Merlin and Arthur* in that both are concerned with the mishaps involved in time travelling. Joseph has wide radio experience and is a popular crime novelist whose detective is a nun in an open order. Her satirical comedy *Go For the Grail\**, directed by David Hunter (R4 27 November 1995), draws on both these interests. Though lasting only an hour it is very intricately plotted. It concerns the fortunes of two women. There is a fourteenth-century peasant named Griselda (Rachel Atkins), a forceful type who dresses as a warrior and believes she is destined to save her village from plague by winning the Grail, by violent means if possible. In modern times there is Cath (Caroline Strong),

---

[11] Lindsay Clarke, *Parzival and the Stone from Heaven: A Grail Romance Retold for our Time* (London: HarperCollins, 2001).

the mistress of an unfaithful businessman. She is keen to attend a salesman-ship seminar (titled 'Go For the Grail') run by Laurence (Garrick Hagon), a high-powered American ('the Genghis Khan of management training'), but she smokes and he is an obsessive anti-smoker. So she goes to a hypnotherapist to get help with kicking the habit. This hypnotherapist is married to an archaeolo-gist. Consequently when Cath is put into a trance she meets, through some unex-plained crossing of temporal wires, Griselda and unwittingly brings her back to modern times. Though vulgar, greedy and smelly, the honest Griselda acts as a catalyst for Cath, showing her the falsity of her lover, and then accompanying her to the seminar, where Laurence's unctuous spiel presents his concept of salesmanship within an extended Arthurian allegory. Salesmen are regarded as knights questing through a forest, their task being to harness the wisdom of the sleeping Merlin. After challenging the crone, they win over the damsel (a non-gender-specific term for the customer), and see what all knights search for. As his acronym explains:

G   Generosity
R   Responsibility
A   enActability
I   Insight
L   Leadership.

Upon hearing this mantra, most of the seminar participants start chanting, 'Grail, grail, grail. ...' Believing that Laurence must possess the true Grail, Griselda tries to get it by attacking him with a sword. This is Cath's moment of transforma-tion. She restrains Griselda, and delivers a scathing condemnation of the futile hypocrisy of the salesman's ideology. There are no certainties, she realises: no guaranteed successes for questers. Though people always need to have ideals, faith and love, 'there is no Grail. There never was.'

Abandoning both her business job and caddish lover, and taking up smoking again, Cath intends to join a practical community project to develop allotments for people to grow their own food, whereas Griselda believes now that her Grail search was in vain, and so returns to the fourteenth century to marry her faithful admirer. The archaeologist later discovers from the local archives, however, that Griselda's village had been spared the plague, ostensibly through the agency of St Edburga, whose 'bright vision' had been restored by Griselda. In the saint's grave had been found a pair of blue-tinted contact lenses. We remember at this point that these lenses were Laurence's and had gone missing – so must have been filched by Griselda. As they were instrumental in protecting the village from the plague, the object of Griselda's Grail quest had thus been achieved. Laurence had indeed possessed a quasi-Grail.

That is a very well-shaped dénouement. What prevented the play from being overly successful, however, was the pervasive superficiality of the dialogue and the weakness of the acting in the medieval parts. By contrast, the modern busi-ness roles were, even though highly stereotyped, much better performed – by Caroline Strong in particular. But only in the seminar scenes did the drama really spring momentarily to life.

Several other burlesque sketches may be noted. *King Arthur and the Knights* *of the Round Table** was a five-minute parody of an Arthurian film supposedly made in yuppie style and concerned with the vogue issue of inflationary real estate values (R2 17 January 1988). News of the Saxon invasion is greeted with the whinge, 'Ooh, there goes the neighbourhood'; while the Coffee Table hero given the task of stopping an evil Black Knight from taking over the upper-class damsel's castle says promptly, 'No sweat. I'm going to gazump him.' Another snooty upper-class damsel in distress features in Tim de Jongh's fifteen-minute *Sir Percival**, a Monty Pythonesque parody of treasure hunt games and BBC news reporting (R5 13 August 1991). Percival reaches the target castle, merely to find himself having to spend three hours carrying out the damsel's belongings, and receiving only an airy wave of her hand as reward. In an Arthurian episode written by Michael Dines ('How Ye Queste was Wonnne'*) for the *Crowned Hudds* series, the comedian Roy Hudd has his considerable talent marginalised among a waste of excruciating puns, scabrous *double-entendre* and now outdated topical allusions (R2 c.1995). Willie Rushton takes the role of Merlin as humorous linking figure in Louise Spencer's *Merlin Lives!*, a ten-part series about British history for schools, in which Richard Pearce features as Arthur (R4 September–October 1989). Merlin appears briefly too in Marcus Brigstocke's *The Museum of Everything*, new series* (R4 18 March 2004), where he histrionically presents a 'history of wicker'. The most adroit satire is probably contained in an episode of Danny Robins and Dan Tetsell's series of literary spoofs, *Paperback Hell* (R4 12 October 2005). Here the relevant quasi-Arthurian episode is *The De Niro Code**, whose simplistic anagrams, historical inaccuracies, national stereotyping, and very short action-packed chapters make it an effective parody of Dan Brown's *The Da Vinci Code*.[12]

The only Arthurian heroine to provide the prime subject of a radio drama, the Lady of Shalott, was featured in two important plays, both of which radically altered her traditional role. The first of these works was also Lucy Gough's first play for radio, a forty-five-minute piece named *Our Lady of Shadows**, which was directed by Richard Wortley, and provided with music by Elizabeth Parker (R3 8 April 1995). Though Tennyson's poem, four verses of which are recited at the outset, provides the immediate inspiration, what Gough defines as her own 'dramatic poem controlled by rhythms' develops very differently. Catherine (Claire Skinner), the central figure, had been left at a nunnery by her father. Years later she accidentally caused an explosion while carrying out a private alchemical experiment. She is therefore confined to a tower on an island, guarded by a mute Hag. As the windows are shuttered she uses a lens smuggled to her by a sympathetic Sister Ignatius (Rosemary Leach) to construct a camera obscura, which projects shadows onto the floor of her room. When the image of the Hag appears she delights in swatting it. She is given paints and vellum to practise illumination of a religious manuscript, but she also uses her own faeces and menstrual blood as pigments to portray more naturalistically her shadow world, which she is desperate to escape. The Knight's horse is steadily heard

---

[12] In another exotic offshoot, Christopher Dawes and Rat Scabies (former drummer of the punk group The Damned) discussed their book, *Rat Scabies and the Holy Grail*, an account of their recent investigations at Rennes-le-Château (R2 15 June 2005).

approaching, pausing only for the rider to dismount and urinate. Catherine is so aroused by the radiant image of the armoured Knight that she tears down the shutters, and poses naked at her window to attract him. When he climbs the stairs towards her, however, the Hag kills him with a log. Catherine is amazed to discover that his armour may be stripped off, and that without it he is no stronger physically than she. With the Hag's help, she dons the armour, and rides off on the horse. Her aim is to

> Circumnavigate the world.
> Discover new lands.
> Fight the Crusades.

This is powerfully charged and highly original in interpretation. Difference and a fascination with body fluids do not necessarily, however, create a wholly successful play. One problem is that the symbolism is too blatant. Even though Gough avers that it is not meant to be 'naturalistic', the listener's doubts about the credibility of the action are not allayed. Catherine's scientific prowess and the Hag's summary killing of an armoured Knight suggest an obsessive personal fantasy rather than imaginative intensity. As this is evidently a parable of an adolescent girl's search for freedom, it is surely redundant and counterproductive to make her a reader of Aristotle and Paracelsus, a calculator of how long it would take to circumnavigate the world, or for her to proclaim herself as God. Secondly, the dramatic action is not well presented in terms of radio. A clearer narrative is needed, for on too many occasions it is difficult for a listener to know what is happening. It was later presented on a conventional stage, and that is probably a more suitable medium for it.[13]

A more satisfactory means of providing contemporary relevance was found by John Fletcher. He had already written a play, *The Death of Arthur*, staged at Plymouth, Dorchester and Gloucester in 1988, which alternated between Arthur's Britain and modern times.[14] For *The Lady of Shalott** (R4 25 August 1997) he chose to reset the medieval tale against 'a series of real events' in a suburb of Victorian London. Produced by Catherine Horn, this ran for ninety minutes in the *Monday Play* series. Edwin Bartlett (Clive Swift) is a lepidopterist and heir to a family grocery chain. Lord Huntley, a tough North Country tycoon, offers to put money into Edwin's failing business if the latter will agree to marry Huntley's illegitimate daughter, Adelaide (Sarah-Jane Holm). As Edwin is fifty-five and Adelaide sixteen it is intended as only a nominal marriage. Adelaide is consequently brought back from Switzerland, where she has been raised, to be rushed through a marriage ceremony and whisked off to Edwin's vast Mordern Abbey. Since he is wholly engrossed with his butterfly collection, they meet very infrequently. Several years pass before a major disruption occurs. This comes in

---

13 It was performed during the Flames Festival of Young Directors at the Studio Theatre, University of East Anglia, Norwich, in March 1996. The text has been published in Lucy Gough, *Crossing the Bar, Head, Our Lady of Shadows*, ed. Brian Mitchell (Bridgend: Seren, 2000), pp. 81–112.

14 See Allen Sadler, 'The Death of Arthur', *Independent* (18 February 1988); Mick Martin, 'Point Taken', *Times Educational Supplement* (25 March 1988); and B. A. Young, 'Arthur's naked combat', *Financial Times* (26 March 1988), Weekend section, p. xix.

the shape of a new vicar, the Reverend Bertram Dyson (Ian Hughes), a fluent preacher and advocate of 'spiritual' values. Much admired by his flock, he is soon invited to tea by Adelaide, and when shown over the extensive garden he sends her into raptures with his enthusiasm for flowers and the poetry of Tennyson. Edwin sees in the vicar not only a suitable companion for his wife but also a stimulating person for himself to debate Darwinian theories with, so invites him to become their lodger. Bertram's avowed Arthurian orientation is prominent. In public sermons, he envisages Christ coming in the mode of a King Arthur to save the world; and strolling privately around the Abbey garden he quotes repeatedly from Tennyson's 'Sir Launcelot and Queen Guinevere'. Regarding him as her Galahad, Adelaide embroiders an appropriate scene of a Knight and his Lady. Eventually during a discussion between Edwin and Bertram on the role of beauty in nature ('Is it merely a question of reproductive attraction?'), the sexually repressed Adelaide can control her feelings no longer, and kisses Bertram passionately. To Bertram's embarrassment, Edwin then suggests that Adelaide and Bertram should make love, and that he, as a student of natural history, will observe their performance. This is enacted to the apparent satisfaction of all concerned, and continues to be so on many other occasions, Bertram reciting 'The Lady of Shalott' before making love to her at one notable picnic at the Devil's Punchbowl in Surrey. Nonetheless, Edwin grows tired of his own virginity, and becomes personally addicted to the chloroform he uses to kill butterflies. Having dosed heavily one night, he tries to enforce his conjugal rights but, when Adelaide resists, there is a struggle, and he is asphyxiated. At Adelaide's trial for murder, Bertram behaves unchivalrously by blaming her for leading him astray. Fortunately for her, a former servant tells a newspaper the story of her upbringing and arranged marriage. This influences the court, she is duly acquitted and will enjoy a rich widowhood. The sting in the tail comes when the scene switches to Wyoming (a location indicated by fake American accents). Miss Adelaide, sixty-eight and a ranch-owner, is enjoying a chat with her young cowhands. Mention of the slaying of a wanted Chicago hoodlum, who has thereby escaped formal execution, leads her to reflect on her own career. The slain hoodlum, she privately opines, was not very 'professional', for a professional does not go round the place drawing attention to himself:

a real killer does it very quietly, very simply. As I did. I killed Edwin. ... I clamped that handkerchief over his face, and made sure it didn't come off until he was good and proper dead.

For Adelaide the Lady of Shalott's awakening to love was an unqualified good, and one not to be given up or allowed to fade away. Love is eternal, 'the centre of things', and Launcelot remains her 'own true-love'. But her own life must also continue to be lived through and fought for. She has followed the trajectory desired by Gough's heroine, and forged a way of life in new lands. And Fletcher's realisation of the process carries the ring of authenticity. The legend is given new vitality.

Apart from an episode devoted to it in the Fife series, the Tristan story was rarely treated in radio drama of this period, and the single work to take up the legend did so only very obliquely. This was Christopher William Hill's dark comedy, *Killing Maestros** (R4 14 August 2003), directed by Liz Webb in the *Afternoon Play* series. Productions of Wagner's *Tristan and Isolde*, we are told, have often been jinxed by mysterious deaths. When the latest conductor falls prey to this curse, his successor, Sergei Bodanov (Bill Nighy), fears for his own life. Convinced that Wagner is trying to kill him, he consults a therapist and, although he proves a hypochondriac pest as patient, Dr Lieberman (Henry Goodman) unwisely rejects a colleague's advice to ditch him. Sergei also meets Lieberman's wife, Ruth (Lorelei King), and the two have a passionate affair set against the background strains of Wagner's opera. Dr Lieberman then seeks manic revenge by bombarding Sergei with telephone calls purportedly from Wagner. His goal seems to have been achieved at the end of the operatic première, when Sergei collapses. In hospital, though, he recovers rapidly and announces that he is cured of hypochondria. The disappointed Lieberman immediately dies of a heart attack himself. A little later we discover that Sergei has resumed his neurotic calls to the therapist's, but the wiser Laura (Sylvestra Le Touzel) has now succeeded Lieberman and simply deletes the messages left on the answerphone. Wagner's opera, of course, merely provides a convenient peg on which to hang a modern comedy of manners. The heart of the play, and its quality, lies not in the enchantments of adultery but in the confrontational dialogue: the fencing between therapist and patient, and the savage bitching between husband and wife:

> SHE: You cured me.
> HE:  Cured you! You're a one-woman psychiatric ward! I could retire
>      and spend the rest of my life treating you!

Generally it is well acted except in the central role. For though Nighy's part requires him to be a great conductor, a neurotic bore and a practised womaniser, it is only in the last role that he convinces.

Overall this quarter of a century had proved the finest period of all for Arthurian radio drama, surpassing the previous peak of the 1950s not only in terms of quantity and quality but also in the rich diversity of styles and interpretations.

# 6

## Conclusion

### The BBC and its Audience

Flourishing under the high-minded direction of Sir John Reith, the early BBC seems to us at this distance to have enjoyed great self-confidence in the belief that the new medium of radio could and should be used as a force for good in the world: 'Nation shall speak peace unto nation' was the vaunted slogan every week on the front page of *Radio Times*. There was a secure belief, too, in the values of the prevailing cultural order. Reith's hierarchical system felt at ease with itself. The BBC presented a clear educational and social model. It laid down rules of pronunciation and grammatical etiquette. Enjoying its monopoly position, it could impose a policy of mixed programming, which was followed on all stations, and was designed to raise the general level of cultural awareness of the entire country. The audience would be regularly exposed to Bach and Beethoven alongside Albert Ketèlbey's light music, in the belief that, even if it did not already like and understand the great classical composers, it would gradually learn to do so: no easy escape could be found on another channel. This cultural acquisition was not, though, left solely to nature and to chance. Authoritative guidance was at hand in the shape of *Radio Times*, which performed a clear educational role in providing helpful introductions and synopses before major productions of opera or drama. Although the audience was socially very diverse, it was regarded as a great and cohesive Middle England, intelligent and eager for self-improvement.

Under this dispensation, key radio programmes could be treated as national occasions, when the nation tuned in to its own quintessential voice. Radio gave, for example, to a play like Bridson's *King Arthur* a public hearing that was hugely unprecedented in theatrical terms. It was presented as a quasi-sacramental state ritual on St George's Day, with a theme adumbrating that of the upcoming coronation of King George VI. It was produced by the Head of BBC Drama, performed by leading actors, its incidental music composed by the young Benjamin Britten (himself only a stop-gap for a more senior composer) and played by the London Symphony Orchestra. It occupied the prime time slot on the National Service, and was repeated on the London Regional the following evening. An audience of ten million was predicted. No Arthurian play in British history had ever received such massive celebratory attention. A heady new era appeared to be dawning for radio drama and for Arthuriana.

Sadly, however, this promised dawn of a regained Camelot was soon clouded over. There were constant attacks on the BBC's policy from several fronts. Many traditionalists had always been unhappy with the medium and its contents.

From the outset the quality of sound reception was not uniformly good, and in early years there were many like the married couple in Bowyer's cartoon who detested having such an ugly modern contraption in their gracious home [**plate 35**]. Evelyn Waugh's Lady Seal had a different strategy for dealing with the apparatus. Her butler brought the wireless into the room only when it was required, and removed it immediately afterwards.[1]

There was besides considerable resistance among the intelligentsia to radio in any form. Benjamin Britten's father refused to buy a gramophone or wireless lest the family should stop making their own music.[2] Arnold Bax may have complained that the BBC did not broadcast his music sufficiently, but had no set himself and did not see the *Radio Times*.[3] Eric Gill carved the wonderful figures of Prospero and Ariel over the entrance of Broadcasting House in the early 1930s, but did not listen to any programmes himself.[4] Even more interestingly, Maurice Gorham, who was editor of *Radio Times* from 1933 to 1941, did not possess a radio at home during the period of his editorship.[5] When Daphne du Maurier's Rebecca and Max de Winter sought privacy on the Continent they tried wireless as an antidote to boredom, but soon abandoned it because 'the noise is such an irritant'.[6] A Nancy Mitford heroine hated the medium, its 'facetiousness and jazz', for it seemed 'a definite and living force for evil in the land'.[7] As late as 1950, the blurb on the cover of an Agatha Christie novel quotes the author as saying, 'I loathe wireless and all loud noises.'[8] Some of us may think she has a valid case, and still shudder at the *Radio Times* advertisements of the 1920s encouraging listeners to buy special aerials and loudspeakers so that they can listen to the radio out in the garden or on the river or on picnics in the countryside.

Down in the servants' hall of Mitford's heroine, the wireless may have been 'blazing away' (p. 125), but not all listeners outside the intelligentsia were pleased with the fare they were getting. The BBC faced continual criticism in *Radio Times* from those who disliked the cultural leavening involved in the policy of mixed programming. These malcontents often turned instead to the overseas commercial station of Radio Luxembourg in search of more dance music. That closed down at the start of the war, but when the BBC's monopoly was broken temporarily by the American Forces Network in 1943, which was given permission to broadcast from London to GIs waiting in Britain to launch the D-Day offensive, the informal announcing style and superior swing bands heard on this station attracted, too, many young British listeners.

Already, in fact, BBC programme planners had started to relax the mixed programming policy. From 1940 channels began to specialise, with the result that

---

1   Evelyn Waugh, *Put Out More Flags* (London: The Book Club, 1943 [1942]), p. 23.
2   Humphrey Carpenter, *Benjamin Britten: A Biography* (London: Faber & Faber, 1992), p. 12.
3   Foreman, *Bax*, p. 276.
4   Fiona MacCarthy, *Eric Gill* (London: Faber & Faber, 1989), p. 245.
5   Martin Baker, *Artists of 'Radio Times'*, p. 18.
6   Daphne du Maurier, *Rebecca* (Harmondsworth: Penguin, 1962 [1938]), p. 9.
7   Nancy Mitford, *Pigeon Pie* (Harmondsworth: Penguin, 1961 [1940]), pp. 53–4.
8   Quoted on the back cover of Agatha Christie, *Appointment With Death* (Harmondsworth: Penguin, 1950).

the largest audience (mainly civilian) belonged to the new Forces Programme, which evolved into the Light Programme and then into Radio 2. In this area of popular music and comedy, few Arthurian items are found. What has been crucial for the continuance of Arthurian programmes, however, was the creation in 1946 of the determinedly highbrow Third Programme (later modulating into Radio 3). This innovation finally brought a much greater intellectual audience to the BBC, for not only did the service afford more scope for classical music and experimental plays, but it fostered closer links with the academic world by encouraging Oxbridge dons to give specialist talks. In this early post-war period there was a widespread hope that social amelioration in the shape of universal free secondary education, easier access to university courses, and publicly funded arts bodies would create a much wider demand for the high culture. It is from this optimistic milieu that arose Third Programme's commissioning of translations by Coghill and Tolkien. Apart from some rare exceptions, however, such as the audience of two million attained by Coghill, the Third's audience figures have remained consistently low in comparison with those of other channels, whereas audiences for those other channels were generally boosted by specialisation and finally peaked in about 1950. At this latter point, BBC radio could justifiably claim to address the whole nation in all its diversity: virtually everyone listened to something. Even until the late 1950s, *Saturday Night Theatre* (HS) was the cultural focus of the week for many millions. It means that Sherriff's *The Long Sunset* must be regarded as the most widely heard of all Arthurian plays in that it started in *Saturday Night Theatre* in 1955, was repeated twice that year, and on Light Programme twice in 1956, besides receiving repeats in HS (1960), and in Radio 4 (1971 [twice], 1984 and 1990). By then being adopted as a set book for school examinations, it must rank as the best-known Arthurian play ever.

But this was radio's high point. By the end of the 1950s it had surrendered supremacy to television. The loss of audience is felt particularly in children's programmes: the influential *Children's Hour*, which had been introduced in 1922, was to close in 1964. Children's television would indeed show three significant Arthurian series between the 1950s and 1980s, but since then children's programmes in that medium have been dumbed right down, and the Arthurian legends now survive there only in burlesque forms. Besides, the BBC's domination of even the radio audience has been severely eroded by the introduction of legal British commercial radio: Classic FM (playing the more popular end of the classical music spectrum) now attracts almost three times as many listeners as Radio 3. Further inroads into the literary sector have been made by the launch of digital stations: the commercial Oneword is, for example, dedicated to readings from books, a field in which the BBC once set the pace. Within this shifting world it is not always easy to establish the size and relative popularity of the Arthurian programmes broadcast, but a recent survey reveals that the BBC has at present only a 58 per cent share of the total radio audience.[9] Listeners tune

---

9   From the outset all listeners were required to buy a radio licence. An extra fee for television was later introduced. From 1971 the separate radio licence was abolished. Radio is therefore

into its services as follows: R2 27 per cent, R1 21 per cent, R4 19 per cent, R5 12 per cent, and R3 4 per cent. In such circumstances, the BBC is fearful of losing market share to its commercial rivals, and these fears are presumably driven by the fact that the BBC still relies for funding on a universal licence fee, which is decided by government, and which must be paid even by those who use only the commercial television channels.[10]

Nonetheless, the genre of radio itself has proved remarkably resilient. Overall listening figures are now rising again rather than falling. Arthurian programmes are still attracting sizeable audiences because Radio 4 is still the country's chief patron of new drama, and its serialisation of novels continues, while there has been a remarkable development of the feature format. Moreover Radio 3 remains a bastion of classical music, and, since it has broadcast round the clock since 1996, it is never off the air. Music in pre-war times was broadcast on non-specialist channels, and would presumably have reached quite a wide audience, but as most classical music has, since the war, been broadcast on TP/R3, it evidently has not matched those numbers. Nonetheless it remains a very significant sector because the Arthurian items are so frequently replayed on this service, its audience probably contains a higher proportion than other channels do of 'devoted listeners' rather than 'casual hearers', and, even if the overall proportion of radio listeners (4%) seems small, the raw numbers are still vastly greater than those for concert or theatre attendance.

## Pioneering a New Medium

Radio has acted as a remarkable pioneer for Arthurian programmes in any of four major interlinked ways.

First, in its role as a news organisation it has functioned like a quality newspaper, and given information about what are regarded as important new happenings. In this way it picks up some of the most significant Arthurian events, which commonly involve the latest music, films, plays or books. The latest Wagnerian productions are regularly brought to our attention. Vinaver's publication in 1947 of his Malory text based on the Winchester manuscript find was promptly signalled by a Third Programme talk. Gwyn Jones's new translation of *The Mabinogion* gave immediate rise to a series of talks and readings in 1950. When Valerie Eliot published her edition of the original transcripts of her husband's *The Waste Land* in 1972, this too was accompanied by complementary radio accounts. As the testimony of the spade was also considered newsworthy, a series of programmes focused attention on the excavations by Alcock at South Cadbury in the late 1960s. Moreover the colourful adventures of the modern Arthur Pendragon were traced in the 1990s as they impinged on important contemporary issues such as access to ancient monuments, the preservation

---

funded now by the television licence and by profits from BBC enterprises such as *Radio Times*.

[10] Data taken from website of RAJAR (Radio Joint Audience Research Limited) for the period ending September 2005.

of the countryside and the rise of neo-pagan religions. In 2005 the Broadway musical *Monty Python's Spamalot* was already receiving attention, well ahead of any promised British production.[11]

Secondly, radio would act as a reviver of previous artefacts. By zealously marking key anniversaries of writers, it would help to create an appropriate climate for its recovery of many poets and musicians. It could follow an established trend or subtly reshape attitudes. Tennyson and Spenser were great beneficiaries of this latter approach. It could also reclaim work by minor and generally forgotten figures, such as the two Edwardian plays by Ernest Rhys, *Enid* and *The Quest of the Grail*, which were revived by the Welsh Service in the late 1930s. Even more notable, was the same service's production of Frederick Cowen's *The Lily Maid* in 1927, a piece that can rarely have been heard since its 1897 concert première. Performance on radio could exponentially widen the audience for a neglected literary work. A case in point is Dennis Potter's story, *Excalibur*, which had appeared only in a little-known American magazine before Radio 4 organised a reading to mark the anniversary of Potter's death. Of works that probably gained a much larger readership, and a deeper understanding, because of broadcasting, David Jones's *In Parenthesis* provides a fine example. Nest Cleverdon is surely correct in attributing its now relative popularity to the continual productions of it by her husband.

Thirdly, radio enjoyed a major role as a munificent go-between, transmitting productions and publications from elsewhere. By so doing it has not only informed but popularised. Music being the easiest art form to transmit, through relay or recording, expectedly forms the largest category. And as the broadcasting of classical music has always been comprehensive, it was a natural consequence that Arthurian items should frequently be played and for these to dwarf, in both number and duration, those from all other genres. Of all Arthurian musical forms, opera has proved the most significant, and among composers Wagner's dominance is constant. This was abundantly reflected in BBC policy and, by transmitting so many live and recorded performances of *Tristan* and *Parsifal*, radio has become a major channel through which these works are more widely heard in whole or in part. In addition to this Wagnerian focus, a vast range of Arthurian music has been broadcast, some for the first time: minor works receiving perhaps only a nonce performance, while others, such as two twentieth-century classics of instrumental music – Bax's *Tintagel* and Messiaen's *Turangalîla Symphony* – receive repeated attention. To a lesser, but not inconsiderable extent, has been the coverage of drama. Initially the plays broadcast were mainly transfers from the conventional stage. Few English plays were Arthurian, but among those that were translated from foreign originals three were highly significant productions. Gracq's *The Fisher King* had not appeared previously on an English stage, nor has it yet been published in English translation. Auden's translation of Cocteau's *The Knights of the Round Table* was to precede stage performance in this country, as would the translation of Schwartz's *The Dragon*.

[11]  The musical opened in London in October 2006.

Nonetheless, a caveat must be entered here, because radio's undoubted successes as a go-between must be weighed against its apparent shortcomings. The focus was, except for music, often surprisingly insular. Though Wagner's influence meant that the Tristan story was traced to its Continental sources in a landmark talk by Geoffrey Grigson and in several later features, the wealth of medieval French and German literature went largely unnoticed until very recently. Post-medieval Continental writing was, but for a sudden efflorescence from the mid-1950s to the mid-1960s, similarly overlooked. Even American literature was, save for Twain, disregarded. Within British literature, too, there are many unexpected gaps. Radio neither adapted the wealth of material that appeared on minor and provincial stages nor co-opted all the notable plays produced in the London theatre, such as Laurence Binyon's *King Arthur* (1923), John Masefield's *Tristan and Isolt* (1927), John Arden and Margaretta D'Arcy's *The Island of the Mighty* (1974), Howard Brenton's *The Romans in Britain* (1980), Christoph Hein's *The Round Table* (1991) and Tankred Dorst's *Merlin* (2001). Nor can I trace any readings from the longer Arthurian poems of John Masefield, Laurence Binyon, Charles Williams, Martyn Skinner or John Heath-Stubbs. Among Arthurian novelists, Edward Frankland, Warwick Deeping, Hannah Closs, Naomi Mitchison and Mary Stewart seem to be missing. Radio's adoption of stage drama and printed literature has been highly selective.

Finally, however, if it has not always chosen to reflect what is happening elsewhere, the BBC has played a substantial role in commissioning new work and creating new forms. The supremacy of the print medium for academic discourse has not been seriously challenged by radio. What has emerged over the last twenty years or so is the radio feature programme, which reflects a commendable range of expert viewpoints, together with appropriate music, on a given topic. This form has proved particularly successful for Arthurian programmes. Comparable television programmes may be superior in their ability to show landscapes, buildings and paintings, but the pace of television narration is customarily laborious and repetitive. By means of adroit editing, radio producers can create a much more flexible array of voices and can introduce music more effectively. The twenty-odd major features, spread mainly over Radio 3 and Radio 4, that have been devoted to Arthurian topics are a substantial contribution to popular information concerning the debate over the historical Arthur, the evolution of the legend and its contemporary application.

As for literary studies, it was, for instance, a very remarkable achievement to have pioneered Coghill's translation of *The Canterbury Tales*, the first major updating of the poem for an adult audience since Dryden's version in 1700. Though the work owed its eventual runaway success to publication in book form, radio can justifiably claim to have nurtured the new growth. Radio can also point to the fact that without its suggestion and persistence Tolkien would never have completed his translation of *Sir Gawain and the Green Knight*. Even though this has never achieved in print the classic status of Coghill's translation of Chaucer, the broadcast remains a landmark event. In music, too, commissions have called into existence new Arthurian works by Phyllis Tate and David Bedford. Though far less known, it has also commissioned a huge amount of incidental music for Arthurian plays, and in doing so has created virtually a new form of the original 'melodrama'. Two scores written by Benjamin Britten for 1930s plays have now entered the modern repertory, but there is too a neglected wealth of incidental music by composers such as Richard Addinsell, Elizabeth Poston, Elisabeth Lutyens, Grace Williams, Humphrey Searle, Steven Faux and David Bedford.

Most importantly, radio drama has made a virtue of its apparent limitations and developed into an important new medium inhabiting an indeterminate zone between private reading and the public stage: among those works commissioned, twenty single plays and four series have been Arthurian. Since radio drama is low-budget, innovation involves little fiscal constraint, and this exemption has paradoxically given creative writers and producers far greater artistic autonomy than their counterparts possess in television and cinema, and allowed them to exploit the freedom and psychological depth of the genre. Their plays have varied in style and time setting, ranged from tragic to comic, and covered a panoply of Arthurian themes: heroic, moral, social, amatory and religious. By introducing so much that is new, radio drama is, in regard to Arthurian material, quantitatively superior to that of the London stage. It might also quite reasonably be claimed that Crossley-Holland's *Arthur's Knight* is the finest twentieth-century Arthurian play in any dramatic genre. Together with the diffusion of Wagnerian opera, this dramatic flowering has been the major achievement of radio Arthuriana. And, as with music, there is no prospect of radio's dominance in this field being threatened by television in the foreseeable future.

## Pro-Arthurian Forces

In terms of the total BBC output, the number of Arthurian items broadcast was minuscule. But if viewed as a discrete mass the catalogue of items is impressive. No other British hero has attracted so much radio attention. Of King Alfred (an indubitably historical hero in war and peace) there is scarcely a mention; and of Boadicea only a thin thread of programmes (although there are recent signs of expansion). Robin Hood is a film superstar, widely known and liked, but he has featured only within children's programmes, and these have been discontinued. St George, who has a magnificent artistic provenance, a reputable literature, ecclesiastical sanction and royal affiliation, used to be the subject of regular homage on his feast day, but this occasion was summarily dropped (not without complaint) from radio recognition about thirty years ago. Presumably his overtly Christian and English associations were judged unsuitable in the BBC's new agenda for multicultural, multifaith Britain. Arthur – who may count as Celtic or British (which incorporates English), Christian or pagan – has therefore no radio rival.

Why then were so many Arthurian programmes broadcast? Many widely differing factors seem to have been responsible.

Numerically the largest number of items stems from Wagnerian opera, which was performed because it was highly valued as music, not because it had an Arthurian connection. But because of the great influence Wagner's *Tristan* had upon other musicians, this led to a host of associated musical works, which were also performed on air, and thus an Arthurian theme was continually regenerated.

Within English literature, certain Arthurian texts were regarded as part of the classical canon, and particularly suitable for children's education. Simplified adaptations of Malory and *Sir Gawain and the Green Knight* have therefore been regularly incorporated into schools programmes or *Children's Hour*. Tennyson's 'The Lady of Shalott' is unusual in that it has served not only as a literary classic for adults but can be recited without adaptation to younger listeners. The academic rediscovery of Tennyson in the 1960s led to major feature programmes that reassessed his role as creator of Arthurian myth. Tennyson's long shadow falls upon much later BBC production, from Brian Patten's investigations at Tintagel to the modern reworking of the legend in three radio plays (Torrance, Gough, Fletcher).

The spirit of place, which has been a powerful agent affecting the Arthurian Revival for the last two centuries, has been carried over into radio by those who have been imaginatively inspired by the location where they were born, had lived or visited. Because of the pervasive Arthurian associations with Wales and the West Country (from Somerset to Cornwall), and the cultural transformation of these into expressions of local (or national) identity, regional stations have produced a steady stream of Arthurian programmes. The first Arthurian radio drama (Buckton's *The Wooing of Guinevere*) stemmed from the Cardiff studio; two of Treece's verse dramas would not have been heard except for the support of the Welsh service; while a comparable concern with Celtic roots has prompted even national programmers to commission features celebrating Cornwall's cultural heritage.

Much has depended, too, on personal taste. Within the BBC, individual producers have often enjoyed considerable latitude over what materials were commissioned. It becomes evident from a scrutiny of the contributors' files at Caversham that certain producers felt a strong attraction towards the Arthurian legends, and these men were instrumental in getting such work on air. Their names include Louis MacNeice, E. J. King Bull, Charles Lefeaux, Dafydd Gruffydd, Terence Tiller, Douglas Cleverdon, John Powell and Nigel Bryant. But the BBC was a broad church, and not all members of staff had similar views. Battle was often joined. P. H. Newby's condign rejection of MacNeice's suggestion for a Gawain play seems, for example, to have reflected a modern novelist's distaste for the mythico-poetical Arthurian subject. Hart and Scott-Moncrieff obviously had no liking for T. H. White's *The Once and Future King*, and summarily turned it down for *Woman's Hour*. On the other hand, the fate of some Arthurian work that was not accepted for broadcasting seems to have rested on more sensitively expressed literary criteria. That Val Gielgud rejected Bradnum's *For the Death of a Beast* cannot be attributed to anti-Arthurian prejudice, for Gielgud had earlier strongly backed Clemence Dane's Arthurian series. Harman Grisewood banished the two Treece dramas to Wales, but gave valid reasons for doing so: he had after all been instrumental in ensuring that David Jones's *In Parenthesis* was kept in the active repertory. Sheer chance could also play its part. Had T. H. White fulfilled his contract to write a Tristram play, the course of radio playwriting in the 1960s might have been very different.

Finally, there is the question of patriotic intent. In pre-war days the BBC was not narrowly party-political, but it normally flew the flag for Britain. *Radio Times* was rather bright and breezy, full of photographs of docks being opened, ships launched, royal overseas tours conducted, all of these activities bathed in an optimistic glow of peaceful, but heartwarming, national pride. Bridson's play fits this cultural milieu. He may have been left-of-centre and not customarily a jingo but a chief motive in his *King Arthur* is undoubtedly the celebration of a new Arthur, a king 'who will rule justly and righteously, and who shall restore to our great country its ancient freedom, its ancient happiness' (p. 61). With the outbreak of the Second World War, government was well aware that in radio it had an important psychological weapon, and the rapid reorganisation of programmes that ensued suggests that a national interest was paramount. This was radio's great opportunity as a news medium, since it was listened to avidly for information about the war fronts and for the morale-building speeches by Churchill. Wisely, perhaps, the propaganda was very delicately handled: on the Forces programme a mood of more entertainment than usual was fostered through dance music and comedy, Hitler being downsized into a ridiculous figure of fun. Home Service was differently addressed. Here matters were treated more overtly and seriously, and there is some evidence that the Matter of Britain, too, was introduced with a very patriotic angle into such programmes as Cleverdon and Felton's West Country travelogue and the 1943 production of Dryden and Purcell's dramatic-opera. The major work in this respect is Dane's *The Saviours*, which was broadcast to a vast audience, in the very eye of the storm, when a beleaguered Britain knew itself in deadly peril of invasion, and when the spirit of Arthur was meaningfully summoned to resist the new Saxon foe. The series' political application is continued well into the post-war period, too, for parts were often repeated to mark commemorative national events right through to the coronation year of Elizabeth II. The propaganda was not always necessarily effective, though; the influential *Listener* critic objecting in 1940 to such exaggerated underlining of a political message. And we should resist too great an alacrity always to equate adoption of the Arthurian legend with manipulative British propaganda. By no means all of its multi-faceted correspondences could be shaped to suit such a purpose. There was, for example, the awkward case of Wagner. Wartime saw a sharp drop in BBC performances of *Tristan* and *Parsifal*. Even if this music was Arthurian, it belonged to the other side.

Comparably ambiguous applications are occasionally evident thereafter. We may suspect that a patriotic purpose informs a play such as Sherriff's *The Long Sunset* (1955), wherein the catastrophes of the fifth century prefigure twentieth-century British crises. Moreover, the legend is made applicable to the Cold War in Schwartz's *The Dragon* (1965), for its heroic Lancelot is clearly intended as an encouragement of resistance to, and victory over, Soviet corruption and repression. Yet in Cooper's *Without the Grail* (1958), the Arthur of Malory's *Morte* becomes a denigrated symbol of British colonial rule in India, and, as Cooper represented the new trend in writing for radio, it was outlooks like his that proved dominant for the next generation. The BBC's ethos has altered radically since the 1950s, and few people would now impute a patriotic intent, except in the case of football, to radio controllers. How then do we explain the resurgence of Arthurian plays and features on air during the 1980s?

The clue lies probably in Britain's ideological ferment within that decade. The previous thirty years had seen an inexorable decline in the country's international power, influence and economic vitality, while the very concept of its separate national identity was acutely challenged. And now, not only was it subject, like most other places, to the global economy's erosion of cultural difference, but it was also experiencing the constitutional loss of political and economic independence through the transfer (for good or ill) of major powers to the European Union. Moreover, the bases of national identity had been called into question by the widespread official fostering of the policy of multiculturalism among the many immigrant communities. Resistance to these internationalising trends was encapsulated in the defiantly pro-British persona of Boadicea, the renaissance of whose potency as a nationalist (and feminist) icon dates from this period, the most significant image of her new avatar being a *Daily Express* cartoon that pictured prime minister Margaret Thatcher as the Iceni Queen in a chariot with luridly sharp spikes on the wheels.[12] Complementary to this heroic revival was a new interest in Arthur. Compared with that of Boadicea, his restored image was generally milder and less frankly combative, more elegiac in tone, as if in acknowledgement that the new Battle of Britain may already have been lost. Nonetheless his myth represented a characterising feature in what was widely canvassed as the national narrative that enables Britons to see themselves historically as a separate community and to read cultural significance into their lives. As part of this national debate, what kind of Arthurian myth has radio then developed?

## The Arthur of Radio

The context of Arthur has been shaped by radio according to the demands of the medium. Initially, with justifiable pride in the quasi-official role of radio as a mass purveyor, the early BBC presents Arthur as a very public national figure in the plays by Bridson and Dane. But that dramatic model has been profoundly modified by a growing appreciation of radio's distinctive technical qualities, for a medium confined to sound cannot hope to rival painting or film in the delineation of the external world of physique, costume, architecture and landscape. It offers little scope for the pageantry of tournaments, the splendour of courts or the beauty of ladies. Nor can it cope with dramatic action. As battles can be intimated only briefly, there can be no protracted fights or hunts. This is reason enough why the Robin Hood legend, which is so dependent upon ambushes in the greenwood, found scant attention as a major radio subject. Likewise the legend of Sir Gawain and the Green Knight may be briefly narrated for children, but would prove difficult to dramatise adequately, and has sensibly been avoided. Because combat must be played down, Arthur cannot be the superhero

---

12   The cartoon is reproduced in Antonia Fraser, *Boadicea's Chariot: The Warrior Queens* (London: Weidenfeld & Nicolson, 1988).

that is possible in films. And because radio cannot employ or adequately evoke a cast of thousands, Arthur's human circle tends to be confined to a chosen few, familial and/or comradely.

The necessity for keeping scenes brief, and in a minor key, has moreover its advantages, for the episodic nature of radio drama is well suited for conveying the whole sweep of the Arthurian story across different locations and the passing years. This fluidity is complemented by another attribute of the medium: its essential privacy and domesticity. Instead of our visiting a cinema or theatre, radio comes to us while we remain in our everyday surroundings, and engage in our usual occupations. Language may be heightened to compensate for the lack of the visual but, between ourselves and the language of the performance, there is no barrier erected by stage set or costuming. The fact that we access radio from within our normal circumstances leads also to our readiness to empathize imaginatively with the dramatic enactment. As the action feels so close it readily embodies the myth of an Arthur who is constantly on the verge of returning to the modern age.

All this has significant repercussions. Since the action is internalised, the focus is psychological. The legend reveals here its immense suitability for radio, as its major personae – male and female, young and old – are extremely diverse in type and complex in nature. Among them memory becomes the main actor, the dominant time is a personal past, the concern is moral, and the mood one of melancholy regret over loss or failure. Characters are most finely evoked when forced into isolation, as prisoners, as exiles, or in the loneliness of approaching death (Treece, Weir, Fife, Crossley-Holland). Soliloquy is endemic, and the use of atmospheric music crucial. Arthur has, of course, to remain a hero – the tradition can allow only a few maverick exceptions (Baldwin) or else the basis of the whole legendary fabric will collapse – but he (and other major figures) are given very human failings (Baczkiewicz) or treated ironically (Joseph). Only Ashton sounds the old publicly upbeat note, but manages to do so by assigning his key action to 1940. Elsewhere success tends to be achieved by saving oneself through private struggles for independence (Gough, Fletcher) or for moral enlightenment (Crossley-Holland, Clarke) rather than by acting as saviour of others. The fragmentation that these plays suggest is an apt reflection of a contemporary Britain that has lost the old acknowledged certainties of national and social order, and is so deeply divided about its direction that it wavers on the edge of dysfunction. We have remade Camelot in our own troubled social image.

This slightly muted Arthur of radio drama is, however, complemented by the very different Arthurian world of the modern feature programme. If the former seems somewhat limited (and British) in scope, this quality is compensated in the latter, for essentially the feature condenses the entire richness of all radio's (and other media's) treatments of the legend. The major features have all revealed that the Matter of Britain has a British core in that it is set in Britain, narrates an heroic British warrior's struggle against an alien invader, and that ever since the end of the Middle Ages this story has been treated far more frequently in this island's present-day language than in any other. That is, however, only one, and not perhaps the most interesting, part of the story. For its national theme is richly supplemented by religious and amatory motifs, and its Celtic origins have long been augmented by Continental cultures, taken over by the English, and are now continuously re-exported and re-imported. Employing the special facilities of radio, and manipulating vast resources of recorded materials, the feature melds history, folklore, landscape, literature, music and commercial appropriation in its exploration of the Matter of Britain. The topic has become so huge and so intricately diverse, and the applications so open-ended, that no simplistic judgement is now acceptable. The story has become the story. That is now the fascination.

Evaluation of radio's effect on the modern development of the Arthurian legend may initially appear problematic. The most potent twentieth-century influences on contemporary treatments of the legend have – I speak without regard to quality – come either from the novelist (T. H. White and Marion Zimmer Bradley) or the cinema (*Camelot, Excalibur* and *Monty Python and The Holy Grail*). Radio's influence has been very much smaller. And even within the culture of radio itself, no single Arthurian programme has achieved the impact of Dylan Thomas's *Under Milk Wood* or Samuel Beckett's *All That Fall*. Nevertheless the cumulative mass of Arthurian programmes suggests that they occupied a significant role in the cultural life of many listeners. As BBC music has profoundly transformed our way of listening to, and knowledge of, music, responsibility for the continuing diffusion of Wagner may be attributed largely to broadcasting. The number of Arthurian programmes shows, too, the extent of penetration consistently achieved by the legend within a modern medium. These programmes continued, preserved and helped to recover an Arthurian tradition in the popular imagination. By adaptation and popularisation they widened access to it among adults and children. The older literary forms of the novel and the play were modified to suit the new medium, and within this a wholly new genre of radio drama was created. The BBC's achievement in all this has been considerable. Over there in Avalon, King Arthur should be well pleased. Radio Camelot has kept his memory green in modern Lyonesse.

# Appendix A
## Major Radio Programmes

| | Opera | Drama, Literature, Criticism and History |
|---|---|---|
| 1923 | | |
| 1924 | | Sharpe *Arthur and the Round Table* T |
| 1925 | Purcell *King Arthur* | Brooks *Spenser's 'Faerie Queene'* T<br>Morgan *'The Faerie Queene'* T<br>Buckton *Wooing of Guinevere*<br>Drury *Vanished Land of Lyonesse* T |
| 1926 | | |
| 1927 | Purcell *King Arthur* (2)<br>Cowen *The Water Lily* | Hewitt *The Legend of King Arthur* T<br>Moffat *Caxton's Malory* T |
| 1928 | Wagner *Parsifal* | Phillips *Paolo and Francesca*<br>Buckton *Avalon* |
| 1929 | | D'Annunzio *Francesca da Rimini*<br>Miles *'Mabinogion' by film producers* S |
| 1930 | Wagner *Parsifal* | Henderson *Tintagel and legend of Arthur* T<br>Riley *Early Romances of West* T<br>Williams *Geoffrey of Monmouth* T |
| 1931 | Purcell *King Arthur* | Dryden tr. Chaucer *The Wife of Bath's Tale*<br>Ege *Depression over Fairyland* |
| 1932 | Wagner *Parsifal* | Fielding *Tom Thumb the Great* |
| 1933 | Wagner *Parsifal* (2) | Watts *In Quest of Arthur* T<br>Ege *Depression over Fairyland* R |
| 1934 | | Worsley *Adventures of Sir Goahead* |
| 1935 | Purcell *King Arthur*<br>Boughton *Queen of Cornwall* | |

|       | Opera | Drama, Literature, Criticism and History |
|-------|-------|-------------------------------------------|
| 1936 | Wagner *Tristan and Isolde*<br>Wagner *Parsifal* | Grigson *King Arthur in the West* T |
| 1937 | Wagner *Parsifal* | Bridson *King Arthur*<br>Rhys *Enid*<br>Fisher *Tristram* F |
| 1938 | Zandonai *Francesca da Rimini* | Rhys *The Quest of the Grail* |
| 1939 |       | White *The Sword in the Stone* S |
| 1940 |       | Dane *The Saviours* S |
| 1941 |       |       |
| 1942 |       |       |
| 1943 | Purcell *King Arthur* |       |
| 1944 |       | Reed *Tintagel* |
| 1945 |       |       |
| 1946 | Wagner *Tristan and Isolde* | Coghill tr. Chaucer *Wife of Bath's Tale*<br>Twain *A Yank at the Court of King Arthur* S<br>Eliot *Charles Williams* T<br>Jones *In Parenthesis* |
| 1947 | Wagner *Tristan and Isolde*<br>Wagner *Parsifal* | Coghill tr. Chaucer *Wife of Bath's Tale* R<br>Bridie *Lancelot*<br>Armstrong *Sir Borloys and the Dark Knight*<br>Powell *Sir Lancelot and Little Hands*<br>Isaacs *Malory* T<br>Gruffydd *Arthurian … Mabinogion* T |
| 1948 | Martin *Le Vin herbé* |       |
| 1949 | Purcell *King Arthur*<br>Wagner *Tristan and Isolde*<br>Wagner, *Parsifal* | Coghill tr. Chaucer *Wife of Bath's Tale* R<br>Gracq *The Fisher King*<br>Treece *The End of a World* |
| 1950 | Wagner *Tristan and Isolde*<br>Wagner *Parsifal*<br>Boughton *Queen of Cornwall* | Treece *The Tragedy of Tristram*<br>Gwyn Jones *Mabinogion* T |
| 1951 | Purcell *King Arthur*<br>Wagner *Tristan and Isolde*<br>Wagner *Parsifal* (2) | Cocteau *The Knights of the Round Table*<br>Gracq *The Fisher King* R |

| 1952 | Wagner *Tristan and Isolde*<br>Wagner *Parsifal* | Malory *The Death of Arthur*<br>Spenser *The Faerie Queene* S<br>Phillips *Paolo and Francesca*<br>White *The Sword in the Stone* |
|---|---|---|
| 1953 | Purcell *King Arthur*<br>Wagner *Tristan and Isolde* (2) | Tolkien tr. *Sir Gawain and Green Knight* S<br>Malory *The Death of Arthur* R<br>Malory *The Quest of the Holy Grail*<br>Jones *The Anathemata*<br>Dane *The Hope of Britain* R<br>Dane *The Unknown Soldier* R<br>*Myth or Legend?* S<br>Cocteau *The Knights of the Round Table* R |
| 1954 | Wagner *Parsifal*<br>Zandonai *Francesca da Rimini* | Twain *A Yank at the Court of King Arthur*<br>Jackson *Who was King Arthur?* T<br>Jones *The Anathemata* R<br>*Boughton and Glastonbury* T |
| 1955 | Wagner *Tristan and Isolde* | Malory *The Quest of the Holy Grail* R<br>Jones *In Parenthesis* R<br>Sherriff *The Long Sunset*<br>*The Historical Arthur* T |
| 1956 |  | Hardy *The Queen of Cornwall*<br>Ratcliff *Tristan of Cornwall*<br>Sherriff *The Long Sunset* R (2) |
| 1957 | Wagner *Tristan and Isolde* (2)<br>Wagner *Parsifal* | Jenkins *The Thistle and the Grail* |
| 1958 | Wagner *Tristan and Isolde*<br>Martin *Le Vin herbé* | Jones *The Anathemata* R<br>Cooper *Without the Grail*<br>*Glastonbury legends and archaeology* T |
| 1959 | Purcell *King Arthur*<br>Wagner *Parsifal* | Bradnum *The Cave and the Grail* |
| 1960 |  | Dickinson *Tennyson* F<br>Sherriff *The Long Sunset* R |
| 1961 |  |  |
| 1962 | Wagner *Tristan and Isolde*<br>Wagner *Parsifal* |  |
| 1963 |  | Bridson *Man to Be Strong* |
| 1964 | Purcell *King Arthur*<br>Wagner *Tristan and Isolde* | Jones *In Parenthesis* R |

| | Opera | Drama, Literature, Criticism and History |
|---|---|---|
| 1965 | Wagner *Tristan and Isolde* | Schwartz *The Dragon* |
| | | Gibbs *King Arthur* T |
| | | D. M. Thomas *The Strait* |
| 1966 | Purcell *King Arthur* | Laughton *South Cadbury* F |
| | Wagner *Tristan and Isolde* | |
| 1967 | | Cocteau *The Knights of the Round Table* |
| | | Palmer *Laureate in Lyonnesse* T |
| 1968 | Wagner *Tristan and Isolde* | Tennyson *Idylls* |
| | Wagner *Parsifal* | Jones *In Parenthesis* R |
| 1969 | Wagner *Tristan and Isolde* | Schwartz *The Dragon* R |
| | Wagner *Parsifal* | |
| 1970 | Purcell *King Arthur* (2) | Twain *A Yankee at the Court of K. Arthur* S |
| | Wagner *Tristan and Isolde* | |
| | Wagner *Parsifal* | |
| | Martin *Le Vin herbé* | |
| 1971 | Wagner *Tristan and Isolde* (2) | Jones tr. *Sir Gawain and the Green Knight* S |
| | Wagner *Parsifal* (2) | Malory *Morte Darthur* S |
| | | Owen *The Grail Legend* T |
| | | Tiller *The Road to Shalott* F |
| | | White *The Sword in the Stone* S |
| | | Sherriff *The Long Sunset* R |
| 1972 | Purcell *King Arthur* | Jones tr. *Sir Gawain and Green Knight* S R |
| | Wagner *Tristan and Isolde* | Tiller *The Road to Astolat* F |
| | Wagner *Parsifal* | Tiller *The Road to Camelot* F |
| | | Eliot *The Waste Land* |
| 1973 | Boismortier *Don Quichotte* | |
| | Wagner *Tristan and Isolde* (2) | |
| | Wagner *Parsifal* | |
| 1974 | Purcell *King Arthur* | Cook *Their Love Shall Drink Its Fill* F |
| | Wagner *Tristan and Isolde* | Gibson *Arthur, Avalon and Sedgemoor* T |
| | Wagner *Parsifal* | Duggan *Conscience of the King* |
| | Martin *Le Vin herbé* | |
| 1975 | Wagner *Tristan and Isolde* | Hartmann *Iwein* S |
| | Wagner *Parsifal* | Orr *David Jones* F |
| | Crosse *Potter Thompson* | |
| 1976 | Wagner *Tristan and Isolde* | Kavanagh *Powys 'Glastonbury Romance'* T |
| | Wagner *Parsifal* | Sherriff *The Long Sunset* R |

| | | |
|---|---|---|
| 1977 | Wagner *Tristan and Isolde* | Spenser *Faerie Queene* |
| | Wagner *Parsifal* | Davenant *Britannia Triumphans* |
| | | Quiller-Couch *Castle Dor* |
| | | Honeycombe *Lancelot and Guinevere* |
| | | Arthur *The Stuff of Legend* T |
| | | |
| 1978 | Wagner *Tristan and Isolde* | Rosen *Rutland Boughton* F |
| | Wagner *Parsifal* | Jones *The Anathemata* R |
| | | White *The Sword in the Stone* S |
| | | Honeycombe *Lancelot and Guinevere* R |
| | | |
| 1979 | Wagner *Tristan and Isolde* | Mann *Tristan* |
| | Wagner *Parsifal* | Torrance *Half Sick of Shadows* |
| | | Vaughan *The Matter of Arthur* F |
| | | |
| 1980 | Wagner *Tristan and Isolde* | |
| | Wagner *Parsifal* (2) | |
| | Whitehead *Tristan and Iseult* | |
| | | |
| 1981 | Wagner *Tristan and Isolde* (3) | Jones *In Parenthesis* R |
| | Wagner *Parsifal* | Jones *The Sleeping Lord* |
| | | Orr *David Jones* T |
| | | White *The Sword in the Stone* |
| | | |
| 1982 | Wagner *Parsifal* (2) | Russell *Gawain in Reading* T |
| | Chausson *Le Roi Arthus* | Billings *In Search of Tristan* T |
| | Martin *Le Vin herbé* | |
| | | |
| 1983 | Purcell *King Arthur* | Priestley *The Thirty-First of June* |
| | Wagner *Tristan and Isolde* | |
| | Martin *Le Vin herbé* | |
| | | |
| 1984 | Wagner *Tristan and Isolde* | Wilson *The Princely Pleasures* |
| | Wagner *Parsifal* | Sherriff *The Long Sunset* R |
| | Martin *Le Vin herbé* | Weir *Passings* |
| | | |
| 1985 | | Salmon *Around the Coast of Cornwall* T |
| | | |
| 1986 | Purcell *King Arthur* | Westwood & Barron *Myths, Legends* T |
| | Wagner *Tristan and Isolde* | Thomas *T. H. White* F |
| | Wagner *Parsifal* | Weir *Passings* R |
| | Blackford *Gawain and Ragnell* | Dauncey *Trystan and Essyllt* F |
| | | |
| 1987 | Wagner *Tristan and Isolde* | Wright tr. Chaucer *The Wife of Bath's Tale* |
| | Wagner *Parsifal* | Ashton *The Peril* |
| | Chausson *Le Roi Arthus* | |
| | | |
| 1988 | Wagner *Parsifal* | Griffiths *Messiaen and Tristan* T |

| | Opera | Drama, Literature, Criticism and History |
|---|---|---|
| 1989 | Wagner *Tristan and Isolde*<br>Wagner *Parsifal* | |
| 1990 | Wagner *Tristan and Isolde*<br>Wagner *Parsifal*<br>Tippett *New Year* | Hartill *Sir Gawain* F<br>Lewis *That Hideous Strength* S<br>Sherriff *The Long Sunset* R<br>Crossley-Holland *The Slumber King*<br>Fife *Arthur the King* S |
| 1991 | Wagner *Parsifal* (2)<br>Tippett *New Year*<br>Birtwistle *Gawain* | Evans tr. Chaucer *The Wife of Bath's Tale*<br>*Tristan and Iseult*<br>Stone tr. *Sir Gawain and the Green Knight* S<br>Fife *Arthur the King* R |
| 1992 | | Evans tr. Chaucer *The Wife of Bath's Tale* R<br>*Tirra Lirra by the River* F<br>Crossley-Holland *The Slumber King* R |
| 1993 | Wagner *Tristan and Isolde* (2)<br>Martin *Le Vin herbé* | Baldwin *Merlin and Arthur*<br>Crossley-Holland *Arthur's Knight* S<br>*The Story of Arthur Uther Pendragon* F |
| 1994 | Wagner *Tristan and Isolde*<br>Chausson *Le Roi Arthus*<br>Birtwistle *Gawain* | White *The Sword in the Stone* S<br>Baldwin *Merlin and Arthur* R<br>Huckvale *Who is the Grail?* T<br>Huckvale *Avalon* T<br>Vaughan *The Matter of Arthur* FR |
| 1995 | Purcell *King Arthur* (3)<br>Wagner *Parsifal* | Wyatt *Fairest Isle*<br>Hooker *A Map of David Jones* F<br>Gough *Our Lady of Shadows*<br>Clarke *A Stone from Heaven* S<br>Joseph *Go for the Grail*<br>Patten *Tintagel on Trial* F |
| 1996 | Chausson *Le Roi Arthus* (2) | Forbes *History of Britain in Six Menus* F<br>Jones *The Once and Future King* F<br>Hooker *A Map of David Jones* R |
| 1997 | Wagner *Tristan and Isolde* (2) | Page *Sir Gawain and the Green Knight* F<br>Fletcher *The Lady of Shalott* |
| 1998 | Wagner *Tristan and Isolde*<br>Wagner *Parsifal*<br>Lerner & Loewe *Camelot* | Matarosso tr. *The Quest of the Holy Grail* S<br>Cleverdon *David Jones* F<br>Potter *Excalibur* |

| 1999 | Wagner *Tristan and Isolde*<br>Wagner *Parsifal* | Page *In Search of Tristan* F |
|------|------|------|
| 2000 | Wagner *Tristan and Isolde*<br>Wagner *Parsifal*<br>Chausson *Le Roi Arthus* | Richards *Glastonbury* T<br>Eldridge *Arthur in Bournemouth* |
| 2001 | Wagner *Parsifal* (2) | Palmer *Spenser's 'Faerie Queene'*<br>Davies *The Lyre of Orpheus*<br>Northam *Monty Python / the Holy Grail* F |
| 2002 | | |
| 2003 | Wagner *Tristan and Isolde* (2)<br>Wagner *Parsifal*<br>Chausson *Le Roi Arthus* | May *The Story of the Story* F<br>Hill *Killing Maestros* |
| 2004 | Purcell *King Arthur* | Noel-Tod *From Camelot to Birkenhead* F<br>Jones *In Parenthesis* R<br>Baczkiewicz & Maye *Arthur* S |
| 2005 | Wagner *Tristan and Isolde*<br>Chausson *Le Roi Arthus* | Malory *The Death of Arthur* S<br>McMillan *First Glastonbury Festival* F |

*Key*

F Feature      S Series      R Repeat      T Talk

## Appendix B
## RT *listings of Wagner and Purcell excerpts, Chausson, Bax, Wright, Messiaen*

| | Wagner *Tristan* excerpts | Wagner *Parsifal* excerpts | Purcell *King Arthur* excerpts | Chausson *Viviane* | Bax *Tintagel* | Wright *Tintagel* | Messiaen *Turangalîla* |
|---|---|---|---|---|---|---|---|
| 1950 | | | | | 1 | 1 | |
| 1951 | | 1 | | | | | |
| 1952 | | | 1 | | 1 | 1 | |
| 1953 | | 2 | 2 | | | | 1 |
| 1954 | | | 1 | | 1 | | 1 |
| 1955 | 1 | | | | 2 | 1 | |
| 1956 | | | | | 1 | | |
| 1957 | 1 | | | | | | |
| 1958 | 4 | | 1 | | 1 | | |
| 1959 | 1 | | | | 2 | | |
| 1960 | 1 | | | | | | |
| 1961 | 3 | 2 | 1 | | 1 | | |
| 1962 | 2 | | 1 | | 1 | | |
| 1963 | 5 | 1 | 1 | | 1 | 1 | |
| 1964 | 1 | | 1 | | 1 | | |
| 1965 | 4 | 3 | 1 | | | 1 | 1 |
| 1966 | 4 | 2 | 1 | | 1 | | 1 |
| 1967 | 5 | 1 | 1 | | 4 | | |

| Year | | | | | | | |
|------|---|---|---|---|---|---|---|
| 1968 | 12 | 3 | | | 2 | 1 | 2 |
| 1969 | 8 | 2 | | | 1 | 1 | 2 |
| 1970 | 7 | | | | 4 | | |
| 1971 | 4 | | | | 2 | 1 | 3 |
| 1972 | 3 | | 2 | 1 | 3 | | |
| 1973 | 1 | | | | 2 | 1 | |
| 1974 | | | | | | 1 | |
| 1975 | | | 1 | 1 | 4 | | |
| 1976 | | | | | 1 | 1 | 1 |
| 1977 | 1 | | 1 | | 3 | | 1 |
| 1978 | 2 | | 1 | | 1 | 1 | 2 |
| 1979 | 1 | | 1 | | 1 | | |
| 1980 | 3 | | | | 2 | 1 | 1 |
| 1981 | 4 | 1 | 3 | | 3 | | |
| 1982 | 3 | | 2 | | | | 1 |
| 1983 | 3 | 4 | 1 | | 4 | | 1 |
| 1984 | 6 | 1 | | | 8 | | |
| 1985 | 6 | 2 | 2 | | 5 | | |
| 1986 | 4 | | 1 | | 3 | | 3 |
| 1987 | 10 | 2 | 3 | 1 | 1 | | 2 |
| 1988 | 4 | 3 | 1 | 1 | 3 | | 5 |
| 1989 | 7 | 1 | | | 5 | | |
| 1990 | 5 | 1 | 2 | 1 | 5 | | |
| 1991 | 7 | 4 | 1 | | 5 | | 2 |
| 1992 | 3 | 1 | 2 | | 3 | | 1 |
| 1993 | 6 | 1 | 4 | | | | 5 |
| 1994 | 15 | 2 | | | 3 | | 2 |
| 1995 | 4 | | 5 | | 6 | | 2 |

| | Wagner Tristan excerpts | Wagner Parsifal excerpts | Purcell King Arthur excerpts | Chausson Viviane | Bax Tintagel | Wright Tintagel | Messiaen Turangalila |
|---|---|---|---|---|---|---|---|
| 1996 | 11 | 7 | 3 | 2 | 2 | | 1 |
| 1997 | 11 | 3 | 2 | 1 | 4 | | 3 |
| 1998 | 13 | 6 | 3 | | 5 | | |
| 1999 | 14 | 5 | 5 | 1 | 2 | | 4 |
| 2000 | 14 | 7 | 5 | | 8 | | 1 |
| 2001 | 12 | 5 | 3 | 2 | 4 | | 1 |
| 2002 | 12 | 5 | 2 | 1 | 1 | | 5 |
| 2003 | 15 | 7 | 1 | 1 | 5 | | 2 |
| 2004 | 26 | 11 | 5 | 1 | 7 | | 3 |
| 2005 | 24 | 6 | 6 | 4 | 7 | | 4 |

## Appendix C
## RT *listings of Tristan theme (excluding Wagner,* Tristan and Isolde; *Bax,* Tintagel; *Wright,* Tintagel Suite; *and Messiaen,* Turangalîla Symphony *and* Cinq Rechants*)*

| | Drama and Literature | Music |
|---|---|---|
| 1923 | | |
| 1924 | | |
| 1925 | | |
| 1926 | | |
| 1927 | | |
| 1928 | | Pengelly *Tristram and Iseult* |
| 1929 | | |
| 1930 | | |
| 1931 | | |
| 1932 | | Boughton *Three Tristram Songs* |
| 1933 | | |
| 1934 | | |
| 1935 | | Boughton *The Queen of Cornwall* |
| 1936 | Grigson *Tristan in the West* T | |
| 1937 | Fisher *Tristram* F | Boughton *3 Songs from Queen of C* |
| 1938 | | |
| 1939 | | |
| 1940 | | |
| 1941 | Miles *The Truth about Tristan* T | |
| 1942 | | |

| | Drama and Literature | Music |
|---|---|---|
| 1943 | | |
| 1944 | Swinburne *Tristram of Lyonesse* | |
| 1945 | Reed *Tintagel* | |
| 1946 | | |
| 1947 | | |
| 1948 | | Martin *Le Vin herbé* |
| 1949 | | Ladmirault *Prelude: Tristan et Iseult* |
| 1950 | Treece *The Tragedy of Tristram* | Boughton *The Queen of Cornwall* |
| 1951 | | |
| 1952 | | |
| 1953 | J. M. White *Tristan and Iseult* T | |
| 1954 | | |
| 1955 | | |
| 1956 | Hardy *The Queen of Cornwall* Ratcliff *Tristan of Cornwall* | |
| 1957 | Arnold *Tristram and Iseult* | |
| 1958 | | Martin *Le Vin herbé* |
| 1959 | | |
| 1960 | | |
| 1961 | Reed *Tintagel* | |
| 1962 | | |
| 1963 | | |
| 1964 | | |
| 1965 | D. M. Thomas *The Strait* | Rangström *Tristans Död* |
| 1966 | | *Lamento di Tristan* |
| 1967 | | *Lamento di Tristan* |
| 1968 | | |
| 1969 | | |

| | | |
|---|---|---|
| 1970 | | Martin *Le Vin herbé* |
| 1971 | | |
| 1972 | | |
| 1973 | | |
| 1974 | Cook *Their Love Shall Drink Its Fill* F | Martin *Le Vin herbé* |
| 1975 | Hogwood *In honour of Cornwall* F | |
| 1976 | | |
| 1977 | Quiller-Couch *Castle Dor* | |
| 1978 | | Boughton *Scenes from Queen of C* |
| 1979 | Mann *Tristan* | |
| 1980 | | Whitehead *Tristan and Iseult* |
| 1981 | | |
| 1982 | Billings *In Search of Tristan* F | Martin *Le Vin herbé* <br> *Sir Tristram* |
| 1983 | | Martin *Le Vin herbé* |
| 1984 | | Henze *Tristan* |
| 1985 | | Ladmirault *Prelude: Tristan et Iseult* <br> Henze *Tristan* <br> Bergsma *Fantastic Variations* |
| 1986 | *Trystan and Essyllt* | Henze *Tristan* (2) |
| 1987 | | |
| 1988 | Griffiths *Messiaen and Tristan myth* T | |
| 1989 | Pruslin *Acquiring Mann's Tristan* T | |
| 1990 | Fife *Arthur the King* (episode) | Martin *Le Vin herbé* |
| 1991 | *Tristan and Iseult* <br> Griffiths *The Lay of Sir Tristram*'T | Henze *Tristan* <br> Bedford *Toccata for Tristan* |
| 1992 | | Bedford *Toccata for Tristan* <br> Bedford *Ronde for Isonde* |
| 1993 | | *Romance of Tristan* (motet) <br> Martin *Le Vin herbé* |
| 1994 | | Henze *Tristan* |

|  | **Drama and Literature** | **Music** |
|---|---|---|
| 1995 | | |
| 1996 | Pearson *A Week in Cornwall* F | |
| 1997 | | |
| 1998 | | Waxman *Tristan and Isolde Fantasy* |
| 1999 | Page *In Search of Tristan* F | |
| 2000 | | |
| 2001 | | |
| 2002 | | |
| 2003 | May *The Story of the Story* F<br>Hill *Killing Maestros* | Mival *Tristan – Still* |
| 2004 | | |
| 2005 | | |

# Appendix D
# RT *listings of The Lady of Shalott/Elaine theme*

|  | Tennyson Reading | Associated Lit. and Drama | Associated Music |
|---|---|---|---|
| 1923 | * |  |  |
| 1924 |  |  | Nicholls |
| 1925 | * |  | Bendall<br>Nicholls (2) |
| 1926 |  | *Many-Towered Camelot* |  |
| 1927 |  |  | Dunhill<br>Spain-Dunk<br>Nicholls |
| 1928 | * | Stobart | Spain-Dunk |
| 1929 |  |  |  |
| 1930 |  |  | Dunhill |
| 1931 |  |  |  |
| 1932 |  |  |  |
| 1933 |  |  | Dunhill (2)<br>Davis |
| 1934 | * |  | Dunhill<br>Nicholls |
| 1935 |  |  | Boughton<br>MacDowell |
| 1936 |  |  | Dunhill<br>Edmunds |
| 1937 |  |  | Boughton<br>Slade<br>Dunhill |

| | Tennyson Reading | Associated Lit. and Drama | Associated Music |
|---|---|---|---|
| 1938 | | | Wright<br>Gibbs |
| 1939 | | | Dunhill |
| 1940 | | | |
| 1941 | | | Dunhill |
| 1942 | * | | |
| 1943 | | | |
| 1944 | | | Jacobson |
| 1945 | * | | Dunhill<br>Wright (2) |
| 1946 | * | | Wright |
| 1947 | | Powell | |
| 1948 | | | Wright |
| 1949 | | | |
| 1950 | * | | Wright |
| 1951 | | | |
| 1952 | * | | Wright |
| 1953 | | | |
| 1954 | | | |
| 1955 | | | Wright |
| 1956 | | | Tate |
| 1957 | * | | |
| 1958 | | | |
| 1959 | | | Tate |
| 1960 | | | |
| 1961 | ** | | Tate |
| 1962 | | | |
| 1963 | * | | Wright |

| Year | | | |
|------|---|---|---|
| 1964 | | | |
| 1965 | | Christie | Wright |
| 1966 | | Mason | |
| 1967 | * | | Sibelius |
| 1968 | | Hallam Tennyson | Wright<br>Bliss |
| 1969 | | | Wright |
| 1970 | | | |
| 1971 | * | Tiller | Wright |
| 1972 | | Tiller | |
| 1973 | | | |
| 1974 | | | |
| 1975 | | | |
| 1976 | | | |
| 1977 | | | |
| 1978 | | | Boughton<br>Wright |
| 1979 | | Torrance | Tate |
| 1980 | | | Wright |
| 1981 | | | |
| 1982 | | | |
| 1983 | | | |
| 1984 | | | |
| 1985 | | | |
| 1986 | | | |
| 1987 | | | |
| 1988 | | | |
| 1989 | | | |
| 1990 | | Fife episode | |

| | Tennyson Reading | Associated Lit. and Drama | Associated Music |
|---|---|---|---|
| 1991 | | | Bliss |
| 1992 | * | *Tirra Lirra* | |
| 1993 | | | |
| 1994 | | | |
| 1995 | | Gough | |
| 1996 | | | |
| 1997 | | Fletcher | MacDowell |
| 1998 | | Christie | |
| 1999 | | | |
| 2000 | | | |
| 2001 | | | MacDowell |
| 2002 | | | |
| 2003 | | | |
| 2004 | | | MacDowell |
| 2005 | | Christie | |

# Appendix E
## Versions for Children

| Retellings of Pre-20th-Century Works | 20th-Century New* and Adapted Works |
|---|---|
| **1923** Badman *Legends of King Arthur* S<br>Chaucer *Wife of Bath's Tale* | |
| **1924** | |
| **1925** Spenser T | |
| **1926** Malory T<br>Hodges *Stories of King Arthur* S | |
| **1927** Williams *Arthurian Heroines* S<br>*Legendary Heroes*<br>Cater *Legend of King Arthur* T | |
| **1928** Stobart *Arthurian Legends* S<br>Stobart *'Faerie Queene'* T | |
| **1929** Kennedy *Kynge Arthur* S | |
| **1930** Gass *Arthur and Round Table* T<br>Eaves, *Gareth*<br>Peach *Knights of the Round Table* S<br>Barber *Stories from Malory* | |
| **1931** Champion *Fairhands*<br>Morgan *Sir Owen* S<br>Morgan *Y Greal Santaidd* | |
| **1932** | |
| **1933** | Worsley *Sir Goahead* S* |
| **1934** *How Lancelot came north*<br><br>Robbie *Arthur and the Round Table* T | <br><br><br>Hughes *Ogof Arthur** |

| Retellings of<br>Pre-20th-Century Works | 20th-Century New* and<br>Adapted Works |
|---|---|
| 1935  Hughes *Arthur* and *Saint Greal*<br>Marsden *Sleeping Knights/Richmond* T<br>Brown *King Arthur in Scotland* T S | Balfour *Watcher of West**<br>Enoch *Magic in Air** |
| 1936 | |
| 1937  Vinden *Sir Gawayne* | |
| 1938  Farjeon *Elizabeth at Kenilworth*<br>Ashmore *Sir Gareth the Fair*<br>Power *Story of Arthur* T<br>Atherton *Gawayne and the Green Knight* | |
| 1939  Thomas *Kenilworth Pageant* | Fry *The Caves**<br>White *The Sword in the Stone* S |
| 1940  Power *Arthur of Britain* T | Phillips *Three Princes** |
| 1941 | |
| 1942  *Tom Thumb* | McGarry *Merlin's Wand** |
| 1943  Watkins *Lady of the Fountain* | |
| 1944  Pyle *Arthurian Legends* S | |
| 1945  Harvey *Jack the Giant Killer* | |
| 1946  Levy *Tom Thumb* | |
| 1947  Jefferson *The Grave of Vortigern* | Uttley *King Arthur's Tree** |
| 1948 | |
| 1949 | |
| 1950  Millar *Gawayn and the Green Knight* S | |
| 1951  *Adventures of Peredur* | |
| 1952  Doolan *King Arthur* S<br>Gwyn *Knights of the Round Table* S | |
| 1953  Millar *Gawayn and the Green Knight* S R | |
| 1954  Lonsdale *Tearne Wadling* | |
| 1955 | |
| 1956 | Clare *Merlin's Magic* S |
| 1957 | |

1958      Masefield *Midnight Folk*

1959   Sutcliffe *King Arthur* T

1960   Millar *Malory* S
Millar *Gawain and the Green Knight* S R

1961      Masefield *Midnight Folk* R
Sutcliff *Lantern Bearers* S

1962

1963   Millar *Gawain and the Green Knight* S R    Garner *Weirdstone...* S

1964

1965

1966

1967   Cavender *Malory* S

1968

1969

1970

1971   Langdon *Tale of King Arthur* S      White *The Sword in the Stone*
Millar *Gawain and the Green Knight* S R

1972      Garner *Elidor*

1973

1974   *Who was King Arthur?* T

1975      Crosse *Potter Thompson*

1976   *Sir Gawain and the Green Knight*

1977   Malory *Le Morte d'Arthur* S

1978   Self *Sir Gawain and the Green Knight* S    Cooper *The Dark is Rising*

1979

1980

1981      White *The Sword in the Stone* S
Cooper *Greenwitch* S

1982   Self *Sir Gawain and the Green Knight* SR    Sutcliff *The Road to Camlann* S
Dickinson *Weathermonger* S

1983

| | Retellings of Pre-20th-Century Works | 20th-Century New* and Adapted Works |
|---|---|---|
| 1984 | | Sutcliff *Lantern Bearers* S |
| 1985 | | Cooper *The Dark is Rising* R |
| 1986 | Blackford *Gawain and Ragnell* | Blackford *Gawain & Ragnell* |
| 1987 | | Sutcliff *Sword and the Circle* |
| 1988 | | |
| 1989 | | Spencer *Merlin Lives*\* S |
| 1990 | Coleman *Gawain and the Green Knight* S | |
| 1991 | | |
| 1992 | | |
| 1993 | | |
| 1994 | | |
| 1995 | | Cooper *Over Sea,Under Stone* S |
| 1996 | | |
| 1997 | | Cooper *Over Sea,Under Stone* S R<br>Cooper *The Dark is Rising* R |
| 1998 | | |
| 1999 | | |
| 2000 | | |
| 2001 | | |
| 2002 | | |
| 2003 | Flynn *King Arthur and the Knights* S<br>*Jack the Giant Killer* | Crossley-Holland *Seeing Stone* S |
| 2004 | | Crossley-Holland *Seeing Stone* S R<br>Crossley-Holland *Crossing Places* S |
| 2005 | | |

# Appendix F
## Arthurian Illustration in Radio Times

| Year | Day/ month | Artist | Subject | |
|------|------------|--------|---------|---|
| 1923 | 7/12 | Fleet | *King Arthur's (K)nights* advert for Polarphone | B |
| 1924 | | | | |
| 1925 | | | | |
| 1926 | 26/2 | Anon | Wagner *Tristan and Isolde* advert for Ediswan Valves | B |
| 1927 | | | | |
| 1928 | | | | |
| 1929 | 29/11 | P. B. | Wagner *Tristan and Isolde* cartoon | B |
| 1930 | 11/4 | Elizabeth Rivers | Wagner *Parsifal* | B |
| | 16/5 | Althea Willoughby | Wagner *Parsifal* | B |
| | 8/8 | Mervyn Wilson | *There were no loud-speakers in Lyonesse* | B |
| 1931 | 14/5 | Donia Nachshen | Wagner *Tristan and Isolde* | B |
| | 11/9 | Eric Fraser | Ege *Depression Over Fairyland* | B |
| 1932 | 25/10 | Anon | Wagner *Tristan and Isolde* | B |
| 1933 | 7/4 | Clixby Watson | Wagner *Parsifal* | B |
| 1934 | 9/3 | Lewis Hart | Worsley *Sir Goahead* | B |
| 1935 | 30/1 | C. W. Hodges | Boughton *The Queen of Cornwall* | B |
| | 11/12 | Anon | Purcell *King Arthur* | B |
| 1936 | 3/4 | K. G. | Wagner *Parsifal* | B |
| | 15/5 | C. W. Bacon | Wagner *Tristan and Isolde* | B |
| | 22/5 | Clixby Watson | Wagner *Tristan and Isolde* | B |
| 1937 | 16/4 | J. R. Hart | Bridson *King Arthur* | B |
| | 19/7 | C. W. Bacon | *Merlin in Brechfa* | B |

| Year | Day/month | Artist | Subject | |
|------|-----------|--------|---------|---|
| 1938 | 21/9 | Carmen | Ashmore *Sir Gareth the Fair* | B |
| 1939 | 11/6–19/7 | Robin Jacques | White *The Sword in the Stone* (6) | B |
| 1940 | | | | |
| 1941 | | | | |
| 1942 | 30/4 | Eric Fraser | Purcell *King Arthur* | B |
| | 11/11 | Eric Fraser | Dane *The Unknown Soldier* | B |
| 1943 | | | | |
| 1944 | | | | |
| 1945 | | | | |
| 1946 | 11/11–29/11 | Anon | Twain *A Yank at the Court of King Arthur* (2) | BP |
| 1947 | 4/4 | Tom L. Poulton | Wagner *Parsifal* | B |
| 1948 | | | | |
| 1949 | 13/4 | Dorothea Braby | Wagner *Parsifal* | B |
| 1950 | | | | |
| 1951 | | | | |
| 1952 | 16/3 | Bruce Angrave | White *The Sword in the Stone* (2) | B |
| | 6/10 | Laurence Scarfe | Phillips *Paolo and Francesca* | B |
| 1953 | 8/11 | Dorothea Braby | Dane *The Unknown Soldier* | B |
| 1954 | 14/8 | Norman Mansbridge | Twain *A Yank at the Court of King Arthur* | B |
| 1955 | 15–23/4 | Douglas Relf | Sherriff *The Long Sunset* (3) | B |
| 1956 | 13/4 | Eric Fraser | Ratcliff *Tristan of Corwall* | B |
| 1957 | | | | |
| 1958 | | | | |
| 1959 | 3/4 | Eric Fraser | Wagner *Parsifal* | B |
| | 12/6 | Eric Fraser | Wagner *Parsifal* | B |
| 1960 | | | | |
| 1961 | 8/11 | Val Biro | Tate *The Lady of Shalott* | B |

| | | | | |
|---|---|---|---|---|
| 1962 | | | | |
| 1963 | | | | |
| 1964 | | | | |
| 1965 | 1/3 | Will Nickless | Schwartz *The Dragon* | B |
| | 13/6 | C. W. Bacon | Wagner *Tristan and Isolde* | B |
| 1966 | 1/8 | Eric Fraser | Wagner *Parsifal* | B |
| 1967 | | | | |
| 1968 | | | | |
| 1969 | | | | |
| 1970 | 27/7 | Barry Wilkinson | Twain *A Yankee at the Court of King Arthur* | B |
| 1971 | 10/1 | Eric Fraser | Malory *Morte Darthur* | B |
| | 13/12 | Eric Fraser | *Sir Gawain and the Green Knight* | B |
| 1972 | 14/1 | Eric Fraser | *The Road to Astolat* | B |
| | 30/3 | Val Biro | Wagner *Parsifal* | B |
| 1973 | | | | |
| 1974 | | | | |
| 1975 | | | | |
| 1976 | | | | |
| 1977 | 24/7 | Roy Ellsworth | Wagner *Tristan and Isolde* | B |
| | 18/12 | Eric Fraser | Honeycombe *Lancelot and Guinevere* | B |
| 1978 | | | | |
| 1979 | | | | |
| 1980 | | | | |
| 1981 | 26/12 | Robin Jacques | White *The Sword in the Stone* | B |
| 1982 | | | | |
| 1983 | | | | |
| 1984 | 15/3 | Ian Pollock | Weir *Passings* | B |
| 1985 | | | | |
| 1986 | 4/8 | Mike Walker | *Trystan and Essyllt* | B |

| Year | Day/month | Artist | Subject | |
|------|-----------|--------|---------|----|
| 1987 | | | | |
| 1988 | | | | |
| 1989 | | | | |
| 1990 | 11/11 | Sven Arnstein | Fife *Arthur the King* | BP |
| 1991 | | | | |
| 1992 | | | | |
| 1993 | 11/12 | Richard Johnson | Baldwin *Merlin and Arthur* | CP |
| 1994 | | | | |
| 1995 | 15/4 | Kim Marsland | Clarke *A Stone from Heaven* | C |
| 1996 | | | | |
| 1997 | | | | |
| 1998 | 25/5 | Clifford Harper | *The Quest of the Holy Grail* | C |
| | 11/7 | Bill Sanderson | Wagner *Tristan and Isolde* | C |
| 1999 | | | | |
| 2000 | 9/11 | John Storey | Wagner *Tristan and Isolde* | C |
| 2001 | | | | |
| 2002 | | | | |
| 2003 | | | | |
| 2004 | 22/10 | Kevin Hauff | Baczkiewicz *Arthur* | C |
| 2005 | | | | |

*Key*
B  Black and white       C  Colour       P  Photograph

# Select Bibliography

*Unpublished scripts for radio programmes*
*(in BBC Written Archive, Caversham Park, unless otherwise stated)*

Armstrong, Anthony, 'Sir Borloys and the Dark Knight'.
Ashton, Dennis, 'The Peril'.
Bradnum, Frederick, 'The Cave and the Grail'.
Bridson, D. G., 'King Arthur'.
——, 'Man to Be Strong: A Profile of William Morris'.
Gracq, Julian, 'The Fisher King', tr. Rollo H. Myers and E. J. King Bull.
Hartmann von Aue, 'The Adventures of Sir Iwein', tr. Susanne Flatauer.
Honeycombe, Gordon, 'Lancelot and Guinevere'. Theatre Museum, London.
Jenkins, Robin, 'The Thistle and the Grail'.
Mason, Ba, 'How I Met the Lady of Shalott'.
Ratcliff, Nora, 'Tristan of Cornwall'.
Rosen, Carole, 'The Glastonbury Ring'.
Russell, W. M. S., 'Sir Gawain in Reading'.
Torrance, Lee, 'Half Sick of Shadows'.
Treece, Henry, 'The End of a World'.
Wilson, Derek, 'The Princely Pleasures at Kenilworth'.

*Published materials*

Alcock, Leslie, *Arthur's Britain: History and Archaeology AD 367–634* (Harmondsworth: Allen Lane The Penguin Press, 1971).
——, *'By South Cadbury is that Camelot...': The Excavation of Cadbury Castle 1966–70* (London: Thames & Hudson, 1972).
Anderson, W. R., 'Wireless Notes', *Musical Times* 76 (March 1935), 223.
——, 'Round About Radio', *Musical Times* 87 (December 1946), 371.
——, 'Round About Radio', *Musical Times* 91 (March 1950), 100.
——, 'Round About Radio', *Musical Times* 94 (August 1953), 359–60
Andrew, Nigel, 'Classic Serial', *Listener* 123 (8 February 1990), 47.
——, 'Thou art translated', *Listener* 118 (10 December 1987), 43.
Appleton, E. R., *Three Kings of Somerset: Song*. Music by Reginald Redman (London: Cramer, 1933).
Aprahamian, Felix, 'Musica Viva', *Radio Times* (12 March 1968), 41.
Armstrong, Anthony, 'Sir Borloys and the Dark Knight', *Strand Magazine* (December 1933), 634–43.
Armstrong, Martin, 'The Spoken Word', *Listener* 36 (31 October 1946), 608.
——, 'The Spoken Word', *Listener* 43 (29 June 1950), 1111.
B., H., 'Triennial Festival: Première a Worthy Spectacular', *Eastern Daily Press* (20 October 1970), 7.

Baigent, Michael, Richard Leigh, and Henry Lincoln, *The Holy Blood and the Holy Grail* (London: Jonathan Cape, 1982).

Bailey, Paul, 'Woe', *Listener* 79 (8 February 1968), 187–8.

Baker, Denys Val, *The Minack Theatre* (London: George Ronald, 1960).

Baker, Martin, *Artists of 'Radio Times': A Golden Age of British Illustration* (Oxford: Ashmolean Museum, 2002).

Bannister, Winifred, *James Bridie and His Theatre* (London: Rockliff, 1955).

Barber, Richard, ed., *King Arthur in Music* (Cambridge: Brewer, 2002).

*BBC Programme Records, 1922–1926* (London: BBC, n.d.).

*BBC Radio Drama Catalogues, 1923–1975*. Microform (Cambridge: Chadwyck-Healey, 1977).

Bédier, Joseph, *Le Roman de Tristan et Iseult* (Paris, 1900).

Beachcomber, 'The Seven Absurdities of Opera', *Radio Times* (29 November 1929), 623.

Benham, Patrick, *The Avalonians* (Glastonbury: Gothic Image, 1993).

Blyth, Alan, 'King Arthur', *The Times* (2 September 1972), 11.

Bradnum, Frederick, 'Norwich Revisited', *Listener* 59 (5 June 1958), 945.

Bridie, James, 'Lancelot: A Play in Two Acts', in *Plays For Plain People* (London: Constable, 1944), pp. 1–78.

Bridson, D. G., *Prospero and Ariel, the Rise and Fall of Radio: A Personal Recollection* (London: Gollancz, 1971).

Briggs, Asa, *The History of Broadcasting in the United Kingdom*, 3 vols (London: Oxford University Press, 1961–70).

Brook, Donald, *Conductors' Gallery* (London: Rockliff, 1945).

Carpenter, Humphrey, *The Inklings* (New York: Ballantine, 1981 [1978]).

——, *W. H. Auden: A Biography* (London: Unwin Paperbacks, 1983).

——, *J. R. R. Tolkien: A Biography* (London: Grafton, 1992 [1977]).

——, *Benjamin Britten: A Biography* (London: Faber & Faber, 1992).

——, *The Envy of the World: Fifty Years of the BBC Third Programme and Radio 3, 1946–1996* (London: Weidenfeld & Nicolson, 1996).

——, *Dennis Potter: A Biography* (London: Faber & Faber, 1998).

Christie, Agatha, *Appointment with Death* (Harmondsworth: Penguin, 1950 reprint).

——, *The Mirror Crack'd from Side to Side* (London: Collins, 1962).

Clare, Helen, *Merlin's Magic*, illus. Cecil Leslie (London: Bodley Head, 1953).

Clarke, Lindsay, *Parzival and the Stone from Heaven: A Grail Romance Retold for our Time* (London: HarperCollins, 2001.

Cleverdon, Douglas, 'David Jones and Broadcasting', *Poetry Wales* 8: 3 (1972), 72–81.

Cocteau, Jean, 'The Knights of the Round Table', tr. W. H. Auden, in *The Infernal Machine and Other Plays* (New York: New Directions, 1967 [1963)), pp. 179–291.

Cole, Hugo, 'Music: *Potter Thompson*', *Listener* 93 (29 May 1975), 712.

Cooper, Giles, 'Without the Grail', in *Six Plays for Radio* (London: BBC, 1966), pp. 126–83.

Cooper, Martin, 'Wagner as Christian or Jungian Myth', *Listener* 61 (29 January 1959), 216–17.

Coulton, Barbara, *Louis MacNeice in the BBC* (London: Faber & Faber, 1980).

Cowen, Frederick Hymen, *The Water-Lily, A Romantic Legend, for soli, chorus and orchestra* (London: Novello, Ewer, 1893).

Crisell, Andrew, *Understanding Radio*, 2nd edn (London: Routledge, 1994).

——, *An Introductory History of British Broadcasting*, 2nd edn (London: Routledge, 1997).

Crompton, Richmal, *William – the Bad* (London: Macmillan, 1984 [1930]).

Cropper, Martin, 'Dangerous ride for a disc-jockey', *The Times* (27 November 1990), 23.

Crosse, Gordon, *Potter Thompson: A Music Drama in one act*. Libretto by Alan Garner (London: Oxford University Press, 1977).

Currie, Tony, *The Radio Times Story* (Tiverton: Kelly Publications, 2001).

Cutting, Tracy, *Beneath the Silent Tor: The Life and Work of Alice Buckton, 1867–1944* (Wells: Appleseed Press, 2004).

D'Annunzio, Gabriele, *Francesca da Rimini*, tr. Arthur Symons (London: Heinemann, 1902).

Dane, Clemence, 'The Men Who Saved Our Land', *Radio Times* (22 November 1940), 5.

——, *The Saviours: Seven Plays on One Theme* (London: Heinemann, 1942).

Dawes, Christopher, *Rat Scabies and the Holy Grail* (London: Sceptre, 2005).

Dent, Edward J., 'Purcell's *King Arthur*', *Listener* 14 (4 December 1935), 1037.

Dexter, Harry, 'Music Over the Air', in *Music 1951*, ed. Ralph Hill (Harmondsworth: Penguin, 1951), pp. 220–32.

Dickinson, Peter, *Marigold: The Music of Billy Mayerl* (Oxford: Oxford University Press, 1999).

Dillon, Francis, 'The BBC Voice', *Listener* 85 (21 January 1971), 91.

——, 'A Modern Malory', *Listener* 85 (25 February 1971), 253.

Driver, David, ed., *The Art of 'Radio Times': The First Sixty Years* (London: BBC, 1981).

Du Maurier, Daphne, *Rebecca* (Harmondsworth: Penguin, 1962 [1938]).

Eliot, T. S., 'The Significance of Charles Williams', *Listener* 36 (19 December 1946), 894–95.

Elizabeth, 'The Knight who was a Scullion', *Radio Times* (16 September 1938), 85.

Eltham, Graham, 'I know that near the stars', *Radio Times* (23 December 1927), 646–7.

'Experimental Play Broadcast: Mr R.C. Sherriff on Roman Settlers in Britain', *The Times* (25 April 1955), 17.

Farjeon, Eleanor, and Herbert Farjeon, 'A Masque of Broadcasting', *Radio Times* (13 May 1932), 399–41.

Fife, Graeme, *Arthur the King* (London: BBC, 1990).

Foreman, Lewis, *Bax: A Composer and His Times*, 2nd edn (Aldershot: Scolar Press, 1987).

F[orster], P[eter], 'At the Court of King Cocteau', *Radio Times* (17 April 1953), 21.

Fraser, Antonia, *Boadicea's Chariot* (London: Weidenfeld & Nicolson, 1988).

Frayn, Susanna, 'The Magic of Arthur', *Radio Times* (10–16 November 1990), 4.

Gielgud, Kate Terry, *A Victorian Playgoer*, ed. Muriel St Clare Byrne (London: Heinemann, 1980).

Gielgud, Val, *British Radio Drama 1922–1956: A Survey* (London: Harrap, 1957).

Gillard, David, 'Unearthly Powers', *Radio Times* (2 February 1990), 72.

Goldie, Grace Wyndham, 'Broadcast Drama: King Arthur', *Listener* 17 (28 April 1937), 12.

——, 'Broadcast Drama: Heroes on Sunday', *Listener* 25 (2 January 1941), 28.

Gough, Lucy, *Crossing the Bar, Head, Our Lady of Shadows*, ed. Brian Mitchell (Bridgend: Seren, 2000).

Graham, Colin, ed., *King Arthur: His Magical History. Based on an Opera by John Dryden. Set to Music by Henry Purcell* (London: Faber Music, 1970).

Gray, Frances, 'Giles Cooper: The Medium as Moralist', in *British Radio Drama*, ed. John Drakakis (Cambridge: Cambridge University Press, 1981), pp. 139–57.

Grevatt, Wallace, *B.B.C. Children's Hour: A Celebration of Those Magical Years*, ed. Trevor Hill (Lewes: Book Guild, 1988).

Grigson, Geoffrey, 'King Arthur and Tristan in the West', *Listener* 16 (9 September 1936), 477–9.

Grisewood, Harman, *David Jones: Artist and Writer: broadcast in the Welsh Home Service, 1 March 1966* (London: BBC, 1966).

Hall, Barrie, *The Proms, and the Men who Made them* (London: Allen & Unwin, 1981).

Hardy, Thomas, *The Famous Tragedy of the Queen of Cornwall* (London: Macmillan, 1923).

——, *Collected Letters*, ed. Richard Little Purdy and Michael Millgate, 7 vols (Oxford: Clarendon Press, 1978–88).

Harker, J. B., 'Our Arthurian days', *Radio Times* (28 June 1929), 661.

——, 'There were no loud-speakers in Lyonesse', *Radio Times* (8 August 1930), 279.

Hart-Davis, Rupert, *Two Men of Letters: Correspondence between R. C. Hutchinson, Novelist, and Martyn Skinner, Poet, 1957–1974* (London: Michael Joseph, 1979).

Helweg, Marianne, 'Merlyn's Magic Again', *Radio Times* (14 March 1952), 6.

Herbage, Julian, 'Dryden's *King Arthur*, Composed by Purcell', *Radio Times* (6 December 1935), 13.

——, 'King Arthur, or the British Worthy', *Radio Times* (16 February 1951), 11.

Hillier, Bevis, *John Betjeman: New Fame, New Love* (London: John Murray, 2002).

Hope-Wallace, Philip, 'Broadcast Drama', *Listener* 36 (28 November 1946), 766.

——, 'Broadcast Drama', *Listener* 45 (15 March 1951), 435.

——, 'Broadcast Drama', *Listener* 45 (31 May 1951), 891.

Horne, Alan, *The Dictionary of 20th Century British Book Illustrators* (Woodbridge: Antique Collectors' Club, 1994).

Hughes, T. Rowland, *Storïau Mawr y Byd* (Aberystwyth, 1936).

Hunt, Tony, 'Ernest Chausson's *Le Roi Arthus*', in *King Arthur in Music*, ed. Richard Barber (Cambridge: Brewer, 2002), pp. 61–89.

Hurd, Michael, *Immortal Hour: The Life and Period of Rutland Boughton* (London: Routledge & Kegan Paul, 1962).

——, *Rutland Boughton and the Glastonbury Festivals* (Oxford: Clarendon Press, 1993).

Hussey, Dyneley, 'Broadcast Music', *Listener* 36 (31 October 1946), 608–9.

——, 'Broadcast Music', *Listener* 37 (12 June 1947), 931–2.

——, 'Broadcast Music: Parsifal', *Listener* 43 (12 January 1950), 83–4.

——, 'Music: "Half Sick of Shadows" ', *Listener* 56 (1 November 1956), 727–8.

Jackson, Kenneth, 'Who Was King Arthur?', *Listener* 53 (17 February 1955), 285–6.

Jacobs, Arthur, '*King Arthur* at Cambridge', *Musical Times* 90 (September 1949), 327–8.

——, 'The BBC's *King Arthur*', *Musical Times* 92 (April 1951), 182–3.

James, Derek, 'Lost in a legend!', *Eastern Evening News* (28 November 1990), 12.

Jenkins, Robin, *The Thistle and the Grail* (Edinburgh: Polygon, 1994).

Jung, Emma, and Marie-Louise von Franz, *The Grail Legend*, tr. Andrea Dykes (London: Hodder & Stoughton, 1971).

K., A., 'Purcell's *King Arthur* at Cambridge', *Musical Times* 69 (1 March 1928), 255–6.

Keller, Hans, '*Tristan* and the Realism of Adolescence', *Listener* 59 (5 June 1958), 957.

*King's Lynn Festival: Eleventh Festival Programme, 22 to 29 July 1961* (King's Lynn, 1961).

Kirkbride, Ronald, *Yuki* (London: Barker, 1967).

Knapp, Bettina Liebowitz, *Jean Cocteau* (New York: Twayne, 1970).

Lacy, Norris J., ed., *The New Arthurian Encyclopedia* (Chicago and London: St James Press, 1991).

Lam, Basil, 'Music: Purcell's *King Arthur*', *Listener* 88 (31 August 1972), 281.

Loomis, Roger Sherman, ed., *Arthurian Literature in the Middle Ages: A Collaborative History* (Oxford: The Clarendon Press, 1959).

MacCarthy, Fiona, *Eric Gill* (London: Faber & Faber, 1989).

Mann, William, '*King Arthur*: Norwich', *The Times* (20 October 1970), 14.

Mazzeno, Laurence W., *Alfred Tennyson: The Critical Legacy* (Rochester, NY: Camden House, 2004).

McNaught, W., 'King Arthur', *Musical Times* 77 (January 1936), 68–9.

——, 'Broadcast Music: Major British Works', *Listener* 29 (13 May 1943), 580–1

Milligan, Spike, *More Goon Show Scripts* (London: Sphere Books, 1974).

Mitchell, Alastair, and Alan Poulter, eds, *A Chronicle of First Broadcast Performances in the United Kingdom, 1923–1996* (Aldershot: Ashgate, 2001).

Mitchell, Donald, and Philip Reed, eds, *Letters from a Life: The Selected Letters and Diaries of Benjamin Britten 1913–1976*, 2 vols (London: Faber & Faber, 1991).

Mitford, Nancy, *Pigeon Pie* (Harmondsworth: Penguin, 1961 [1940]).

N., C., 'Cocteau's Camelot', *Radio Times* (18 May 1951), 10.

Nastali, Daniel P., and Phillip C. Boardman, *The Arthurian Annals: The Tradition in English from 1250 to 2000*, 2 vols (Oxford: Oxford University Press, 2004).

*Norfolk and Norwich Twenty-Fourth Triennial Musical Festival. Programme for Friday Evening, October 6, 1893* (London: Novello, 1893).

Northcott, Bayan, 'Last Week's Broadcast Music', *Listener* 88 (7 September 1972), 315.

'On the Cliffs: A Cornish Drama Festival', *The Times* (11 August 1951), 8.

Orel, Harold, *The Final Years of Thomas Hardy, 1912–1928* (London: Macmillan, 1976).

Ottaway, Hugh, 'Radio Notes', *Musical Times* 97 (December 1956), 646.

Owen, D. D. R., *The Evolution of the Grail Legend* (Edinburgh and London: Oliver & Boyd, 1968).

Palmer, David, 'The Laureate in Lyonnesse', *Listener* 77 (31 May 1967), 815–17.

Peach, L. du Garde, *Knights of the Round Table: Five Plays from the Arthurian Legend*, illus. Evelyn Simpson (London: Pitman, 1940).

Philip, Neil, *A Fine Anger: A Critical Introduction to the Work of Alan Garner* (London: Collins, 1981).

Phillips, Stephen, *Paolo and Francesca: A Tragedy in Four Acts* (London: John Lane The Bodley Head, 1899).

Porter, Andrew, 'Norwich: *King Arthur*', *Musical Times* 111 (December 1970), 1250.

Purcell, Henry, *King Arthur and the Saxons: An Operetta or Cantata*. Designed and arranged by W. Gillies Whittaker and Jane Dawkins (London: Oxford University Press, 1951).

*Quest of the Holy Grail, The*, tr. Pauline Matarosso (Harmondsworth: Penguin, 1969).

Reel, Jerome V., 'A Listing of Arthurian Music', in *King Arthur in Music*, ed. Richard Barber (Cambridge: Brewer, 2002), pp. 161–90.

Reid, Charles, *Thomas Beecham: An Independent Biography* (London: Readers Union, 1962 [1961]).

Reynolds, Gillian, 'Unearthing Arthur', *Daily Telegraph* (10 November 1990).

Rodger, Ian, 'Norfolk Orpheans', *Listener* 62 (16 July 1959), 111.

Rowlands, John, *T. Rowland Hughes* (Cardiff: University of Wales Press, 1975).

Sadie, Stanley, 'Lively Children's Opera', *The Times* (10 January 1975), 11.

Schwartz, Yevgeny, *The Dragon*, tr. Max Hayward and Harold Shukman, in *Three Soviet Plays*, ed. Michael Glenny (Harmondsworth: Penguin, 1966), pp. 135–218.

Scott-Sutherland, Colin, 'Patrick Piggott (1915–1990), an introduction', *British Music* 23 (2001), 11–39.

Self, David, *Sir Gawain and the Green Knight* (London: Macmillan Education, 1979).

Selvon, Samuel, *The Lonely Londoners* (London: Longman Drumbeat, 1979 [1956]).

'Sermons that ruined the carrot crop', *Listener* 21 (23 February 1939), 407–8.

Sherriff, R. C., 'When the Legions Left Britain', *Radio Times* (15 April 1955), 4.

——, *The Long Sunset: A Play in Three Acts* (London: Longmans, 1960).

——, *No Leading Lady: An Autobiography* (London: Gollancz, 1968).

Skelton, Geoffrey, *Wagner at Bayreuth: Experiment and Tradition* (London: Barrie & Rockcliff, 1965).

Smith, A. H. W., 'Update: A Supplementary Bibliography of Twentieth Century Arthurian Literature', *Arthurian Literature* 10 (1990), 135–60.

Spark, Muriel, *The Prime of Miss Jean Brodie* (Harmondsworth: Penguin, 1965 [1961]).

Stallworthy, Jon, *Louis MacNeice* (London: Faber & Faber, 1996).

Steegmuller, Francis, *Cocteau: A Biography* (London: Macmillan, 1970).

Steinbeck, Elaine, and Robert Wallsten, eds, *Steinbeck: A Life in Letters* (New York: Viking, 1975).

Street, Sean, *A Concise History of British Radio 1922–2002* (Tiverton: Kelly Publications, 2002).

Sullivan, Arthur S., *Kenilworth, A Masque of the days of Queen Elizabeth as performed at the Birmingham Festival*. Words by Henry F. Chorley (London: Chappell, 1865).

Swan, Michael, 'The Spoken Word', *Listener* 66 (21 September 1961), 443.

Tennyson, Alfred, *A Selected Edition*, ed. Christopher Ricks (London: Longman, 1989).

Tennyson, Hallam, 'The *Idylls of the King*', *Radio Times* (2 February 1968), 61.

Thomas, D. M., 'The Strait', in *Penguin Modern Poets 11* (Harmondsworth: Penguin, 1968), pp. 118–23.

——, ed., *The Granite Kingdom: Poems of Cornwall* (Truro: Barton, 1970).

Thomas, L. Edith, *The Book of the Words of the Kenilworth Castle Pageant* (Leamington Spa, 1939).

Tolkien, J. R. R., tr., *Sir Gawain and the Green Knight, Pearl and Sir Orfeo*, ed. Christopher Tolkien (London: Allen & Unwin, 1975).

Tooke, Barry, and Mat Coward, *The Best of 'Round the Horne'* (London: Boxtree, 2000).

Treece, Henry, 'The Tragedy of Tristram', in *The Exiles* (London: Faber & Faber, 1952), pp. 13–39.

Trevilian, M. F. Cely, *Defendamus: A Pageant of Taunton, 1928*. Music by Laurance E. Tanner (Taunton: Goodman, 1928).

Trewin, J. C., 'At the Play', *Punch* 221 (22 August 1951), 216.

——, 'Broadcast Drama', *Listener* 47 (17 April 1952), 647.

——, 'Broadcast Drama', *Listener* 48 (16 October 1952), 655.

——, 'Broadcast Drama', *Listener* 52 (19 August 1954), 299.

——, 'Drama', *Listener* 53 (28 April 1955), 767–8.

——, 'Drama', *Listener* 55 (26 April 1956), 526–7.

Uttley, Alison, 'King Arthur's Tree', in *Uncle Mac's 'Children's Hour' Book*, ed. Derek McCulloch (London: Purnell, [1947]), pp. 8–19.

Vaughan, David, *Frederick Ashton and his Ballets* (London: Black, 1999).

W., S., 'Purcell: Master of Texture', *The Times* (18 October 1969), III.

Wakeman, Rick, *The Myths and Legends of King Arthur and the Knights of the Round Table* (New York: Triangle Music Corporation, 1975).

Walker, Roy, 'Three in One', *Listener* 59 (23 January 1958), 173–4.

Warner, Sylvia Townsend, *T. H. White: A Biography* (London: Jonathan Cape and Chatto & Windus, 1967).

Westrup, J. A., *Purcell* (London: Dent, 1937).

White, Jon Manchip, 'A Verse Play from the Lumber Room', *Radio Times* (3 October 1952), 11.

Whitehead, Kate, *The Third Programme: A Literary History* (Oxford: Clarendon Press, 1989).

Wildman, Carl, 'With Cocteau in Camelot', *Radio Times* (24 August 1967), 42.

Williams, Stephen, 'The Legend of the Grail', *Radio Times* (15 April 1949), 6.

Wilson, Keith, *Thomas Hardy on Stage* (London: Macmillan, 1995).

Young, Francis Brett, *The Island* (London: Heinemann, 1944).

Zehnder, Martin, ed., *Something Rich and Strange: Selected Essays on Sam Selvon* (Leeds: Peepal Tree Press, 2003).

# Index

# ARTHURIAN STUDIES